THE GUINNESS BOOK OF POLITICAL BLUNDERS

GEOFFREY HINDLEY

GUINNESS PUBLISHING

Published in Great Britain by Guinness Publishing Ltd.
33 London Road, Enfield, Middlesex EN2 6DJ

"Guinness" is a registered trademark of Guinness Publishing Ltd.

This Publication Copyright © Guinness Publishing Ltd., 1996

The Work Copyright © Geoffrey Hindley 1996

The right of Geoffrey Hindley to be identified as the Author of this Work has been asserted in accordance with the Copyright, Design and Patents Act 1988.

All rights reserved. No part of this publication may be reproduced, stored in a retrieval system or transmitted in any form or by any means, electronic, mechanical, photocopying, recording or otherwise, without the prior permission of the publishers and copyright holder.

ISBN 0-85112-545-X

A catalogue record for this book is available from the British Library.

Designed by Cathy Shilling and Rob Burns

Printed and bound in Great Britain by The Bath Press, Bath

Front Cover Illustration
US President Richard M. Nixon; British premier Neville Chamberlain, brandishing his Munich agreement with Adolf Hitler; Benito Mussolini; (background) the 1990 London riots against the poll tax.

Picture Acknowledgements
Guinness Publishing would like to thank The Hulton Deutsch Collection for permission to use the illustrations in this book.

The Author
Encyclopedist, historian, author on royalty, lecturer and broadcaster, Geoffrey Hindley has written some 20 books, mostly in the field of social history, as well as film and TV scripts. For over 10 years, Geoffrey Hindley was a regular question setter for BBC's *Mastermind*. Now living in France, he teaches at the University of Le Havre.

CONTENTS

INTRODUCTION	1
CHAPTER 1: SCANDALOUS BLUNDERING	5
CHAPTER 2: THE GREASY POLE	19
CHAPTER 3: BLUNDERS OF PRINCIPLE	35
CHAPTER 4: BLUNDERING ESTABLISHMENTS	55
CHAPTER 5: PARTY MATTERS AND PARTY LEADERS	71
CHAPTER 6: ELECTION BLUNDERS	86
CHAPTER 7: FOLLIES OF PRIDE AND OVERCONFIDENCE	98
CHAPTER 8: PROBLEMS OF LEADERSHIP	114
CHAPTER 9: FOOT IN MOUTH	126
CHAPTER 10: FAULTS IN FOREIGN FIELDS	136
CHAPTER 11: BLUNDERS OF MISPLACED TRUST...	152
CHAPTER 12: BLUNDERING ROYALS	163
CHAPTER 13: BLUNDERS OF DESTINY	171
INDEX	185

To politicians, who provide much entertainment and without whom we would have nobody to blame.

INTRODUCTION

'I reject the cynical view that politics is inevitably or even usually a dirty business' – President Richard Milhous Nixon. 'The French people are incapable of regicide' – King Louis XVI of France in 1789, four years before he was sent to the guillotine. 'The Chancellor's position is unassailable' – Margaret Thatcher on her finance minister, Nigel Lawson, shortly after she had appointed Sir Alan Walters, an economist who consistently and publicly assailed Lawson's policies, and shortly before Lawson himself resigned in October 1989.

The spectacle of public figures saying silly things which they later have, or should have, cause to regret is an innocent entertainment for the populace at large. From time to time politicians say or do things which land their own careers in trouble and this, too, meets with plaudits from the citizenry. At the time of the election for the leadership of the British Conservative Party in 1995 one government minister confided, in the semi-articulate argot that passes for modern English, that he would be voting for John Major as 'the least worst prime minister we have'. Weeks after Major's convincing victory in the contest, this same minister announced that he would be leaving politics at the next general election. Sometimes, however, politicians actually do things which have repercussions on the lives of their compatriots, and then the joke may pall.

Attaining power in 1979 just as North Sea oil came on stream, Britain's new Tory government made no attempt to harvest this windfall resource for long-term investment in the nation's future. Rather, they encouraged full exploitation, which certainly boosted Britain's balance of payments position but also hiked sterling's exchange rate as a petro-currency. Businesses which, in the late 1970s, had planned investment on the basis of a pound–dollar rate around the $1.50 mark, now confronted a rate nearer $2.40. With exports rendered uncompetitive by government policy and manufacturers denied the kind of preferential prices allowed by American administrations to US companies using US oil, British industry foundered, losing 20 per cent of productive capacity in the first three years of the new administration. Overseas competitors were even able to buy hi-tech plant and machinery which were being auctioned off by Britain's broken industrial sector at bargain prices. The resulting unemployment was paid for thanks to the non-renewable liquid black gold being pumped from the ocean bed.

A decade and a half later Tory ministers, seeking re-election for yet another term of office, were boasting Britain as the enterprise centre of Western Europe. The country's manufacturing base, after years of decline, was indeed expanding in some areas – thanks to inward investment from Pacific Rim nations seeking cheap labour and the advantages of a virtually deregulated labour market. This outcome, in so far as it was not the result of inadvertence but rather of rigorously applied economic and political ideology, was not

A Conservative government is an organized hypocrisy.

BENJAMIN DISRAELI, IN A HOUSE OF COMMONS SPEECH, 17 MARCH 1845

INTRODUCTION

perhaps a blunder in the normal sense of the word, but to those among Britain's work force putting in longer hours than people of any other European country and who were in the least protected and most insecure labour market of any advanced economy, it must have seemed that someone somewhere had erred.

Of course, authors of books such as this have the luxury of hindsight. It is too much to suppose that one will avoid such indulgence always or even perhaps often – it is too tempting. However, it must be acknowledged that what may now seem obvious blunders, could, at the time, have seemed to be the outcome of wise, or at least democratic, statesmanship.

When, in 1936, German troops marching on Hitler's orders reoccupied the Rhineland territories assigned to French protection by the Treaty of Versailles, only a very small minority of people criticized the failure of Britain and France to challenge the action. Hitler's own generals had certainly expected retaliation and had been dismayed when the Führer told them of his intentions. After all, such an initiative would mean ripping up the treaty which the victor nations, politicians and people alike, considered the great prize for all the blood, sweat and agony of the First World War. It seemed obvious to the German high command that if they let their soldiers loose on this internationally guaranteed territory Germany, at that time quite unprepared for major military action, would be invaded and humiliated once more.

But it was Hitler, and not the generals, who had judged the mood of the democracies aright. Historians like to castigate the decision-makers of those times as weak-willed. Winston Churchill made the same charge at the time. But there were powerful counter-arguments. The French government was weak at home; British public opinion was increasingly opposed to the Versailles settlement on grounds of fairness, believing the document to have been an act of vindictive greed; and many pointed out that the Rhineland was, after all, German territory. And as for Churchill, he was notorious in his own party as a maverick who had twice changed his party allegiance and had always been free with his criticism of government. If it is the business of democratic governments to enact the will of the people, it is hard to find fault with the decision not to risk war again, barely 15 years since victory in the 'War to end all Wars'.

Two years later, Germany presented the democracies with another test. Much has been written about the Munich Agreement of 29 September 1938, signed by Hitler for Germany, Daladier for France and Neville Chamberlain for Great Britain, which effectively handed the defences of Czechoslovakia to the Wehrmacht. The figure of the British Prime Minister at Croydon airport, brandishing his 'piece of paper' – Hitler's personal guarantee to him that there would be no more demands – his gaunt face and prim moustachioed mouth seeming to hint at a smile of triumph, is a documentary-maker's cliché guaranteed to awaken indignation and contempt.

At the time reactions could not have been more different. In terms of international diplomacy it was a triumph. Europe had seemed once more on the brink of war and then, suddenly, miraculously, 'the clouds dispersed, the sky was blue, the sun shone'. The miracle was universally attributed to

Is it not beautiful? The only central European city not destroyed. And all my doing.

EDWARD BENES, PRESIDENT OF CZECHOSLOVAKIA WHO ACCEPTED THE ANGLO–FRENCH MUNICH CAPITULATION TO HITLER IN 1938, LOOKING OUT ON PRAGUE FROM THE PRESIDENTIAL PALACE IN 1945

INTRODUCTION

the statesmanship of one man. In the words of one observer, 'The aged Prime Minister of England had saved the world.' Speaking of Chamberlain's earlier visit to Berchtesgaden that year, the Irish leader, Eamon de Valera, said admiringly: 'This is the greatest thing that has ever been done.'

In France only one non-Communist deputy voted with the Communists in the National Assembly against the Munich Agreement. This was the Count of Paris, the royalist movement's champion. The movement castigated him for venturing to criticize the peace deal and some even accused him of Communist sympathies. In the country at large a public subscription was opened to buy Britain's prime minister a country estate, complete with trout stream, fishing being his passion.

If it is true that 'a week is a long time in politics', then Chamberlain enjoyed his triumph with London's right-wing media for an eternity. On 15 March 1939 London's humorous weekly *Punch* carried a cartoon, showing John Bull waking up with relief as a nightmare, 'Danger of War', flies out of the window. That day the Germans marched into Prague. A London daily had taken to printing on its masthead the slogan, 'There will not be war this year, next year, nor in the foreseeable future' and continued to do so until August. In September Germany launched its invasion of Poland, and Great Britain and France declared war.

Chamberlain was a man in touch with the feeling of his contemporaries who worked for an objective both he and they approved – peace. Reluctantly, he was obliged to go back on that objective and declare war. But there are, of course, pledges made to win elections and broken by their makers once the election is won. The secret here is smoke-screening and

Praise be to God and to Mr Chamberlain. I find no sacrilege, no bathos in coupling these two names.

GODFREY WINN,
COLUMNIST,
DAILY EXPRESS,
SEPTEMBER 1938

Neville Chamberlain on his return from negotiating with Hitler terms which he believed would hold the peace in Europe. His principal blunder was to pursue the policy of appeasement favoured by the majority of his contemporaries.

INTRODUCTION

> *We did not - repeat, did not - trade weapons or anything else for hostages, nor will we.*
>
> PRESIDENT RONALD REAGAN, COMMENTING ON ALLEGATIONS RELATING TO THE IRAN–CONTRA HOSTAGE AFFAIR IN NOVEMBER 1986

weasel words. When George Bush pledged not to raise taxes in the US presidential election of 1988, he gave himself no let-out and insisted on the sincerity of his commitment by inviting people to 'read my lips'. When, as president, he did raise taxes, the US electorate saw the breach of promise as too blatant. They remembered it in 1992, when they voted Bush out of office.

John Major's use of the same ploy was much more adroit. In Britain's 1992 election campaign he assured the voters with all the sincerity he was then credited with, that 'We have no plans to widen the scope of VAT'. Assuming, no doubt rightly, that few people listen at all closely to what is said at election times but react to what they want to hear, Major was able to make what may have been a perfectly accurate statement. In hindsight, however, the statement begins to look deceptive. Increasing indirect taxes, such as VAT, facilitates the reduction of income tax and thereby boosts the Tory claim to be the party of low taxation. With the 1992 election safely – if surprisingly – won, the Tories brought in a bill to extend VAT to domestic electricity, gas and coal. While the Tories may not have actually drawn up plans for this extension of VAT before the election, people got the general impression that they had pledged *not* to extend it.

In October 1995 a public opinion survey revealed that among the national institutions the highest trust rating was still accorded to the Church (some 54 per cent) while government came in at just 13 per cent. As for politicians, a mere 5 per cent of the sample admitted to believing them. Maybe it is because they have a way with words that exploits normal usage with intention to deceive. Apart from lowering their standing in public perception, the habit does not appear to do them serious harm.

Even outright absurdities can be brushed aside. In March 1995 Britain's Chancellor of the Exchequer, Kenneth Clarke, aiming to trumpet the flourishing state of Britain's economy, commented on a local radio station that in the nearby town of Consett 'you have got one of the best steelworks in Europe. It doesn't employ as many people as it used to, because it is so modern.' Unfortunately, the works in question had been closed for 20 years. A few days later, having been informed of his mistake, the Chancellor announced 'Consett ... is also one of the major centres in Western Europe for disposable baby nappies.' The factory in question had closed in 1991. Michael Howard, Home Secretary in the same administration, was frequently censured by the courts for breaking the law or exceeding his powers, or failing to follow proper procedures. In other countries it is almost unheard of for the Minister of the Interior, custodian of law and order, to come before the courts. In Britain he was, during the mid-1990s, best described as a recidivist. But these gross lapses of professional competence have had, so far as can be seen, no impact at all on his career in office.

> *It sort of settled down to trading arms for hostages.*
>
> PRESIDENT RONALD REAGAN COMMENTING ON ALLEGATIONS RELATING TO THE IRAN–CONTRA HOSTAGE AFFAIR IN MARCH 1987

As will be seen, then, it may be difficult to determine what can be properly called a political blunder. For our purposes it is taken to be some act with a consequence that actually disadvantages the perpetrator or his party; or that should disadvantage him or her; or that damages the country or society where he operates with or without his intention. It may also, on occasion, denote any error which entertains the onlookers or provides an improving moral or diverting story.

CHAPTER 1: SCANDALOUS BLUNDERING

In politics a scandal of any kind is a blunder. The dictionary definition of scandal – 'A thing or person causing public outrage or indignation' – expresses the point perfectly. It matters not whether the outrage is justified or merely conventional. The saying that no publicity is bad publicity is matched in politics by the other clichés, 'no smoke without fire' and 'throw enough mud and some is bound to stick'. For the real objection to scandal is that it is uncontrolled publicity. Since the highest art of the politician is to avoid, if possible, answering any question, even when publicly put, it is obvious that information of any kind vouchsafed without clearance is problem material. In this chapter we look at a number of *causes célèbres*, some of which involved criminality or near-criminality and all of which caused more or less serious political trouble.

The Affair of the Diamond Necklace

The books written to explain the origins of the French Revolution would fill a library. Theories range from the political to the economic, from the social oppression of the peasantry to the political philosophy of Jean-Jacques Rousseau. Those who prefer more personal interpretations of history point to the weakness and indecision of King Louis XVI and the influence and reputation of his wife, Marie Antoinette. In the opinion of Napoleon, the beginning of the Revolution dated from the Affair of the Diamond Necklace which broke on the world in August 1785. The main players implicated by the scandal were a lovelorn Cardinal de Rohan, the court jewellers and the Queen. That the business ever came to public knowledge flowed from some regrettable mistakes by people in the highest places.

As daughter of the Empress of Austria, Marie Antoinette brought to her marriage with the future Louis XVI of France in 1770 a distaste for the French court and a distrust of de Rohan who, as French ambassador to Vienna, had passed Austrian state secrets back to Paris. She never won the hearts of the French aristocracy, withdrawing from court life with a small band of favourites which tended to exclude, and so antagonize, the leading families of France.

The Queen became a target of intrigue and scurrilous pamphlet campaigns, accusing her of unbridled debauchery and naming in turn virtually every eligible male at Versailles. If the royal children could be bastardized, the way to the succession was open to others, among them King Louis's own brother, favoured by court factions. The feverish atmosphere of politicking destabilized the royal family's standing and so played a part in the cataclysm

SCANDALOUS BLUNDERING

Above: the Diamond Necklace, which in 1786 was the focus of the court intrigue which became a nationwide scandal. In the opinion of Napoleon, it lit the fuse to the French Revolution three years later.

Right: a lampoon of Louis XVI in 1792, now a citizen king as a consequence of the Revolution, wearing the Phrygian cap, the revolutionaries' 'symbol of liberty'.

which was to come. By the summer of 1785 the Queen's reputation was in tatters. The events of August were to destroy it.

That month Cardinal de Rohan, duke and peer of France, Archbishop of Strasbourg and Grand Almoner of the Realm, was arrested in Versailles on the sensational charge of using the Queen's name to procure a fantastically expensive diamond necklace from the court jeweller without paying for it. The arrest was made on the responsibility of the Marquis de Breteuil, Minister for the Maison du Roi and one of the Queen's favourites. Unfortunately, years earlier he had been ambassador to Vienna until displaced by de Rohan, since when the two had been involved in a personal feud. This seems to have robbed Breteuil of his judgement. All the courtly de

Rohan wished for was to regain the favour of the Queen. What he got was indictment on a charge of scandalous peculation, the case to be heard in public forum.

He had in fact been conned by an impoverished lady in collusion with a professional jewel thief. The self-styled 'Comtesse de la Motte', equipped with forged papers, persuaded the Cardinal that she was a secret emissary of the Queen who had set her heart upon the necklace. If the Cardinal would only pledge his credit to acquire the jewel from the court jewellers, he would be restored to the royal favour. The money would be forthcoming before the first payment became due.

A brief nocturnal interview with the 'queen' in the gardens at Versailles convinced the infatuated de Rohan that he was indeed once more in favour. The 'queen' later turned out to be a Paris prostitute in disguise. The jewel thief took the necklace out of the country and sold the stones and when the court jewellers demanded their money, the Cardinal Archbishop of Strasbourg found himself obliged to divulge that the Queen had let him down.

The Cardinal begged the King to conceal the scandal for the sake of the de Rohan family name, but Louis was in a 'white rage' and ordered him confined to the Bastille, leaving Breteuil to arrange the details of the prosecution. This, he decided, should be heard before the *parlement de Paris*.

The *parlement de Paris*, which had feuded for more than a decade with royal ministers to defend its privileges and profitable legal jurisdictions, had old scores to settle with the court party. It was the worst possible tribunal in which to hear the case, if indeed the case had to be heard in public at all. In more adroit hands than those of Breteuil, the matter would have surely been side-tracked down one of those obscure avenues of legal process and bureaucratic procrastination so beloved of the *ancien régime*.

The trial which ensued dragged the Queen's name through the mire of public gossip with the scum of society. De la Motte was condemned to be flogged, branded and imprisoned for life. The Cardinal was acquitted by the *parlement*, banished from court and fêted by the public. The Queen, according to the gossip (and in court matters there is nothing more powerful) was alleged to have offered to sell her favours for a necklace of diamonds but then to have gone back on the bargain.

Most historians would agree in principle with Napoleon's judgement. By discrediting the Queen in full public view the affair undermined the foundations of the monarchy itself. Public opinion was learning to talk republican language even before it had thought republican thoughts. For centuries court scandals had been hushed up or at least confined to polite society, whose instincts for self-preservation led it to shut out the prying gaze of bourgeoisie and populace. Now a court scandal had been played out on the national stage. It set in motion a vortex of events which would swirl away the once substantial pageant of aristocratic privilege. Had Louis been less touchy, or had Breteuil not been so politically naïve as to set the case before a tribunal composed of the most bitter enemies of the monarchy, the court might have contained the nuisance. As it was, blunders by king and minister conjured a political catastrophe from a society intrigue.

Corruption at the Treasury?

The first term of the US presidency (1869–77) of Ulysses S. Grant was marked by scandal and corruption. The President had come to power on a wave of euphoria as the military hero of the North in the Civil War. But the failure of his administration to restrain the adventurism and embezzlement, rife at all levels of society and in government itself, and its resultant failure to establish a moral tone, tainted his reputation.

The nadir was reached early with the events of 24 September 1869, known as Black Friday. During the preceding weeks two financial speculators, James Fisk and Jay Gould, had been building a corner in gold. At a time when the precious metal was still used as currency, the rocketing price caused by Fisk and Gould's dealings impacted on the finance market. They further enhanced the value of their holdings by starting rumours that the government was set against the selling of its gold reserves. Many a business in need of gold to finance its operations but unable to afford the price was ruined.

Then, on Friday 24 September, George S. Boutwell, Secretary of the Treasury, sold $4 million worth of federal government gold. Thanks to Fisk and Gould he got an artificially high price. Few people doubted that the government advisers had been privy to the speculators' plans. Inevitably, Grant and his administration were seen as cynical profiteers at the expense of the nation's business community. In fact, it appears that the Secretary had

General Ulysses S. Grant (1822–85), who led the Union army to victory in the US Civil War, photographed in his HQ at City Point, in June 1864. Four years later he swept to victory as Republican president and held office for two terms. One historian considered him one of the most ill-fitted men for the office and his administrations were certainly marked by extraordinary corruption and mismanagement.

had no idea of what had been going on. It was a classic case of a policy blunder flowing from inadequate information.

A Scandal to Religion

The case of the British MP Charles Bradlaugh and the parliamentary oath, one of the longest-running scandals of the later 19th century, sparked a series of sensational by-elections in which the electors flouted the religious conventions supposed to dominate Victorian provincial society, while Parliament proved itself a bastion of reaction.

Starting life as a London messenger boy, Charles Bradlaugh served in the army and then in 1853, at the age of 20, he became a solicitor's clerk. Spare-time lecturing and pamphleteering against Christianity under the name of 'Iconoclast', together with the impact of his journal *The Free Thinker*, made him a high-profile anti-establishment campaigner and contributed to his election as a Radical member for Northampton in 1880.

Before taking his seat, a member was obliged to pledge loyalty to Crown and Parliament. Bradlaugh claimed the right to make an affirmation of allegiance in place of the parliamentary Bible oath. His atheistic views were of course well known and shocking to most of his parliamentary colleagues. But there was no law that required a member of Parliament to be a Christian and it was not even clear that the statutes governing the matter obliged members to swear in the words of the Bible oath. The case raised complicated legal issues which only judges were competent to decide. The immediate question, however, as Bradlaugh stood at the bar of the House waiting to take his seat, was for the Speaker of the House, Sir Henry Brand, to decide. He blundered and set in train a series of events which came to constitute a *cause célèbre* of parliamentary history.

The Speaker of the House of Commons is sovereign within its walls. Sir Henry could have given Bradlaugh permission to affirm allegiance in the form he wished while warning him that he might find himself sued for penalties in the courts. Instead, he referred the question to the House, which referred it to a select committee, which in its turn decided by a majority of just one vote against the right to affirm.

Even so, the position was stable as Bradlaugh, having made his protest, was prepared to swear in the ordinary way. He had made his stand as an atheist against what he saw as the flummery of religion. But if it took a meaningless ritual to inaugurate him into his duties as an MP, he was quite prepared to play the game. Now, however, the Speaker made a still more egregious blunder. Whereas it was his duty to safeguard the clear right of a duly elected member, he allowed a debate to develop which ended in the adoption of a quite arbitrary amendment, debarring Bradlaugh from both making affirmation and taking the oath.

A bully-boy group of young Conservative members, led by Lord Randolph Churchill, immediately saw the opportunity for harrying the Liberal government of Prime Minister Gladstone. A devout churchman, Gladstone was also passionate in his defence of tolerance and fairness, but on

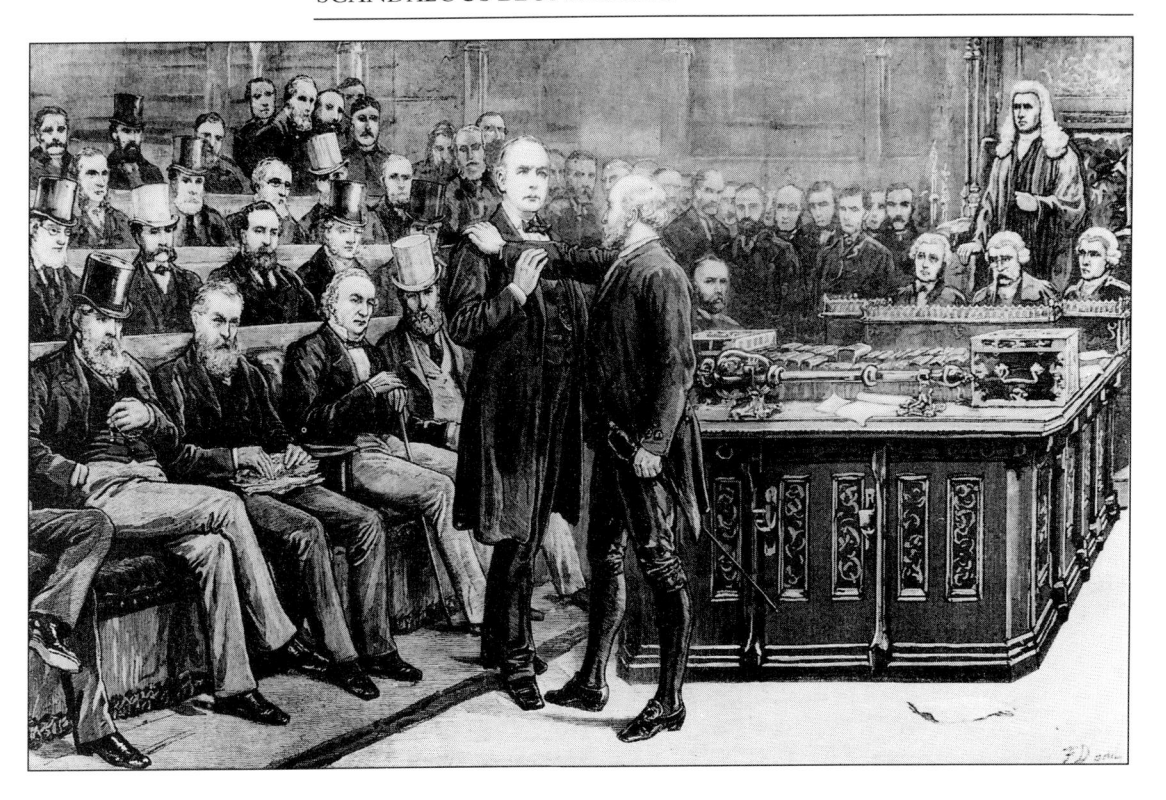

House of Commons, Westminster, 1881. The Sergeant-at-Arms, acting on the Speaker's warrant, arrests Charles Bradlaugh. The latter was duly elected MP for Northampton, but as an atheist refused the right to affirm rather than swear the oath of allegiance.

this issue he could not command a majority. The forces of establishment and hypocrisy, coupled to unscrupulous tactics by Churchill, had full play. In contrast Bradlaugh, who three times went back to the electors of Northampton and was three times returned by handsome majorities, was committed to the parliamentary lock-up known as the Clock Tower, forcibly ejected from the House by the police and subjected to merciless abuse. The controversy raged in press and pamphlets; Gladstone's majority was divided whenever the question came to a vote and Bradlaugh was finally pilloried in a manifestly absurd judgement by the Court of Appeal.

Throughout, he was willing to take the oath in the normal way, but six years elapsed before he was able to sit in the House of Commons as of assured right. In 1886 the new Speaker, Peel, peremptorily put an end to the scandalous saga by refusing to permit any member to interfere between another member of the House and the oath. This sane and historic ruling immediately overturned the original weak decision of Speaker Brand and nullified all the fevered rhetoric on the matter over the previous five years.

A Baronet in the Divorce Courts

But of course, then as now, sex and marriage were the preferred themes of real British scandal. Divorce was obtainable at law from the year 1857 (before that time a special act of Parliament was required), but it was in most people's eyes an unspeakable disgrace and it was not until 1887 that Queen Victoria would allow even the innocent party of a divorce at court. It was a decade when the cult of the home and domesticity reigned supreme and its theme song 'Home, Sweet Home' by Sir Henry Bishop (whose wife had, as a matter of little-known fact, years before eloped with a French harpist), became almost a second national anthem.

Thus, when Sir Charles Dilke, a brilliant Liberal tipped by many as a future prime minister, found himself cited as co-respondent in the divorce courts he would have been wise to move rather more circumspectly than he did. The judge in the case of *Crawford v. Crawford and Dilke*, while granting the decree against the respondent, had dismissed with costs the petition against Dilke as co-respondent with the observation that there was 'no evidence worthy of the name against him'. In fact the only evidence was Mrs Crawford.

It seemed that Sir Charles had come out of the episode with a clean bill of health. But there was a public outburst because, whereas the respondent had made these serious charges of adultery against him, he had not gone into the witness box to refute them. In the weeks that followed, far from dying away, public speculation and agitation intensified. Dilke himself reopened the case by petitioning the Queen's proctor to intervene, presumably hoping to show that the husband and wife had acted in collusion and had cited him to deceive the court. It was a disastrous blunder. Since the case had been brought by the proctor and not by Sir Charles, the court held that he was no longer a party to the trial but only a witness. This meant that during the week-long trial, in July 1886, he had to listen powerless to intervene as the charges were repeated and was incompetent to take issue against them as affecting himself. So he suffered new and more serious damage to his reputation without gaining any chance to reply.

There is debate to this day as to whether or not Sir Charles Dilke was indeed guilty of the adultery as accused. But his contemporaries gave him little benefit of doubt. His political career was to all intents and purposes wrecked. He had been left out of the cabinet while the first trial impended; he lost Chelsea, his parliamentary seat, in the February election of 1886, four months before the second trial, and remained an exile from the political world for six years. He never held government office again, even though he was returned as MP for the Forest of Dean in 1892 and sat in Parliament until his death in 1911.

The Case of Parnell – Tragedy and Blunder

Throughout the 1880s Charles Stewart Parnell embodied the cause of Irish Home Rule. Son of an Irish Protestant landed gentleman and an American mother, he was a tall, startlingly handsome man with the blue eyes, black hair and the full beard of a Celtic patriarch, but with the haughty reserve and disdainful bearing of the English aristocrat. Gladstone was his only rival for the ascendancy on the Westminster scene, while he dominated the Irish Party effortlessly. His charismatic bearing and supreme self-assurance seized the imagination of the British public and no doubt played its part in the conversion of Gladstone to the cause of Home Rule.

As the decade drew to its close, that cause seemed on the verge of triumph.

The disaster which struck it down sprang from a mixture of personal motives and passions and political miscalculations, which make it not only one of the most tragic but also one of the most intriguing episodes in British history.

In April 1887 *The Times* published a facsimile of a letter apparently by Parnell which condoned the Phoenix Park murders in which two government ministers had been hacked to death in sight of Dublin's Viceregal Lodge by members of an extremist Irish nationalist group five years before. The letter featured among a series of articles a piece entitled 'Parnellism and Crime', which aimed to show that the great Irish patriot secretly supported such terroristic acts. British public opinion was shocked. Parnell declared in Parliament that the letter was a forgery but took no further action.

The government, however, set up a commission to inquire into the charges in the articles. This found that the letter was indeed a forgery. When in February 1890 the commission published its conclusions, entirely clearing Parnell, *The Times*, which had paid £30,000 in acquiring the original material, was fined the sum of £250,000.

Much more importantly, British public opinion surged back in favour of Parnell and the cause of Irish Home Rule. Had there been a dissolution of Parliament in the first half of 1890, there can be little doubt that Gladstone would have been returned with an overwhelming Home Rule majority. But no election was called and by the end of the year the cause was dead for a generation. The principal reason for the disaster was a scandalous divorce case. If falling in love can be called a blunder, Parnell himself was the guilty party.

On 17 November 1890 the Divorce Court granted a provisional decree (a decree *nisi*) to Captain W. H. O'Shea, of the Irish Huzzars, in a suit against his wife Katharine O'Shea (*née* Wood), a daughter of the English establishment, Parnell being cited as the co-respondent. The passionate affair between the politician and Kittie O'Shea was some ten years old. There were those in the political world who knew of it but the general public were quite unprepared. The fate of Sir Charles Dilke, four years before, had been a warning to English politicians to keep out of the divorce courts. How a similar scandal might affect the standing of Ireland's champion in Protestant England and Catholic Ireland was about to be discovered.

Parnell made no defence against the citation. How could he? Not only had he and Mrs O'Shea lived as man and wife since 1881, she had borne him three daughters. The O'Sheas' marriage had died some years before the advent of Parnell, but they had continued to keep up appearances rather than offend Kittie's aunt, the aged and extremely rich Mrs Benjamin Wood of Eltham in Kent. Captain O'Shea lived mostly in a London apartment, paid for by the old lady's allowance to his wife, but was a frequent and ostentatious visitor to the little house at Eltham in Kent, where Kittie lived with their children, within walking distance of the grand house of Mrs Wood whom she assiduously nursed.

When Parnell discreetly established himself at Eltham, the good Captain, far from protesting, took advantage of the great parliamentarian's liaison with his wife to further his own political career. In February 1886 he obtained the by-election candidature at Galway City and one of his rivals sneered that it was merely because the Captain's wife was Parnell's mistress.

THE CASE OF PARNELL – TRAGEDY AND BLUNDER

The remark was kept out of the papers, but most leading figures on the Irish political scene had the same suspicions.

Parnell himself swore to friends that there was nothing dishonourable about his dealings with the lady – on the face of it an extraordinary claim but one which may be explained by the fading presence of Mrs Wood. It seems the Captain accepted the transfer of his wife's affections and the three of them accepted the liaison as a true marriage, at least in the sight of God. The *ménage à trois* was adopted as a temporary makeshift until Mrs Wood should die – any hint of divorce before then and the old lady would surely will her money elsewhere. As she was 89, the rather exceptional arrangements would not have long to run before the O'Sheas could divorce and Kittie marry again as Mrs Parnell.

In fact Mrs Wood lived to be 97 and, while she left £144,000 to her niece, the plan encountered new difficulties, for the will was contested by other members of the Wood family. O'Shea, who for 20 years had to all intents and purposes lived off his wife, demanded £20,000 as the price of appearing as the guilty party in the divorce case. With Kittie's assets frozen and Parnell unable to raise a loan of that size, O'Shea proceeded to sue for divorce against his wife, with the effect that among other things he gained legal custody over Parnell's two surviving daughters, an opportunity for further blackmail which he did not hesitate to use.

With his private life in ruins, Parnell had to face up to the possibility of political annihilation. At first the situation seemed manageable. He decided to retain the leadership of the party and nearly all his colleagues backed his decision at a meeting of the National League in Dublin. A group on an American deputation also cabled support. But in England things were threatening. Gladstone, himself a devout churchman, relied heavily on the support of the Nonconformist bodies, strict in their conventional morality. They made it plain that they could not continue to be associated with the Irish Party unless it changed its leader. Gladstone wrote a private letter to Parnell, to be delivered by an intermediary, in which he made it plain that, unless the Irish Party changed its leader, he would resign as leader of the Liberals. Without Gladstone the cause was lost, without Parnell its realization would be delayed but not necessarily impossible.

'Illustrations of the O'Shea–Parnell Divorce Case' from the Illustrated Police News *of November 1890. The ruin of Charles Stewart Parnell was a tragedy in the history of British–Irish relations but undoubtedly meant a field day for the press. For years he and Mrs Kitty O'Shea lived a secret life as husband and wife at her house in Eltham, with her husband's knowledge, but also with various stratagems to keep up public appearances. To the left, below, the artist depicts O'Shea leaving the love-nest by rope ladder.*

The situation was clearly dire. Nothing had as yet been heard from the Irish Catholic hierarchy whose views on divorce, even the divorce of a heretic, would surely be negative. There was just the possibility that if Parnell retired from public life for six months or a year, if he ate humble pie in short, he might be able to return to the political scene. However, the delivery of Gladstone's letter was fatally delayed and the Irish Party went ahead and formally re-elected Parnell their leader.

Now he was unbudgeable, but Gladstone and his advisers decided to make the letter public. The decision has been described as one of the greatest blunders the grand old man of English politics ever made. Publication transformed the letter from private advice to Parnell as to possible future scenarios to a public ultimatum to him and the Irish Party for a change of leader. Parnell was not the man to bow to such pressure. The party faced the humiliating prospect of being forced to change leaders at the behest of Westminster. When, on 30 November, the Irish hierarchy came out with a denunciation of Parnell, good Irish Catholics could be in no doubt now where their allegiance should lie. Even so, the Irish Party at Westminster were reluctant to ditch their leader. After twelve days of debate the party split. Out of 72 members only 26 stayed loyal to Parnell. Almost immediately afterwards a by-election at Kilkenny put the issue to the voters. Parnell had a good candidate and campaigned for him vigorously. However, in only one district did he win a majority of the votes – it was the only district in which the parish priest supported the Parnellite. In June 1891 Parnell married Mrs O'Shea, a natural step, no doubt, but one which only worsened his standing with the hierarchy. In July he campaigned for, and lost, two further by-elections. On 27 September, suffering a bout of rheumatism, he addressed an outdoor political rally in the pouring rain. Afterwards he sat for hours in his damp clothes. He returned to his wife at their Brighton home, rheumatism threatening his heart. On 6 October he died. His death was mourned by the Irish nation – and with good reason. Their cause had been set back 30 years by a sequence of incidents in which passion, politics and miscalculation had all played their parts – and the Irish question remains unsolved to this day.

A Fatal Blunder for a Campaigning Journalist

Journalists, it is generally agreed, are the bane of politicians. They have destroyed many a career by raising rumour and scandal to the level of comment and analysis. The modern French political establishment views with benign contempt the periodic upheavals caused at Westminster by sexual peccadilloes and marital infidelities. Today France's politicians can indulge their disdain safe behind strict privacy laws banning publication of their indiscretions. In 1913, however, they were liable, from time to time, to burst into the public domain to startling effect. In the case under consideration, this was because for once the victim struck back. The tale of the French left-wing finance minister Joseph Caillaux, Madame Caillaux and the editor of the right-wing daily *Le Figaro* proved, if nothing else, the superiority of the French farce to the Whitehall variety.

A FATAL BLUNDER FOR A CAMPAIGNING JOURNALIST

Caillaux, who first became French minister of finance in 1899 at the age of 36 and who was to hold the post on four subsequent occasions, was brilliant, ambitious, conceited and deeply disliked by most French politicians, whether of left or right. When in 1909 he proposed France's first income tax, he extended the ranks of his enemies to virtually the entire male bourgeoisie.

This was a blunder in the popularity stakes bound to be committed sooner or later by a modern finance minister. Much worse was to come, however, when, as prime minister in 1911, Caillaux succeeded in defusing the Agadir crisis, which nearly led to war with Germany over colonial rights in North Africa. The compromise settlement he and the German foreign minister worked out to save the peace infuriated nationalist war-mongers in both countries. Caillaux had to resign the premiership in January 1912.

The following year the talented Caillaux was back at the ministry of finance. Tension with Germany had continued, with the French government determined to match mounting German military preparedness by extending the period of military service from two to three years. Caillaux opposed the measure and earned the general hatred of the right; this he contrived to intensify when the measure was duly passed, by reviving his income tax proposals as the means of paying for it.

In Janary 1914 *Le Figaro* opened a new line of attack, charging the minister with having used his influence to divert public funds into his party's accounts and to quash corruption convictions. The paper made an even greater sensation when the editor, Gaston Calmette, decided to mix its political campaigning with scandalous revelations about the minister's private life. This he achieved rather unusually by publishing love letters between Madame Caillaux and Monsieur Caillaux. But the Madame Caillaux in question was his second wife, who, when the letters had been written during her husband's first marriage, had been his mistress.

Caillaux had had a complicated love life. When he met his first wife, Berthe, she was married to an artist. When the latter learnt of their affair, he promptly divorced her. In her new role, Berthe proved a brilliant political hostess with a nose for intrigue. Experience taught her that her husband might need watching; indeed, forcing his desk, one day late in 1909, she came across perfumed letters signed 'Riri' (a pet name for Henrietta), the wife of a theatre critic and mother of a teenage daughter, and a letter in her husband's hand to 'ma Riri adorée' signed 'Ton Jo'.

Confronted with the evidence, the minister found himself in a quandary. Elections were due the following year. The department of Sarthe where he was *député* was strongly Catholic and a divorce would have wrecked his prospects. With a friend as witness, he accordingly made a formal renunciation of his liaison with 'Riri'. Overcome by the gesture, Berthe burnt the letters then and there and received a gushing letter of gratitude from her husband, which, for all that, was careful to date the day of the conflagration, as if trying to certify beyond question, in the manner of officialdom, the disappearance of the documents.

'Never say never' is a favourite motto of politicians, but there is surely one absolute prohibition which all in the trade should observe: 'Never write love

The second Madame Joseph Caillaux who, in 1914, shot the editor of the Paris newspaper Le Figaro *because of his scurrilous campaign against her husband, a government minister. Caillaux (right) resigned to defend his wife and got her acquitted. His career continued into the 1940s.*

letters,' and – if you ever do make the mistake of writing them – make sure you keep them. It so happened that, before the drama of that boudoir holocaust, Berthe Caillaux had taken the precaution of photographing the evidence in case of future need. When Joseph learnt about the photographs, a messy divorce ensued and at last he was free to marry Henrietta. But the first Mrs Caillaux nursed the grudge and found in Monsieur Calmette, editor of *Le Figaro*, an enthusiastic collaborator.

If publication of the copies of the offending letters caused a sensation, its consequence caused a still greater one. Henrietta Caillaux was mortified at the appearance of these intimacies in print and still more so that her daughter should read of her mother's past in the press. On 16 March 1914, after an early, and rather unsatisfactory, lunch prepared by her cook in her apartment on the rue Alphonse-de-Neuville, she ordered out the family limousine and had herself driven to a domestic agency where she placed a request for a new cook. Next, she drove to the fashionable gunsmiths Gastinnac-Renette and bought an automatic pistol. Not being familiar with the use of such weapons, she went down to the test range in the basement and emptied the five-round chamber in the direction of the target silhouette.

Three shots found their mark. Having been shown how to load the gun by a reluctant shopman, she rehearsed the drill and the operation of the safety catch in the car while being driven to her bank, the Crédit Lyonnais, where she had some business to transact. From there she returned home to write a letter to her husband and to change into afternoon attire. That done, she betook herself to the offices of *Le Figaro* and shot Calmette. Again, she emptied the chamber of the automatic and this time found to her satisfaction that all the bullets hit the target.

The editor was rushed to hospital where he died the same day. But at least he had achieved his objective, for Caillaux did resign as minister of finance – to defend his wife on a charge of murder. He got her acquitted, the jury being persuaded that Calmette's death was caused not by the actual shooting but by botched treatment in hospital. One imagines that many a modern celebrity has pondered wistfully on the *affaire Caillaux*.

A Night on the Town

Caillaux who, on his record, should surely have sunk without trace under the weight of scandal, triumphantly turned the tables on fate. Others do not quite have the knack, it would seem. In 1994 it was revealed that, the year before, the chairman of the Swedish Confederation of Professional Employees paid a visit to a high-class Stockholm porno club, along with two girls. When the story was published, he claimed that he had at first supposed the club was an ordinary night club until, as the evening progressed, he realized that the waitresses were unusually scantily dressed – wearing in fact high heels and nothing else. Anticipating a significant intake of champagne, he wisely hired a chauffeur-driven limousine rather than risk a run-in with Sweden's draconian drink-drive laws. The bill for the evening's entertainment, limo included, came to some 5000 Kr (£425), which the chairman charged to the Confederation's credit card. This turned out to be a mistake. In the outcry that followed the disclosure, he had to resign not only from the Confederation but from his numerous other public appointments.

A Housing Scandal

For years the Gaullist-controlled council of Paris let the most choice addresses on its HLM (i.e. council housing) register to politicians and friends at greatly reduced rents, in some cases as much as 50 per cent below market value. During his term as mayor, Jacques Chirac was advised to sell off the homes, but he refused, no doubt because they were a valuable asset with which to reward party faithful. No doubt, also, because such arrangements were common in town halls of all political persuasions throughout the country.

But common practice has a habit of becoming a scandal when it becomes common knowledge. For years British MPs had, as a matter of course, been taking money from interested parties to ask parliamentary questions. It was only when a journalist, posing as a company executive, was able to produce chapter and verse in the case of two named Conservative MPs (David Tredinnick and Graham Riddick) that public opinion was alerted. The members' claims that they had been doing nothing out of the ordinary merely served to lower Parliament's reputation still further.

In 1993, the Gaullist politician Alain Juppé, then director of finances at the Hôtel de Ville (or Town Hall), authorized costly renovation work and a 15 per cent rent reduction on a prestige apartment which was then let to his son Laurent. A routine piece of what one might call internal management, it began to look rather like a blunder in June 1995. Juppé had recently been appointed prime minister in the wake of Chirac's victory in the French presidential election and details of the HLM deals began to appear in the press. For example, the satirical weekly *Le Canard Enchaîné* revealed that the Juppé family enjoyed no fewer than five top-class apartments on very favourable terms. The paper's cartoonist depicted the prime minister, his hand on his son's shoulder, commenting philosophically: 'You know, Laurent, our code has ethical subtleties ordinary people just can't appreciate.'

A companion article revealed also that in 1980 the city authorities had decided to build council accommodation in one of the smarter quarters of the capital. The local resident were dismayed. After all, the regulations governing the selection of tenants for council housing specified families of modest means, earning not more than 11,500 francs a month. Fortunately, the locals' fears were groundless. This council development turned out to comprise 22 spacious apartments, each with garage space for two cars.

It was true, as the paper observed, that the architects had failed to provide for servants' quarters, but the new tenants were, even so, hardly the type to lower the tone of an area. Mayor Chirac's office selected, for example, Gaullist party government ministers earning 40,000 francs and more, university professors, and rich political widows. All had protested that they were being charged double the rent of an ordinary council tenant – in other words just 50 per cent of the inflated rents charged by the private sector in this quarter. 'From now on,' concluded the *Canard* in businesslike tones, 'applicants for council accommodation know what they have to do: achieve top grades in the élite administration exams or join the government.'

In June 1995 the new Mayor of Paris, Jean Tiberi, whose family also benefited from the scam, proposed to sell the controversial apartments at auction. Prime Minister Juppé published a spirited defence of his actions, while the right-wing paper *Le Figaro* published the names of left-wing personalities who had benefited from France's system of 'grace and favour' residences.

A cartoon depicted the Socialist and Communist leaders Lionel Jospin and Robert Hue sitting demurely on a couch as Marianne, personification of the Republic, reads the list. 'Well, then!' she is saying. 'It seems privileged accommodation in Paris isn't the exclusive preserve of the Right.' 'It's a slander,' protest the two politicians. 'A more thorough report would reveal that the Progressives, true to their principles, always choose apartments to the left as one leaves the lift!' But by this time the Chirac-Juppé administration, buffeted also by foreign policy problems, was ending the shortest honeymoon period of any French presidential team in the history of the Fifth Republic.

As always, the principal blunder committed by Juppé was to be found out. He was, however, fortunate when the case actually did come to court, since the judge ruled that if he should be out of the apartments in question before the end of the year, no further action would be taken. The prime minister had already announced his intention of leaving the premises within the permitted deadline, so everything turned out to be in order. Within days of the judge's ruling the French were riveted by the information that the judge himself also enjoyed such privileged accommodation.

CHAPTER 2:
THE GREASY POLE

It was the opinion of Benjamin Disraeli that politics is for most of its practitioners a perpetual struggle to climb to the top of the greasy pole of public life and stay there. David Lloyd George held that success in politics was the sign of a well-disciplined conscience while Alan Clark, British Conservative minister and political diarist of the 1990s, confided the endearing image of himself and his colleagues as sharks, circling and waiting for traces of blood to appear in the water.

Today, convention requires that the talk be always of principle and that the king shark maintain the traditional stiff upper lip. It was not always so. In 18th-century Britain, when ministerial appointments depended on royal patronage and advancement on more or less open bribery, there was little attempt to maintain appearances. In a letter of March 1754, Horace Walpole, son of Britain's first prime minister and a mordant observer of the political scene, reported the arrival at court of Thomas Pelham Holles, Duke of Newcastle, on attaining prime ministerial office for the first time. The Duke was so overcome by his gratitude to King George II, that when the door of the royal apartment opened, he 'flung himself at his length at the King's feet, sobbed and cried, "God bless your Majesty! God preserve your Majesty!" and lay there howling and embracing the King's knees, with one foot so extended that my Lord Coventry, endeavouring to shut the door, caught his Grace's foot, and made him roar with pain'.

Yes, I have climbed to the top of the greasy pole.

BENJAMIN DISRAELI,
PRIME MINISTER, 1868

Bribery, Corruption, Peerage and ... Cider

Indeed, views differed on the subject of Newcastle, seven years Whig prime minister of Great Britain. No one doubted his whole-hearted pursuit of power and influence, nor his unscrupulous skills as political operator. However his, like ours, was an age when public life was based on the principle that politics was the road to financial profit for oneself and one's family, and he earned the contempt of the fashionable world by quitting the political arena £300,000 poorer than he had been when he entered it.

He was regarded as something of a buffoon. Newcastle it was who at the funeral of King George II nearly brought down the Duke of Cumberland by inadvertently standing on his train. The following year, at the coronation of the King's grandson and successor George III in Westminster Abbey, the young Queen Charlotte had been provided with 'a retiring chamber, with all conveniences prepared behind the altar. She went thither, in the *most* convenient, and what found she there but ... the Duke of Newcastle!'

Yet for all his social gaffes, Newcastle was for years arbiter of the political

I have lived long enough in the world, Sir, ... to know that the safety of a minister lies in his having the approbation of this House.

ROBERT WALPOLE,
BRITISH PRIME
MINISTER, 1739

Right: William Pitt the Elder (1708–78), English statesman, in his robes as 1st Earl of Chatham. A national hero of wars against France, 'the Great Commoner' lost much popular affection by accepting a peerage in 1766. Winston Churchill among others reckoned this a blunder and himself never moved to the House of Lords.

scene, deploying royal funds and royal influence to purchase the rotten boroughs in which to return MPs favourable to his interest and to manipulate the corrupt world of placemen which served for a government. Essential to his control of the House of Commons was his alliance with William Pitt the Elder, called the Great Commoner and probably the most admired man in England. However, a blunder by Newcastle broke the partnership.

The new king, young George III, believing that the royal power had been much diminished by his grandfather's minister, was determined to restore it as far as he could. He turned to his former tutor Lord Bute, a Scottish Tory, as his chief adviser. At first Bute had to be content with the modest title of a royal household official, the Groom of the Stole (or 'stool', interestingly enough the very position that Newcastle himself inadvertently seemed to be occupying in the Queen's convenience at the coronation!). But King George wanted him made a full Secretary of State. Keen as always to oblige the King, Newcastle agreed the appointment, but without informing Pitt.

It was a blunder. The chief minister of the Crown had certainly pleased his monarch, but he had infuriated his ally in the Commons. Pitt charged him with double-dealing, and the rift between the two was never properly closed. Bute pressed his advantage by persuading George III to deny Newcastle use of royal funds and influence in the up-coming general election. Drawing on his own immense wealth, Newcastle was able, in fact, to buy himself a majority in the new parliament – but not for long. The backdrop to all this political manoeuvring was Britain's conflict with France in what became known as the Seven Years War. The quest for peace proved to be Bute's way to power.

Pitt dominated domestic politics by his successes and popularity as war leader. Indeed, some at Westminster considered that he was willing to protract Britain's involvement in the war to maintain his ascendancy. In the autumn of 1761, he advocated declaring war on Spain and continuing Britain's subsidy to Prussia. Bute opposed him on both points and Newcastle made no effective move in support of Pitt. On 5 October Pitt resigned. With Pitt removed from the scene, Newcastle discovered, too late, how important his great ally in the Commons had been and realized that he had played into Bute's hands; six months later he, too, had to resign. His appointments for years past were cancelled and his nominees expelled from their sinecures.

Thanks to Newcastle's blundering treachery, he and Pitt were never fully reconciled. Newcastle, now in his seventies, was finished as a political force and, while Pitt was to continue active in Westminster for another decade and for two years head his own administration, he lost his heroic charisma to become just another politician.

Regarded by the court as an over-mighty and overbearing servant, William Pitt the Elder had for years towered over the English domestic scene and awed his continental contemporaries. 'One has to admit,' wrote Frederick the Great of Prussia, 'that if England has been long in labour and if she has suffered much to produce Mr Pitt, she has at last been delivered of a man.'

In English popular opinion he was hero-worshipped not only as England's champion against France but as a commoner of independence

Our supreme governors, the mob.

HORACE WALPOLE, 1743

BRIBERY, CORRUPTION, PEERAGE AND ... CIDER

> Sir Robert Walpole, prime minister (1721–42), who claimed to know the price of every man in the House of Commons except three, observed that
>
> *It was fortunate so few men could be prime ministers, as it was best that few should thoroughly know the shocking wickedness of mankind.*
>
> WALPOLIANA, HORACE WALPOLE.

and dignity in a corrupt world of courtly politics, peopled by scheming aristocrats like Newcastle and by sycophants looking for promotion to aristocratic status. He alone, 'the Great Commoner', was the one politician who could not be bought ... Or so it was believed, until he left office and accepted a pension for life of £3000 a year and the barony of Chatham in her own right for his nobly born wife.

Popular reaction was bitter and hostile. The Londoners immediately dubbed the new baroness 'Lady Cheat'em'. All politicians, it seemed, were dirt. Even a cynical courtier like Horace Walpole, son of the founding father of English corruption politics, was startled. 'Am I not an old fool,' he wrote, 'at my years [he was 46] to be a dupe to virtue and patriotism? I who have seen all the virtue of England sold six times over ... I adored Mr Pitt ... in fact this immaculate man has accepted the barony of Chatham for his wife with a pension of three thousand pounds a year. What! to ... blast one's character, for the comfort of a paltry annuity, and a long-necked peeress ... !' Five years later Pitt completed his betrayal of his popular image, entering the House of Lords as Earl of Chatham.

At a time when the vote was confined to a scattering of property owners and householders, public opinion was not the force it was to become when Britain achieved something approaching popular democracy in the later 19th century. Moreover, if any politician deserved the rewards of office, it was surely William Pitt who did not for a moment consider his earldom or his pension to be political blunders. Even so, the mass of his countrymen felt they had lost a hero and some 200 years later, when that other great war leader, Winston Churchill, finally left office, his decision to remain a commoner was greatly influenced by the 18th-century public's reaction to Pitt's elevation to the peerage.

As for Lord Bute, he was popular with the King, but he never was so with the country, being accused of taking French bribes for negotiations leading to the Peace of Paris in 1763. Administratively incompetent and a poor judge of other men's abilities, he compounded his problems by appointing as Chancellor of the Exchequer Sir Francis Dashwood, better known as a debauchee and founder of the 'Hell Fire Club'. Dashwood's own comments show that he was as bemused by this astounding appointment as was the rest of London's social and political world. The country at large received a more unpleasant surprise when the wine-bibbing chancellor imposed a cider tax. Bitterly opposed, it increased the Bute administration's unpopularity and in 1763, after just one year as the King's chief minister, he had to resign.

An Ambitious Deputy

Labour's landslide victory of 1945 brought scores of new members into the House of Commons on what, up till that point, had been the Opposition benches. Clement Attlee, leader of the comparatively small parliamentary party for the past six years was now, it could be argued, without a truly democratic mandate from the majority of socialist MPs. At least this seems to have been the way in which Herbert Morrison, second in the party's rankings, saw the situation. He and Ernest Bevin were with Attlee in his room in the House of Commons when the phone call came from Buckingham Palace, requiring the party leader to attend the King so that he might be inaugurated as prime minister. Morrison urged Attlee to ask for a postponement on the grounds that his leadership should be confirmed by a renewed vote of the parliamentary Labour Party, much enlarged by the election landslide. King George VI may have thought he knew who the leader of the new majority party was, but the party's second in command obviously had other ideas or at least ambitions.

Attlee seemed to be considering the suggestion when Morrison was called away to take a private phone call. As soon as he had left the room, Bevin said: 'Clem, go to the palace straight away.' Attlee did so, but nothing was said to Morrison who only learnt that his attempted putsch for the leadership had failed when he read the evening papers.

Unassertive and supposedly ineffectual, Clem Attlee was often underestimated. Given the general astonishment in Labour as well as Conservative ranks at the electorate's ousting of Churchill and his party within weeks of victory in World War II, it is perhaps just possible that, had Morrison pressed his case, Attlee might have agreed to a leadership vote. That slight chance evaporated the moment he left the room. It is a measure of the strength of Attlee's position that he allowed Morrison to stay on as his deputy for the next five years. The fact was, though he himself never seems to have grasped it, that Morrison was simply disliked by most people who came to know him.

Dirty Tricks – Watergate

It sometimes seems that so long as one is not found out, nothing is barred in the struggle to climb the greasy pole. Early one June morning in 1972, police arrested five men inside the Democratic Party's national headquarters in the Watergate, a complex of offices, hotels, and apartments in Washington, DC. Their capture was hardly surprising, given the blundering manner in which they went about their business. For these men were not professional burglars, and others, much higher than they, had blundered far more seriously. The Five and two others found to be implicated were in fact on the staff of President Nixon's campaign organization, the incredibly named CREEP – Committee for the Re-election of the President. In January 1973 the seven were found guilty of conspiracy, burglary, and electronic eavesdropping. Two months later James McCord, one of the convicted burglars, wrote a letter to Federal Judge John J. Sirica, who had sat during the trial, alleging there had been an attempted cover-up of the burglary by persons 'at the highest level' of the executive. President Nixon solemnly declared that he had possessed no knowledge of any such attempts at cover-up.

But then things began to go wrong. Reporters Bob Woodward and Carl Bernstein of the *Washington Post* led a classic campaign of investigative journalism which was to expose much more than a cover-up. In May 1973 the Senate set up a Select Committee into Presidential Campaign Activities

My opinion is, that power should always be distrusted, in whatever hands it is placed.

SIR WILLIAM JONES, 1782

under Democratic Senator Sam J. Ervin Jr. of North Carolina. The televised hearings gripped the nation. Chief among the witnesses was former presidential adviser John Dean III, who testified that former Attorney-General John N. Mitchell had authorized the burglary with the connivance of White House Chief of Staff H. R. Haldeman and adviser John Erlichman, and that the President himself had approved the subsequent cover-up operation.

Concurrently with the hearings of the Senate Select Committee, law professor Archibald Cox was presiding as special prosecutor at another investigation. This would place Watergate in the context of a network of political corruption within which wiretaps and bulging suitcases of cash off-loaded directly into CREEP's wall-safes came to seem as almost engaging gaucheries. After all, illegal fund contributions which by-passed tedious accounting procedures were hardly a novelty in American electioneering. Nor, as it would later emerge, was the somewhat startling revelation made to Senator Ervin's Committee. This was that for some two years, and by Presidential order, the White House had been routinely and clandestinely bugged.

This turned out to have been not only devious but also a serious blunder. Special Prosecutor Cox immediately demanded all such records bearing on the Watergate affair. In October 1973 President Nixon returned a formal refusal and followed this up by ordering Cox's dismissal. The incumbent Attorney-General resigned in protest and now the House of Representatives took the first step towards impeachment proceedings. With a nation in uproar, Nixon appointed as the new Special Prosecutor Texan lawyer Leon

Members of the Judiciary Committee Impeachment panel in Washington, DC, which in July 1974 decided to recommend the impeachment of President Richard Nixon.

Jaworski and, reluctantly, had the tapes made available to Judge Sirica. All, that is, except two which it was claimed had never existed, and 18 minutes of recording erased from a third.

By April 1974, fighting for his political life, Nixon submitted to the House Judiciary Committee typewritten transcripts, wiped clean of the foul-mouthed vernacular that seems to have been his standard private idiom and of much else beside. In June the Supreme Court ordered the handing over of the tapes relating to the cover-up which by now most people assumed had been put in place with White House connivance. In July the House Judiciary Committee adopted three articles of impeachment against President Richard Milhous Nixon. On 5 August Nixon admitted knowledge of the attempted Watergate cover-up and personal involvement in hampering inquiries into the burglary by the FBI. Recommendation by the House that he be tried and his subsequent conviction by the Senate now seemed certainties.

On 9 August 1974 Nixon resigned, the first president to do so. Succeeded by Vice-President Gerald Ford, he quickly received a pardon for any crime which he might have committed while occupying the presidential office. It was issued without any form of inquiry or any admission of guilt by Nixon. (A blunder on Ford's part, it would seem, for many held it against him when he sought election as president 18 months later.) In January 1975 Haldeman, Erlichman and Mitchell were duly convicted of involvement in Watergate. Their boss, who had headed the criminal conspiracy against constitutional government, went free. Conventional wisdom avers that the shame involved in such fall from high office is itself a severe penalty. For those able to feel shame, this may well be true. But for men whose vocabularies do not recognize the word, such a sanction is empty. To the end it seems that Nixon felt guilty only of breach of the Eleventh Commandment – 'Thou shalt not be found out'.

Whenever any mother or father talks to his child, I hope he can look at the man in the White House and, whatever he may think of his politics, he will say: 'Well, there is a man who maintains the kind of standards personally that I would want my child to follow.'

RICHARD MILHOUS NIXON IN TV PRESIDENTIAL DEBATE WITH JOHN F. KENNEDY IN 1960

Just Rewards for Treachery – Monkeys, Snakes and Others

In a career notorious for what the French media dubbed *les zigs zags*, President Jacques Chirac has swerved from classic conservative attitudes to something approximating to socialist-style social reform, from extreme xenophobia to Euro-enthusiasm. Asked by a puzzled interviewer during the 1995 presidential campaign whether he was not, after all, a left-winger, the founder of the new Gaullist party jovially replied, 'Am I left wing? Of course, I eat sauerkraut and drink beer.'

Yet, before the European elections of 1979, in language to delight a rabid national-fronter, he had dismissed Europe as 'an empire of traders' that wanted France as a vassal state and the pro-European Socialists as 'the foreigners' party' who wanted 'the abasement of France'. He had in fact misread the French public mood of the time and the Gaullists were defeated at the polls. Such outspoken blunders were not to be repeated. He supported the Maastricht Treaty in France's 1992 referendum on the Treaty in statesmanlike, rather than demagogic, terms and in his presidential campaign speeches balanced his appeals to the pro- and anti-Europe wings of the divided Gaullist party in masterly fashion.

He had reason to be circumspect. It was his third try at the presidency. Defeat by François Mitterrand in the 1988 campaign had been a devastating blow. France was already tiring of socialism and Mitterrand was held to have abandoned his principles and to have broken his promises as a socialist and he was, moreover, 72 against Chirac's 55. The latter should have won easily but was, just as easily, outmanoeuvred by his wily opponent. Chirac's campaign displayed some mistakes of presentation. Against the regal style of Mitterrand, Chirac *'le bulldozer'* seemed less like the traditional lugubrious French statesman, more like a bustling busybody. Dynamism was out of style in a line which numbered De Gaulle, Pompidou, Giscard d'Estaing and Mitterrand himself.

But Jacques Chirac *was* dynamic. At that time, his wife Bernadette recalled, 'I always had the impression I was attending the launch of an Ariane space rocket.' Helicopter rotors idled, noisily impatient for take-off, doors slammed as official cars accelerated away from one meeting to be sure the candidate kept to his schedule for the next. Here was a man on the move, but dignity was the prime quality to be expected of a president of France. For the 1995 election his daughter and campaign manager, Claude, ordered chauffeurs to maintain a sedate pace even if her father was running a little late. This, and the carefully studied body language of slow expansive arm gestures, lent *gravitas* to his manner.

In an age when even in France television is central to politics, Chirac had the misfortune not to elicit immediate viewer enthusiasm. There is a depth of kindliness in the eyes which is somehow belied by the wooden body language. One aide commented during the 1995 election, 'If our man could shake every French voter by the hand, he would take 98 per cent of the vote.' But his wife woundingly observed: 'At heart, perhaps, the French don't much like my husband.' More seriously, he could not rely on the loyalty of even his closest advisers.

Among these Nicolas Sarkozy de Naga Bocsa, of Hungarian noble extraction, was one of the brightest. Hungarians say that they are the only people who can enter a revolving door behind you and come out ahead. If it is the exception that proves the rule, Sarkozy has tested this one to destruction. In 1983, aged just 28, he made a brilliant launch to his political career when he was elected mayor of the *très snob* Paris suburb of Neuilly. French mayors still wield considerable power in local affairs and the *mairies* of Paris and its smarter *banlieues* are valuable bridgeheads to power in national politics. Friendship with Claude Chirac won him entry to the Chirac circle and *'le wonderboy'*, as the French media called him, was virtually adopted as the son the presidential candidate never had. At his suggestion, a team of whizz-kids and spin doctors were recruited as the *'antenne présidentielle'* for the coming campaign. Old stagers objected to this 'band of *zozos*'. Their suspicions were to be justified in at least one instance.

Following the election triumph of France's right-wing parties in 1993, President François Mitterrand appointed the Gaullist Edouard Balladur to be prime minister. Chirac had no objections as he and Balladur had already agreed that the latter should accept the premiership and leave the former unopposed as the right's candidate for the 1995 presidential elections. On the same basis of understanding Chirac also made no objection when his protégé Sarkozy accepted the post of budget minister under Balladur. He assumed he could trust in both his and the prime minister's support when the presidential elections came along in due course.

In fact many Chirac aides considered this presidential electoral pact a grotesque miscalculation. They warned that Balladur would use his position to plot a bid for the presidency. Chirac replied that he and the PM had a gentleman's agreement – an irony as things turned out since, whereas Chirac was not 'of family', Balladur certainly had pretensions in that respect. For his part, Sarkozy found himself in an increasingly ambiguous position. One of his jobs would be to field questions as to whether or when the prime minister was indeed going to announce his candidacy for the presidency. Balladur had certainly impressed with his early performance as prime minister and seemed increasingly likely to succeed if he should stand for the presidency. By the winter of 1993 the Chirac camp were convinced that the brilliant 'Sarko' had defected. They were right and he had blundered.

Many other Chirac 'loyalists' were to follow suit and Chirac later claimed that his increasing political isolation during 1994 'led me to dominate my temperament'. But almost from the moment he actually came out into the open as a candidate running for the highest office, Balladur's ratings began to falter (for reasons discussed on page 80).

When the first-round polls closed on the evening of 23 April, St George's Day, it was found that just one in five of the voters had chosen Chirac, the lowest first-round score of any French president. Much was made of this but, on the other hand, Balladur was out altogether. In the second round, two weeks later, Chirac was returned with some 52 per cent of the vote.

Many political pundits were wrong-footed by these results. Amateurs of Vietnamese astrology, on the other hand, had no cause to be surprised: 1995 was the year of the pig, famously a fortunate conjunction for those born – like Chirac – in the year of the monkey. However, the pig is notoriously unfriendly to those born in the year of the snake which is, rather astonishingly perhaps, the year sign of Edouard Balladur. As to Sarkozy, though confident that one day he would be back, he was obliged for the time being to content himself with such trappings of office as the elegant *mairie* of Neuilly had to offer.

The last Gombeen Man

He rose from the less than glamorous ranks of provincial Irish dance-hall management to establish a highly successful family business and ascend to the office of Taoiseach, or prime minister, but in 1994 crashed a brilliant and important political career with a sequence of blunders never satisfactorily accounted for. For, while Albert Reynolds had achieved power as head of Ireland's Fianna Fáil, traditionally the party of government, he had had to agree to coalition with the Labour Party, led by Dick Spring. Trusting cooperation, it would appear, was not one of his strong suits, but his devious attempts to manipulate his coalition partner now seem as unnecessary as they were unsuccessful.

Maybe Reynolds owed his success to the fact that he embodied a classic figure of Irish folk culture, the gombeen man, the local fixer with a finger in every pie. No doubt he owed his fall to the fact that he deployed its basic tool, the cunning untruth, once too often. The cynic might argue that this is merely the tool of politicians everywhere, that anyone who reaches the top of Disraeli's greasy pole must be a gombeen man, whatever the local term may be. But the golden rule of politics, not to be found out, always applies and this rule Reynolds was to break.

The origins of the crisis, which was to bring about his downfall, lay in November 1994 with the Taoiseach's decision to appoint Judge Harry Whelehan, former Attorney-General, as President of the High Court. This was the first blunder, for the Labour Party were vigorously opposed to the appointment. For nearly two years the coalition government – its 36-seat majority in a Dáil of 166 the largest in Ireland's history – had enjoyed some success, notably in its dealings with the Northern Ireland question where Reynolds in particular had contributed importantly to developments which had culminated in the IRA cease-fire of September 1994. Now it seemed the Taoiseach had snubbed his coalition partners.

Labour's reaction to the Whelehan candidature was not just a question of hurt pride. They considered him too conservative on social questions; he had recently won Europe-wide notoriety by refusing permission for Miss X, a 14-year-old rape victim of her best friend's father, to leave the country for an abortion in Britain. Eventually, however, in the interests of the coalition, Spring was prepared to agree the appointment, on condition that Labour have an effective veto as to when it should take effect.

The deal was barely struck before it was under threat from a new scandal, this one involving a Catholic priest, Father Brendan Smyth. Charged with paedophile offences in Northern Ireland, he had eventually given himself up to the authorities there, had been tried and was at this time serving a prison sentence. The case came at a time when the Catholic Church in Ireland was troubled by many sex scandals, and public opinion south as well as north of the border had been dismayed by what seemed an epidemic of revelations. Smyth, for example, had admitted to offences over a period of 30 years, during which time his ecclesiastical superiors had done nothing to discipline him.

It was, it soon transpired, a scandal to rock Church and State. For it now emerged that before the priest had surrendered himself, the North's Royal Ulster Constabulary had issued nine extradition warrants over a period of seven months, none of which had produced action from Dublin's Attorney-General. Why had he been so dilatory? Dick Spring demanded explanations. In due course, Whelehan explained that the extradition requests had posed complex legal questions without precedent. Meanwhile, ignoring Labour's dissatisfaction with the state of affairs, Prime Minister Reynolds formally laid the Whelehan nomination as President of the High Court before cabinet on Friday 11 November.

Incensed, Spring led his colleagues from the room in a walk-out protest. He assumed that the Prime Minister, realizing that he had gone too far, would drop his proposal. Later Reynolds was to claim that he thought Labour were merely making a political gesture and would return to the cabinet table once the Whelehan issue was out of the way. In fact, he may well have believed this; after all, such negotiating gestures were part and parcel of a gombeen man's *modus operandi*. In any case, Reynolds pressed ahead, and thereby compounded his initial blunder with a catastrophic miscalculation. The farce of failed communications rapidly blossomed into an exotic political disaster.

Continuing with their agenda, the Fianna Fáil cabinet members duly confirmed the appointment of High Court President Whelehan and went on to nominate Eoghan Fitzsimons to the now vacant post of Attorney-General. Conscious of a good day's work well done, all now adjourned for a cup of tea. The rattle of cups was interrupted by a message from President Mary Robinson to the effect that if the new officers of state were to be formally inaugurated into their appointments this side of the weekend, they had best come up to Phoenix Park, the presidential residence, forthwith. This they and the Prime Minister accordingly did, lamenting only that they would not have time to don the top hat and tails customary for such formalities. The situation was a good deal more serious than they realized.

Hardly had the ministers set out for the Park than a call came through to the Taoiseach's office from Dick Spring. Being informed of what was in train, he of course assumed that the majority party in the coalition were determined to present Labour with a *fait accompli*. Crisis point had been reached.

Over the next five days Dublin's political world was in turmoil. On Tuesday Reynolds persisted in his support of the Whelehan candidacy for the High Court in a speech in the Dáil. The session had ended in uproar but that evening, as he worked to cobble together a survival formula, Reynolds began to believe it might be possible. The basis for the new deal was new information from Fitzsimons, the new Attorney-General, discovered while conscientiously reading himself into his new duties: Whelehan's explanation of the delay in the Smyth extradition case was untrue. Far from the case being unprecedented, it was virtually identical to another case that Whelehan himself had processed in 1992. Faced with this, Reynolds admitted to his Labour colleague that he had been wrong. Whelehan would have to go. As the English historian Macaulay said of Lord Burghley, chief minister of Elizabeth I of England, it would seem that the Taoiseach 'never deserted his friends until it was very inconvenient to stand by them'. Now he proposed that he, along with the Fianna Fáil chief whip and justice minister, would make speeches of grovelling apology to the Dáil and that he, Reynolds, would repeat his admission of error and Spring's soundness of judgement on the floor of the House. Working into the small hours of Wednesday, he and his advisers finalized a document which was presented to Spring at 10.00 a.m. that morning. At 10.22, Spring reluctantly put his name to a new coalition agreement but insisted that it would only become operable after he had heard and approved the three speeches.

Barely ten minutes later the Dáil resumed in stormy session. Almost at once, Reynolds asked for an adjournment on the grounds that party managers needed time to agree the day's business. In fact, the speeches which were to woo Spring's agreement had yet to be written. After some wrangling, the House adjourned. Spring, 'itching' uneasily that 'there was something that just didn't seem right', returned to his office and, shortly after 11.00 a.m., put a call through to Fitzsimons, asking for further clarification on the new development which he himself had heard about on Tuesday evening. Specifically, he wanted to know when the Taoiseach had been informed. 'Monday,' came the uneasy reply.

This bombed the just-signed new deal out of the water. Reynolds had known the reality behind the Smyth case when he made his Tuesday endorsement of Whelehan's candidacy for the High Court. The entire new deal with Spring and his colleagues was, in the words of one of them, 'based on a lie'. When the Dáil resumed its session that afternoon, Reynolds went through with his planned volte-face. He was greeted by gasps of astonishment. He was followed by Spring who made a merciless denunciation of the Prime Minister's manoeuvrings and concluded with the announcement that he and his colleagues would resign their cabinet posts and vote against the government. He sat down to applause from the Opposition benches. The coalition fell and with it a man who had embodied the less admirable features of what some hoped were old-style Irish politics. The gombeen man had gone that final fib too far ... and been found out.

A Gambler at Number 10

On 22 June 1995 at an apparently routine press conference in the rose garden at Number 10 Downing Street, John Major, Britain's Conservative prime minister, attacked for years by anti-European Tories, announced his resignation as party leader. He was, he said, tired of the sniping criticism of himself and could not allow it to continue to weaken the government and party any longer. He called a leadership election, nominations to be in by 29 June, the vote to be on 4 July.

For a man generally derided as weak and indecisive, it was a bold coup. The party's constitution allows for an annual leadership election by sitting Conservative MPs each November, provided that candidates have the backing of a specified number of parliamentary colleagues. But now Major's opponents found themselves facing the life-and-death decision far sooner than they had expected, and the time available for their manoeuvres drastically curtailed. For it was unlikely that any victor would permit another leadership challenge in November. They were taken off guard and unnerved. Norman Lamont, vengeful ex-chancellor sacked by Major, went pale at the news. A pro-Major cabinet minister, by contrast, was reported to be jubilant: 'Anyone able to do joined-up writing will back the Prime Minister.'

But there were risks for Major who may have made an initial miscalculation himself. He apparently thought he would be re-elected unopposed and at first it seemed a reasonable assumption. All his cabinet colleagues bar one

It is folly of too many to mistake the echo of a London coffee-house for the voice of the kingdom.

JONATHAN SWIFT, 1711

pledged their support, as did Baroness Thatcher herself; on 23 June Foreign Secretary Douglas Hurd, the *bête noire* of the Euro-sceptics, announced his intention to retire from office once the leadership was decided, as if to remove one reason for Major's opponents to vote against him.

But there was soon talk of opposition if only a stalking-horse. Minor ministers and obscure back-benchers talked solemnly of being prepared to stand if called upon to do so. If Major had been hoping that any nomination would fail for want of sufficient backers, he miscalculated. Whereas in 1990 some 30 MPs had had to declare themselves openly for the challenger against Margaret Thatcher, the leader in place, the situation in 1995 was quite different. Thanks to Major's resignation, the position of leader was vacant and any would-be contestant needed only a nomination and a seconder to put his or her name forward. One right-wing opponent of the Prime Minister summed it up: 'Major is mad. We did not get the signatures to mount a challenge last year. We would not have got the 33 signatures this year either. Most back-benchers are cowards and Major has made it easy for them. We need just two signatures. There are no hard-core Majorites the way there were Thatcherites.' However, as the results of the election would show, this was the first of many miscalculations by the anti-Major camp.

For more than three years, John Major's premiership had been weakened by almost unrelenting attacks from within the ranks of the Conservative Party and the Tory press. The ringleaders were Lady Thatcher, bilious with anger at her overthrow as Party leader by Major himself; Norman Lamont and Norman Tebbit, like the other two fiercely anti-European. The Tory press was taken aback by the rose garden announcement, for it had been looking forward to months more of speculation, tittle-tattle and conspiracy as right-wing and left-wing challengers readied themselves for a contest which should replace Major with a leader to take the Tories into the next general election, due by June 1997.

Principal contenders were Michael Heseltine and Kenneth Clarke on the left and Euro-sceptics like Michael Portillo and – according to some – Norman Lamont on the right. The question at issue was who would be least likely to lead the party to anticipated electoral disaster at the hands of the 'new' Labour Party under its glamorous young leader, Tony Blair. It was widely believed that the Tories would require a leader of far greater charisma than John Major if they were to have any hope of surviving, let alone winning.

Over the next ten days the country was regaled with a cabaret of political gaffes and miscalculations and unbelievable voting commitments for the forthcoming secret ballot. 'How do you tell when a Tory MP is lying?' quipped one newspaper. Answer: 'When he moves his lips.' The debate was conducted in terms of issues such as British policy towards Europe, the level of public expenditure and the need to cut taxes so as to win votes and yet maintain a low inflation rate. However, the real issue for the nervously calculating electorate of Tory MPs, according to themselves the most sophisticated in the world, was whether or not they would be able to hold on to their seats at the next election.

By Saturday 24 June Lamont had become the frontrunner in speculation as to the possibility of a 'heavyweight' challenge, while the position of John Redwood, Secretary of State for Wales and the one cabinet member who had failed to pledge loyalty, was attracting increasing interest. He announced that he would declare his position the following Monday. There was talk that if Redwood did challenge, other cabinet members might resign to join the contest. Press commentators reckoned that Major's gamble was looking riskier by the hour. They foresaw a wave of abstentions in the first round so that the contest would have to go to a second round in which Major would withdraw and the leadership be fought over by senior cabinet colleagues.

When Monday came Redwood, surrounded by a group of oddball right-wingers whom his own campaign manager would unflatteringly describe as 'nutters', duly announced his resignation from the cabinet and his candidacy for the leadership. That morning Major had left London to attend a European summit at Cannes and inevitably comparisons were made with Margaret Thatcher's absence in Paris at the time of the leadership vote which ousted her (see p. 124). But this time there was still a week's campaigning to run. Many suspected that Redwood would be used as a stalking-horse to force a second round, while some theorized that he had collaborated in such a scenario from the outset – a 'Super Stalking-horse'(!). No-one expected an outright Redwood victory.

Equally few expected a convincing win for John Major either. Right-wing MPs claimed that his campaign had peaked and was now on a downhill slope. Lord McAlpine, a former Tory Party Chairman, described his resignation as 'one more slick trick without honour'. Tactical voting would be the order of the day. This seemed to explain Margaret Thatcher's baffling expression of support for Major at the outset. After years of leading the wreckers against Major, her endorsement only made sense as a tactical manoeuvre to block Michael Heseltine. As such it was gross miscalculation on her part.

The basic misunderstanding on the right was as to the nature of John Major himself as an ineffectual, fumbling Mr Nice Guy punching above his weight. But Major, whose tenure had already outlasted that of five 20th-century premiers, had all the selfish tenacity required of a top politician. He had been a competitor since childhood. Once, when asked when the iron entered his soul, he replied briskly, 'At the age of seven.' The rules for the Tory leadership were complicated but devised in such a way as to ensure that any candidate who won according to the formula would be undoubtedly the winner. In the 1990 election Margaret Thatcher stood down, having failed by four votes on the first round to meet the criteria. No one doubted that had she fulfilled the electoral requirements by even the slimmest of margins, she would have remained in office. But it was the general assumption in July 1995 that John Major would retire, even if he won according to the rules, if the margin was not considered sufficient.

While others blundered, Michael Heseltine, whose initial challenge in 1990 had precipitated the fall of Margaret Thatcher and who was of all men the one most hated by the right and Thatcher herself, coolly weighed the chances of his winning an all-out leadership struggle against the divisive effects of such a struggle on the party's morale. 'He was not sure that there would be a party to lead,' a friend commented later. He decided to cut his losses, to back Major and urge his own supporters to do the same, thus guaranteeing a Major victory so far as possible and to bargain the best deal for himself in the reshuffled cabinet.

On the morning of 4 July, the day of the vote, the right-wing *Daily Mail* carried the headline 'Time to Ditch the Captain'; that afternoon, in Committee Room 12, Heseltine marked his cross against the Prime Minister's name and showed the open paper to the scrutineers before folding it and placing it in the ballot box. Between 3.30 and 5.00 p.m. that afternoon more than 20 known Heseltine supporters cast their votes with similar openness.

The vote was decisively in Major's favour: Major 218, Redwood 89, spoiled papers 20, abstentions 2. The Redwood camp received the result in stunned silence. Their candidate's total would have been adequate had he really been a stalking-horse. The contender himself was dismayed. 'I thought I was going to win ... They have spent the last two years pleading for a lead and policies based on principle. When it's offered them they don't vote for it.' He was convinced that another ten votes for him would have forced John Major to resign.

A basic miscalculation made by the Redwood team was as to the solidarity of the right-wing vote. Where the centre-left vote held firm, the right split several ways. Some voted for Major because they feared a Heseltine win on a second ballot, or because of pressure from their constituencies, or because they were Portillo supporters and so feared that a Redwood victory would terminate all hopes of their candidate for the leadership.

Journalists in the rose garden of Number 10 Downing Street at a news conference on 22 June 1995 at which Prime Minister John Major, back to camera, announced his resignation as leader of the Conservative Party and his intention to fight a leadership election. The snap decision provoked blunders among his numerous rivals. Major won the contest.

The final miscalculation on the right was to suppose that Major would be magnanimous in victory. In fact the post-election reshuffle established the control of the centre-left in cabinet and marginalized the right wing. Kenneth Clarke remained as Chancellor of the Exchequer, while Michael Heseltine was installed as a powerful deputy prime minister at Number 10 Downing Street, in a palatial office and with direct access to the PM. One right-wing minister who had followed instructions on voting tactics muttered unattributably to a journalist: 'We were told to vote for Major to keep out Heseltine, so we did. Now Heseltine is chief executive of UK plc.' Other appointments followed the pattern with the right-wingers being confined to departments with little influence on the vital European debate. Michael Portillo, for example, was made Secretary of State for Defence. 'Major has put him in a box and nailed down the lid,' commented one unnamed source. During the run-up to the ballot most observers expected the Prime Minister to retain Redwood in cabinet, should his challenge fail. In fact he was returned to the back-benches.

On the Tory right it was clear that someone had blundered, but who? The right was split. Was it John Redwood who had precipitated the split by deciding to stand or was it Michael Portillo for refusing to do so? Right-wingers like Portillo, Peter Lilley or Michael Forsyth who had held back were held to be tarnished by having been seen to put their careers before their convictions. 'We have been stitched up,' snarled one Redwood supporter at Portillo supporters who cast tactical votes in favour of Major. Another Redwood adviser consoled himself with the thought that his man would inherit the leadership of the party when it was 'finally rid of Major after the next election'.

Reflecting on Neville Chamberlain's blunders in his assessment of public and party attitudes in the summer of 1939, his contemporary, the Tory politician Alfred Duff Cooper identified three blunders which prompt parallels with the situation Redwood found himself in. First Chamberlain believed that public opinion was what *The Times* told him it was; secondly, he believed that Conservative opinion was what the Chief Whip said it was; thirdly, and as a result he came to make the fatal error of relying on the right-wing of the party, believing that they represented the party. Quoting Shakespeare, Cooper had titled his memoirs *Old Men Forget*. Not only old men, it would seem...

CHAPTER 3:
BLUNDERS OF PRINCIPLE

This chapter is by way of being a surprise as much to the author as it may be to the reader. According to the polls, public opinion rates politicians in single-figure percentage points barely ahead of journalists. According to Charlie Chaplin, his profession of clown counted for more than that of the politician, and according to many politicians of the more cynical variety principles come a bad second to manipulating opinion. Yet this view is surely mistaken. Electors may be hypocrites – expecting for example tax cuts but complaining of bribery when offered them – but they cannot be duped all the time. Once they have identified a public figure as devious, he or she is lost.

Hillary Clinton, America's glamorous first lady, once famously said, 'If I want to knock a story off the front page, I just change my hairstyle.' But she had not always been glamorous. When Bill Clinton first won the governorship of Arkansas in 1978, she was very obviously Hillary the feminist with her heavy rimmed glasses, hairdo's-from-hell and frumpy dress sense. A woman of formidable intellect, she was in the view of some too clever by half.

Her husband's failure at the polls at the next gubernatorial election led not only to a change in hair style but also a less abrasive, sweeter-looking lady. During the 1992 presidential campaign she had to trim her sails once more to the winds of public opinion when she raised a storm by criticizing political wives content to stay at home and 'bake cookies'. The career feminist *persona* being definitely *non grata* with the mass of the electorate, Hillary softened her presentation. With the presidential race astonishingly won, she emerged very definitely as a working first lady, a one-woman think-tank and a force to be reckoned with, who chaired policy discussions and dictated personnel and staff appointments.

Admiring his wife's talents and believing in the principle of women's value in government, President Clinton gave Hillary the prestigious health portfolio, the flagship policy of their presidential campaign. Her triumph seemed assured. However, two years later, her reforms having been demolished on the floor of the House of Representatives, her failure was perceived with equal clarity. From being his boasted 'twofer' she became her husband's greatest liability, her appointment his greatest blunder. Accompanying him on his triumphant trip to Ireland in November 1995 she was content to appear once more as the first lady and even described herself as a household feminist – with the rather startling result that she was considered 'conservative' by Irish feminists whose country, while it boasted a woman president, had at the time yet to legalize abortion or divorce.

It is of course difficult for democratic politicians to hold to principles – usually it is dangerous. In a democracy political parties are coalitions and can

Why, Sir, most schemes of political improvement are very laughable things.

SAMUEL JOHNSON, 1769

only hope to win power by appealing to the widest range of views possible in the band of the spectrum where they lie. By definition extremists are not in the majority so the art of political leadership is to hold the middle ground while persuading the fringes that one understands, even sympathizes with their point of view. Harold Wilson, Britain's four-times Labour prime minister, was a classic practitioner, with the ability 'to convince the left that he was on their side when they knew that he would not follow their policies'.

The Principle of Religious Cleansing

The most notorious achievement of King Louis XIV of France poses in particularly acute form the question: What is a blunder? There are acts of political will or statecraft which achieve exactly what the framer intended. If that intention itself was misguided, is the act itself to be considered a blunder or the perpetrator to be considered a blunderer for getting his or her priorities wrong?

When on 18 October 1685 Louis promulgated the Edict of Fontainebleau, he had a quite specific purpose in mind – the abolition of the Protestant presence in France – and he achieved it. Fontainebleau reversed the Edict of Nantes, promulgated by King Henry IV in 1598, which had allowed freedom of religion to all the French and also granted the Protestants, known as Huguenots, protected status amounting to a state within a state.

Henry, the best-loved of all France's kings and originally a Protestant, had won the plaudits of French Catholics when he converted, to assure a peaceful succession to the crown 'Paris', he famously remarked, 'is worth a mass.' So long as the king confessed the Catholic faith, the hierarchy could live with such jovial cynicism. When he translated it into tolerance of his former co-religionists, plaudits turned to complaints. When he was assassinated in 1614, the future for French Protestantism darkened.

The persecution of the Huguenots reached its climax with the revocation of the Edict. For pious Catholics it was, in the words of Bishop Bossuet, 'the miracle of our times ... by which heresy no longer exists. God alone could accomplish this marvel.' Few government acts have been so successful. Apart from the prolonged revolt of fugitive Huguenots, known as the *Camisards*, in the wild country between Gard and Lozère in the south – terrible and cruel for the region involved but isolated from the rest of France – the Protestant presence in France was suppressed for a century.

If we judge the Edict of Fontainebleau by its intended results it must be viewed as one of the most successful acts of any French government. It had other consequences, however, which were only a little short of disastrous. According to the duc de Saint Simon who observed the effects, it 'depopulated a quarter of the kingdom, ruined its commerce, and weakened it in all its part'. Charles Sorel Sieur de Souvigny reckoned that by this one act, Louis had lost more than he could have gained by the most successful war or than could have been extorted by enemies as the price of the most disastrous peace.

It has been estimated that in spite of efforts to close the frontiers to those flying from persecution, possibly as many as 800,000 Huguenots escaped abroad – 200,000 of these in the months immediately following Fontainebleau. The Protestants of France were generally far better educated than the Catholics, every household possessed a vernacular bible in daily use which strengthened not only piety but literacy. Protestantism was strongest among the artisan classes and among the merchants and manufacturing classes; it numbered also some of the most talented of the military. On the military front, indeed, it could be said that Louis XIV's legislation contributed to a major set-back for the Catholic cause in Europe, the very cause which, after the glory of France, he most earnestly wished to promote. The great Protestant champions were the Anglo-Dutch William of Orange, King William III of Great Britain, and his wife Queen Mary II, who had displaced the Catholic King James II when he fled England in 1688. In 1690 James attempted a come-back with a landing in Ireland; however, his cause was lost in defeat at the Battle of the Boyne in 1690 in which a Catholic army, comprising mainly Irish and French, opposed a Protestant army, comprising Dutch and English and more than 1000 French emigré Huguenot officers under the command of the 75-year-old Marshal duc de Schomberg, who was killed in action. The victory ensured the Protestant ascendancy in Ireland for two centuries.

Louis XIV's success in cleansing France of heresy also brought immense

Louis XIV signs the Revocation of the Edict of Nantes, 18 October 1685.

cultural and commercial benefits to France's Protestant neighbours, the Dutch Republic and Prussia, as well as England, with the emigration of leading figures in the economic, social and intellectual fields. In Prussia alone some 20,000 Huguenots boosted the manufacturing sector of that impoverished territory and significantly contributed to the foundations of its future greatness. It is said that at the end of his reign, King Louis regretted the expulsion of the Huguenots. And yet ...

As a boy, Louis had vowed to drive heresy from France and with the Edict of Fontainebleau he had come as close to realizing that aim as it was humanly possible to do. The blunder, if such it was, lay not in the act, but rather in the objective which it achieved.

The Principle of Oppression

Few heroes of the English socialist tradition enjoyed greater respect than the six Dorset Methodist farm labourers, sentenced in 1834 to deportation for attempting to organize a trade union, known to history as the Tolpuddle Martyrs. The 'martyrdom', unmerited and unnecessary, was the product of official stupidity raised to the level of political blundering. The intention was to oppress, the effect was to create an icon of liberation. Law-abiding Christians moved only by their religious principles to work for the betterment of their own lot and that of their fellows, they found themselves for a time demonized as felons and subversives, a collective threat to the realm.

For 1834 was also the year in which the Welsh mill owner and philanthropist Robert Owen inaugurated the Grand National Consolidated Trades Union (GNCTU). A philanthropic visionary, he dreamed of a world in which workers, organized in their respective crafts, would exchange their products on the basis of the labour value employed in their production and, ultimately, come to control the economic machinery and thence the political organization of the state. Such views, unsurprisingly, caused alarm among the governing classes. The more so as, within a matter of weeks, the GNCTU, inconceivable and probably illegal in the post-Thatcherite Britain of the 1990s, had attracted half a million members.

The men of Tolpuddle had looked forward to joining this great national movement, once their own union was properly launched. Anxious to ensure solidarity among the membership, they devised a solemn ceremony of initiation which involved the administering of a secret oath. It was this that gave the local magistrates their opening. There was at that time no law against the forming of a union, but the administering of secret, and therefore possibly subversive, oaths was illegal (except, of course, such oaths or ceremonies as led to membership of a Masonic Lodge). The martyrs were duly arraigned and sentenced to seven years' deportation. They appealed. But the cabinet of Lord Melbourne seem to have taken the view that these sober non-conformist rustics constituted a threat to the constitution so severe that only the most repressive measures could avert it. They upheld the sentence.

The decision was a blunder both in the immediate and the long term. The 'martyrs' behaved with dignity and courage and public opinion was

A Trade Union rally in favour of the Tolpuddle Martyrs in Copenhagen Fields, London, 21 April 1834.

indignant at the government's severity. The sentences were thought excessive by many even among the landed gentry while, far from intimidating the working classes, the case produced a monster popular petition to parliament. In 1836 the men were pardoned and eventually were brought back to England at public expense. Working-class solidarity found practical expression in subscriptions to a fund which raised enough money to provide five of the martyrs with farms in Essex; the sixth choosing to return to Dorset.

The ultimate fate of the Tolpuddle Six was perhaps not so grim as the hagiography made out – the Essex contingent eventually sold up and emigrated to Canada – yet their 'martyrdom' long remained a socialist rallying call. It was a left-wing icon of great potency created by a blunder of the establishment: it only lost its power when, in the early 1990s, socialism itself was jettisoned from the baggage of Britain's official left by Tony Blair's 'new' Labour Party.

The Principle of Sobriety

In 1872 Henry Austin Bruce, the Liberal Home Secretary, introduced Britain's first Licensing Bill to the fury of the liquor trade and pub landlords. They were not alone in seeing it as a tyrannical limit on the liberty of the subject. The bishop of Peterborough averred: 'I would see England free better than England sober,' and there was actual rioting in several towns. Contemporary commentators reported evidence that the measure and the reactions to it had direct impact on the electoral fortunes of the Liberal Party. For the next two years virtually every public house in the United Kingdom was to all intents and purposes an active committee room for the Conservative Party. And when his Liberal government was defeated at the polls in February 1874, Prime Minister Gladstone had no doubt about 'the principal operative cause. We have been borne down in a torrent of gin and beer.'

But there were more far-reaching consequences too. Up till that time the liquor industry, like most other industrial interests, tended to support the Liberal Party as the party of free trade, free enterprise and class emancipation, while the Tories were seen as the party of privilege and the landed gentry. But the widening of the franchise with the reform bills of 1832 and 1867 weakened these ties and also meant that Tory funds, traditionally by the landed interest, were increasingly inadequate when compared to the financial support for the Liberals from commerce and industry.

From 1872 onwards, to quote one 19th-century historian, 'Money and support of every kind flowed to the Conservative Party from the liquor trade.' This was the time when the party machines were beginning to be built up and large supplies of cash were needed on a regular basis. It has been suggested that without the money from the brewers and distillers, the Conservatives would have had real difficulty surviving as a modern political party. Certainly, the party's finances were greatly benefited by its opponents' principles.

The Principle of the Secret Ballot

With his reform bill of 1867, the Tory prime minister, Benjamin Disraeli, extended the franchise within the United Kingdom of Britain and Ireland, to a large part of middle and lower class voters. If it was intended to win the Tories an enlarged majority through the gratitude vote, it was a blunder. The new electorate, regarding the Tories as the party of privilege, voted not for their benefactor, but for the Liberals, and Disraeli's great rival Gladstone came to power.

Many traditionalists of both main parties saw Gladstone's Ballot Act of 1872 as a much greater threat to the stability of society, for it made the ballot secret for the first time in British experience. With voting up till now done by public show of hands, local big men reckoned they could control the way votes were cast. It certainly seemed obvious that no one would vote openly for known revolutionaries and this was assumed, by many, to explain why British politics were so free of agitators, socialists and revolutionaries. But, once a man (at this time of course all voters were men) could make his choice in the privacy of a voting booth, free of intimidation of boss or local squire and their bully-boys then, so ran the argument, Parliament would be flooded with trouble-makers of all kinds.

As so often, the English ruling classes misread the mood of their coun-

THE PRINCIPLE OF THE SECRET BALLOT

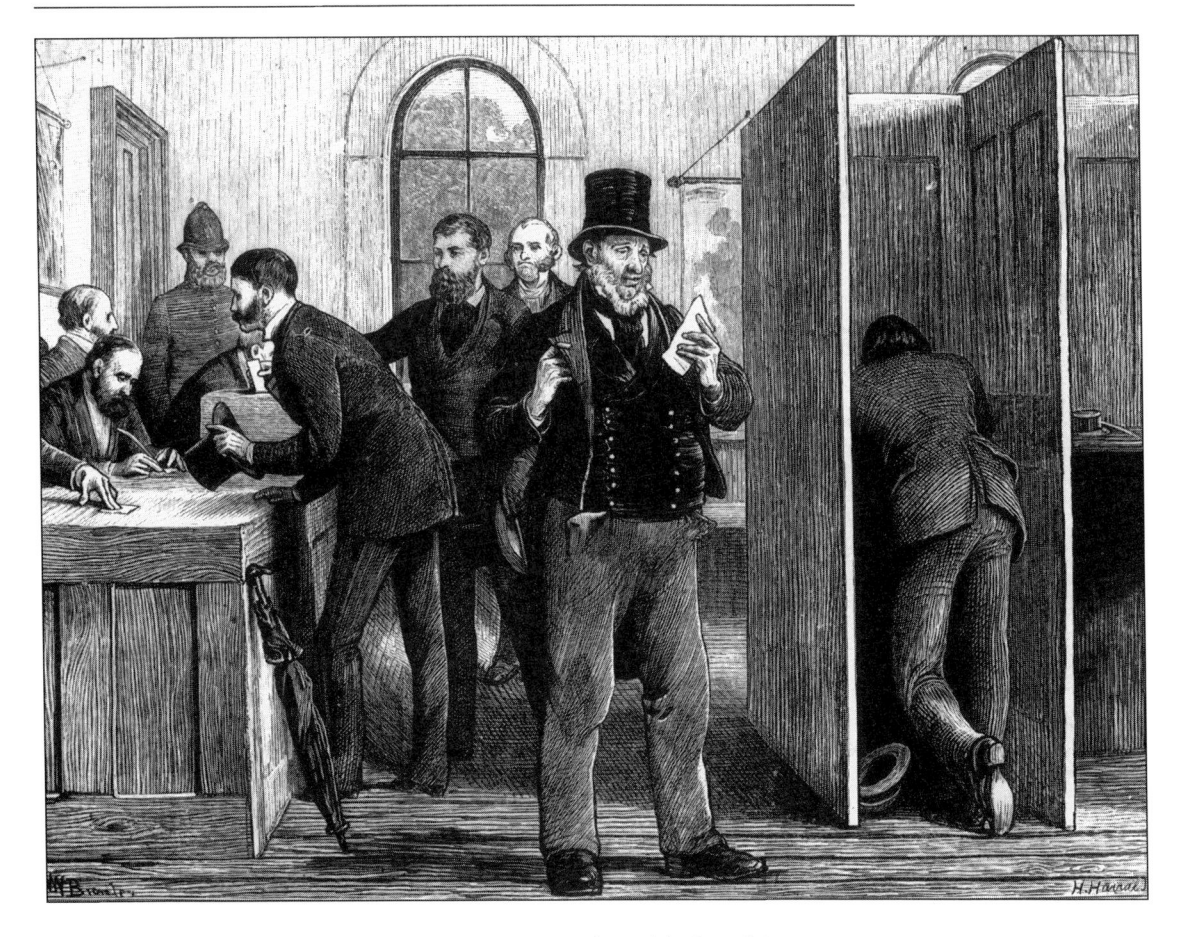

A polling station in 1874, with booths to allow for the new-fangled secret ballot.

trymen. However, in the sister kingdom across the Irish Sea things were different. There, an oppressed tenantry had reason to vote back to Westminster whomever their usually absentee landlord favoured, and that would be a member of one of the two Westminster parties. In 1874 the voting booth revolutionized the situation in Irish politics; as, with a flash of insight, a 26-year-old landowner from County Wicklow had foreseen that it would. 'What is wanted is an independent Irish party, free from the touch of English influence. Now something can be done if full advantage is taken of this Ballot Act.'

The prophesy was dramatically fulfilled at the general election of 1874 when the four-year-old Irish Home Rule Movement of Isaac Butt carried 59 seats. A year later the young Wicklow landowner was returned to Parliament in a by-election and soon supplanted Butt as leader of the Irish cause. He was Charles Stewart Parnell, who was to dominate Westminster and the Irish question for a decade and who would be the cause of Gladstone's defeat on the issue (see pp.11–14).

In the longer perspectives of Gladstone's career, the 1872 Ballot Act can be classed as a heroic if unwitting blunder. It had none of the consequences feared for England but by politicizing the Irish question and ushering in the greatest of Irish champions, it led to final defeat for the prime minister who had presided over its birth.

The Principle of Loyalty

By October 1936 Winston Churchill had been in the political wilderness for the best part of six years, ever since his resignation from the shadow cabinet on the issue of Indian independence back in 1931. Yet he had gone on 'intriguing and making speeches', wrote his friend Duff Cooper, 'in the same spirit, I suppose, that my mother-in-law goes on painting her face and wearing a wig'. But even bad habits may produce results and in the autumn of 1936 Winston was beginning to attract allies in a campaign against the government on the issue of Germany as a threat to the peace.

His group 'The Focus', with its slogan 'Arms and the Covenant [of the League of Nations]', won miscellaneous and in some cases eccentric support from bodies to the left and right of the political spectrum. To many in the Tory Party it appeared as just another manoeuvre in his perennial campaign to force his way back into government. Others considered his support of Edward VIII against Prime Minister Baldwin during the abdication crisis as part of the same manoeuvre. The two were to share a common fate.

When Churchill spoke on 3 December at a rally in London's Albert Hall on 'Defence of Freedom and Peace', it seemed that the somewhat ill-focused movement was indeed beginning to make its mark. But it was on that day, too, that the British public first heard of their King's desire to make an American divorcée, a Mrs Wallis Simpson, his queen. Days later Churchill's carefully constructed alliance lay in ruins, thanks to his own unaided blundering.

When, in mid-November, Duff Cooper had told him of the King's intentions, Churchill had reacted indignantly. He thought that if men had given their lives for the sake of the country during the Great War 'so must the King be prepared to give up a woman'. This would be the view of many when the Edward–Wallis Simpson affair became public knowledge some two weeks later. But by that time Churchill was arguing that the government should defend the King.

Some thought he had been persuaded to change his attitude by the press tycoon Beaverbrook, others that Churchill had decided that the crisis could be used to destabilize Prime Minister Baldwin. When Baldwin consulted him along with the leaders of the two main opposition parties, Attlee for Labour and Sinclair for the Liberals, these two said they would not form an administration should the King ask them. Churchill's response was ambiguous. That Baldwin should put the question to him showed how far his campaign to restore his political fortunes was succeeding. Some of Baldwin's more excitable ministers even envisaged a nightmare scenario in which Edward invited Churchill to form an administration with his 'friends' which then called an election on the issue of the King's marriage.

On 6 December Churchill published a statement that 'No ministry has the right to advise the abdication of the sovereign.' The following day, Baldwin told the House of Commons that the King had been given a few more days to decide between his throne and his intended wife. Churchill now sought to intervene with a supplementary question to the Prime Minister. Twice he was called to order by the Speaker while cries of 'Drop it' and 'Twister' came from all parts of the packed chamber. The veteran parliamentarian, used to dominating debates, had lost his command of the House and he sat down silenced, white-faced and shaken. In the words of one observer: 'In three minutes his hopes of return to power and influence were shattered.'

In fact, apart from misreading the mood of Parliament, he had made every possible political blunder. He misjudged public opinion. There were, it is true, some demonstrations in favour of the King outside Buckingham Palace; one was even mounted by communists and fascists uniquely united in a common cause. But such demonstrations represented a largely middle-class minority. While sympathetic with Edward's dilemma as a man, most people in the country believed he should do his duty as a king. His former popularity as Prince of Wales turned out to be as impermanent as that of a film star who angers his fans. The abdication was almost forgotten by the time George VI was crowned on 2 May 1937.

Churchill also miscalculated the King's resolution in his fight with the establishment. Ideally, Edward wanted to marry Mrs Simpson and remain on the throne. If he saw the abdication crisis as a means to overthrow Baldwin and his government, Churchill had again horribly miscalculated. If he acted from a chivalrous intention to help the King, he had merely hardened opinion in the House of Commons against him. Either way, Churchill had blundered once more into the political wilderness and it would have been a bold man who would have predicted a return to power for the discredited 62-year old.

The Brilliant Blunderer

The youngest cabinet minister in 170 years, holder of an unmatched record of four general election wins, Harold Wilson has a good claim to be the most complete British politician of the century. At his best he was unbeatable, whether in debate in the House of Commons, in manoeuvring for advantage in election campaigns, or in maintaining an appearance of unity among the coalition of ideological coteries which called itself the Labour Party in the 1960s.

And there were solid achievements, rare enough among politicians. By presiding over the birth of Britain's Open University, the world's first to be based on the electronic media, he maintained the socialist ideal of improving the social conditions of his fellow citizens. And by refusing to commit Britain to the US war in Vietnam, he proved almost unique among post-war British PMs in resisting the phoney allure of the 'special relationship' and spared his country hundreds of futile deaths and a thousand more heartbreaks.

His humanity, wit and kindness were acknowledged by political opponents as well as friends, while he is probably the only chief executive this century to relinquish power voluntarily. His resignation on 16 March 1976, of which only the Queen had had prior warning and which stunned the public also made him the only Labour prime minister to be succeeded in post by a member of his own party. Yet for all that, few politicians before the

If he ever went to school without boots it was because he was too big for them.

IVOR BULMER THOMAS, TORY MP, ON HAROLD WILSON

time of John Major had such a mixed press while in office, and none perhaps have suffered more denigration of their achievements after leaving it. As no one would dispute, both facts owed much to some majestic blunders on the part of the protagonist. But the two major mistakes of his premierships, the failure to devalue on first coming to power and the renunciation of force in the struggle with Ian Smith's Rhodesia, sprang, it can be argued, from the underlying principles of his political motivation.

In October 1964 Wilson led the Labour Party to its first victory in 13 years. But the majority was a mere four seats. Every government decision was overshadowed by the imperative to win a larger mandate as soon as possible. The situation would seem to have been tailor-made for Wilson's quick-thinking short-termism as a politician. The man who famously observed 'a week is a long time in politics', was adept, none more so, at surfing the headlines. In the opinion of many, this skill on the breakers dazzled him to deeper perceptions and possibilities.

The economic situation bequeathed by the outgoing Tory government of Alec Douglas Home proved, on analysis of the treasury books, to be yet more dreadful than had been expected. The triumphant socialists faced a sickening dilemma. Devaluation offered the obvious, 'quick fix', economic solution. Wilson, who was not only an adroit short-term political operator but also a trained economist, rejected the option.

A small group of Labour's high command believed that devaluation was the right policy in economic terms. To some Labour supporters in the country it also seemed politically the obvious thing to do. The voters had questioned the British superstition that government belongs to the right and were prepared to recognize that the Conservatives had caused the economic crisis. A bold devaluation would surely be seen as a policy forced on Labour by its predecessors and be accepted as necessary if it was to begin implementing the social policies it believed to be so important for the nation's long-term prosperity.

In the 1990s, when a Conservative government effected a 10 per cent devaluation of the pound to a chorus of approval from the Tory press, it is difficult to understand the mystical, almost hysterical, awe accorded to the currency in the 1960s. Then, it was Labour who were known as the party of devaluation since Britain's last devaluation in 1947 had been at the hands of a Labour government, ruthlessly attacked by the Tory press for its pains. Harold Wilson, President of the Board of Trade in that government, was convinced that a repeat performance would utterly discredit Labour. Many others in the Party believed that only devaluation would meet the underlying economic realities, but conceded that the drastic measure would have to wait until a new election should deliver that longed-for mandate.

The debate became more intense when, following a brilliant election campaign master-minded by Wilson in spring 1966, Labour found itself with a massive 97-seat majority. Now the argument for devaluation seemed unanswerable to leading ministers – even for a time the Chancellor of the Exchequer. But Prime Minister Wilson held firm, determined to plough the furrow of financial orthodoxy and so lay the ghost of Labour as the irresponsible party. The decision, which seems now to have been a repeat of

'And why do I speak about the Navy?' Heckler in the crowd: 'Because you're in Chatham!'

HAROLD WILSON CAMPAIGNING IN 1964 AT CHATHAM, HOME OF BRITAIN'S PRINCIPAL NAVAL DOCKYARD the initial blunder of '64 on a massive scale, belies the image of Wilson the opportunist. He may have determined on financial virtue to establish his party's credentials with the electorate, but holding the line on the strong pound did not come any cheaper. In fact, because he prominently identified with the policy, it cost him dear.

In November 1967 a run on sterling all but wiped out the Bank of England's reserves and the government was forced to devalue, and by the large margin of 14.3 per cent. So Labour was the party of devaluation after all, and Harold Wilson was responsible. His reputation nose-dived. When in his television broadcast explaining his decision, Wilson observed that the pound's devaluation on the international money market would not affect the 'value of the pound at home, the pound in your pocket', he made a rod for his own back.

The analysis was technically correct. A devaluation inflates prices on the home market in the long term, as the rising cost of imports works through to the market place, but there is no immediate effect. This did not prevent the right-wing press from jeering at the man who in the same broadcast, as he announced a large cut in the value of the pound, assured the public that they would not be affected.

But though it is possible to defend the 'pound in your pocket' comment, it was undoubtedly a political blunder in so far as Wilson was never allowed to forget it. Much more serious for the course of events, however, was his handling of the rebellion by the white population of Southern Rhodesia

British Prime Minister Harold Wilson on the campaign trail in September 1964, his audience apparently distracted by a heckler.

(now Zimbabwe). They were determined to resist all moves by Westminster towards eventual black majority rule and their wily leader Ian Smith outmanoeuvred the British Prime Minister by the simple expedient of going back on the solemn agreement reached in negotiations dramatically held on board a British warship, HMS *Tiger*, in December 1966.

It was perhaps a forgiveable blunder for Wilson to trust his devious opponent. It was a startling miscalculation to renounce, in public, the use of force against the rebel regime. For this is what Wilson did. He said that defence chiefs had told him that logistics ruled out the military option. Later they were to claim that such advice had never been given or asked for. At the time there was talk of possible army mutiny in the event of orders to make war on the white 'kith and kin'. Perhaps Wilson merely aimed to placate right-wing opinion at home and foster any moderate opinion in Rhodesia. But, having decided that negotiation and diplomacy offered the only course, it was surely a classic blunder to throw away the negotiator's principal weapon – the opponent's uncertainty about one's intentions.

In fact, despite his reputation for Machiavellian wiliness, Harold Wilson had an almost engaging naïveté. Like a good boy at school, he wanted to earn brownie points by guarding the currency. Like an honourable peace-loving man, he could not contemplate initiating hostilities. In short, he played by the book. In the case of the currency, he misread the text: in the case of Rhodesia, he published what should have been censored. Either way he blundered.

Flagship Principle: The Blunder Supreme

Despite the assurance by the Minister for Local Government that the poll tax would be a vote winner for the Tories, on 18 October 1990 the Liberal Democrats, in the traditionally Conservative constituency of Eastbourne, overturned a Tory majority of 17,000 to win the by-election with a majority of 4550. 'Thatcher's poll tax' was virtually the sole point of debate in the campaign. On 22 November, following a leadership election during which she had rejected any suggestion that she should do 'something substantial' about the tax, Margaret Thatcher, having failed to win the required majority, announced her resignation as leader of the Conservative Party. On 28 November she left office as prime minister, to be succeeded by John Major. One of his first acts was to order a fundamental review of the tax.

A poll tax (literally 'head tax', from Middle English *pol*, 'a head') is one that it is levied on every adult. It may be assessed on a graduated or flat rate. Up to the 1980s the last time a flat-rate poll tax had been levied in England was in 1380, only beggars being exempt. It was immediately and violently unpopular. Collectors were seized and forced to swear to abandon their work; evasion was massive – on the evidence of the returns for 1381 and those for a similar but much lower tax of 1377, one would have to deduce a fall of one-third in the adult population in four years. It was a main cause of the Peasants' Revolt which forced the abandonment of the tax and during which the government's finance minister was beheaded by the rebels.

The Community Charge is a courageous, fair and sensible solution. Far from being a vote loser ... it will be a vote winner.

MICHAEL PORTILLO, MINISTER FOR LOCAL GOVERNMENT, SPEAKING AT THE CONSERVATIVE PARTY CONFERENCE AT BOURNEMOUTH, 11 OCTOBER 1990

Flat-rate poll taxes as such are generally considered socially unfair because a fixed rate obviously bears more heavily on the poor than on the rich. In 1381 a married farm labourer, lucky indeed if he earned a penny for a day's work, was faced with a tax bill for 24 pennies (i.e. two shillings). The Earl of Suffolk, who led the suppression of the peasants in East Anglia, paid the same for himself and his countess. In 1990 a couple of old-age pensioners, living on limited savings in a modest flat in the borough of Westminster, would pay a poll tax of £390, while a married property owner in the same borough's privileged Belgravia district, who formerly paid thousands of pounds in rates, now paid the same £390 for himself and his wife.

The glaring inequity was justified by the argument that since the central exchequer contributed heavily to local government expenditure, the rich paid proportionately more than the poor through their income tax. Economically questionable, the idea was politically crass. Told that Mrs Thatcher had brought in a flat-rate tax Paul Volcker, a former head of the US Federal Reserve and a keen admirer of hers, found the report incredible.

Incredible, but true. How Mrs Thatcher, a politician to her finger tips, came to agree a policy which represents the greatest blunder this century in British domestic politics is puzzle enough. Why she should have compounded her mistake by claiming the policy as her personal 'flagship', is beyond all understanding.

Before the introduction of the poll tax or, to give it its official name, the 'community charge', in 1988, reform of local government taxation had been for years a subject for debate and controversy. The traditional system of a rate on property values dated back to before the suffrage reforms of the 19th century to a time when, if property ownership entailed the obligation to pay local taxes, it also carried with it the privilege of voting on their expenditure. Once the right to vote became general and independent of property ownership, decisions as to the spending of local taxes became subject to an electorate of which a substantial proportion did not pay them.

Rates were assessed on property rather than people, so a single person owning a comfortable house might pay as much in local rates as a neighbouring family where parents and perhaps two or three children were in paid employment. If the single person was a pensioner, the disparity between incomings and outgoings for the two properties would be still more marked and the obvious unfairness of the system more obvious. Furthermore, as the services expected from local government became more numerous and expensive, an ever larger proportion of local expenditure came to be financed from central government: local finances became a national issue. In the 1980s the reform of the rating system would become a central topic of political debate and the name of Margaret Thatcher would become linked with a pledge to abolish it in favour of some fairer system.

What that fairer system might be, however, was far from clear. Considered simply as a method of raising revenue, the rates had important advantages. They were well established, well understood, easy to assess, easy to raise and difficult to evade. By 1982 three main alternatives were mooted – a local sales tax, a local income tax and, least favoured of all, a poll tax. The arguments against it had not changed since the disastrous experiment

> *I don't mind how much my ministers talk – as long as they do what I say.*
>
> MARGARET THATCHER, BRITISH PRIME MINISTER, 1987

six centuries earlier. Given the Thatcher government's enthusiasm for traditional standards in education, it might be thought that some knowledge of history would have come to their aid. The more so as the junior Home Office Minister William Waldegrave, who pioneered the initial studies that led to the poll tax proposals, bore the family name of Sir Richard Waldegrave, Speaker of the House of Commons and a poll tax commissioner in 1381.

However, as often before, British respect for tradition proved of little practical value. Waldegrave, aided by another ambitious and able young minister, Kenneth Baker, recruited an intellectually brilliant team, among them Lord Rothschild who, rightly as it turned out, prided himself on having no political judgement. There were no consultations with local government bodies, since they were considered to be the problem. To maintain an open mind the team even avoided consulting Sir Frank Layfield who, as chairman of a civil service review of local government finance in the mid-1970s, was the most knowledgeable man in the field. More influential seem to have been the views of local Tory Party constituency committees, many of whom were pensioners, often single pensioners, the people most vocal on the injustices of the rating system but by no means a majority of the electorate.

It seemed reasonable that all those who used local services should contribute to them directly by some form of per capita levy, though not necessarily a single-rate poll tax. Prime ministerial approval first had to be obtained, for Margaret Thatcher did not, as often supposed, actually originate the poll tax. By March 1985, however, she and the Party needed a policy proposal for the reform of the rates system. The previous month a rates review for Scotland conducted during 1984 had been presented and it meant severe increases for householders. Local Tory associations 'went berserk', according to one MP.

Accordingly, on Sunday 31 March 1985, Mrs Thatcher and half her cabinet convened for an all-day session at Chequers, the Prime Minister's country residence, to resolve on a policy to meet the danger of a rates rebellion by Tory voters. The objectives were simple enough: to reduce the rates burden on their supporters in the country; to do this as soon as possible; and to do it without raising income tax. The poll tax proposals, as formulated by Waldegrave and Baker, were supported by the Party Chairman Lord Whitelaw and Scottish Secretary George Younger. Slick presentation sold them to Thatcher as a real alternative to the rating system. Details, such as the rate at which the new tax should be levied, what groups of people were to be exempted (students, for example?), over how long a period should the revolutionary system be phased in, and the degree of treasury support to subsidize the less well-off losers, remained to be settled. And the Chancellor of the Exchequer was absent. But, if we are to accept the record of Baroness Thatcher herself in her book *The Downing Street Years*, the poll tax 'was born' at this Chequers meeting.

For his part, Chancellor Lawson was 'horrified' at what he considered to be 'a colossal error of judgement' and 'grotesque political blunder'. He was assured that things were not so far advanced as he feared and that he would be able to present his objections before any final decision was taken. A month later he did so in cabinet committee, only to have his arguments brusquely dismissed by the Prime Minister herself.

It being now clear that she was committed to the poll tax principle, any cabinet colleague with a view to a future career either kept out of the way or supported the proposal. On 9 January 1986 it was put to full cabinet for the first time – and passed in just 15 minutes. Lawson did not waste his breath on arguing the case against a second time. There was one other man who might have made an effective opposition to the proposals had he not, at an earlier point on the agenda, left the cabinet room, the meeting and, as it in fact transpired an hour or so later, the very government.

For this was the same cabinet meeting at which Michael Heseltine, Minister of Defence, departed over the Westland helicopter controversy. The conflict in government over this financially troubled company had been building over the past several weeks. Where Margaret Thatcher and Trade and Industry Secretary Leon Brittan favoured a takeover by the American Company Sikorski and, it was rumoured, were less than scrupulous in their manoeuvring, Heseltine was 'batting' for a European consortium and had angered the Prime Minister by his outspoken public statements.

The affair had riveted public attention, for there were suspicions that Mrs Thatcher, aiming to undermine Heseltine's position, had prompted the Solicitor General to write a letter to him, critical of his analysis of the situation and then arranged for the letter to be leaked. Her reputation for straight dealing was tarnished and the dramatic resignation of the Defence Minister in mid-cabinet seemed almost to endanger her position as prime minister. As Heseltine enthralled a hastily convened press conference with an account of his resignation and grievances, cabinet members were taking their leave of a meeting where a decision had been taken which was fraught with dire long-term consequences for the Prime Minister.

The Heseltine resignation masked any chance of the poll tax decision making the news; the publication on 26 January of the green paper 'Paying for Local Government' which opened public presentation of the sensational new levy, was also overshadowed, this time the headline news being the catastrophic explosion of the US space shuttle *Challenger*.

Three days later, however, London's heavyweight press detonated a series of fire-crackers under the proposed 'community charge' replacement for the rates. *The Times* attacked as 'verbiage' attempts to conceal the reality with misleading terminology, pointing out that a true 'charge' is one which gives the prospective payer the option of paying or not, according to whether services are used or not. The *Financial Times* called for an updated property tax while the *Economist*, concluded that 'the big losers on the new tax, young singles and couples, are floating voters'. A dangerous point at election times. Worse still was to come. By 1990, when the tax was implemented, opinion polls showed up to 70 per cent against the tax, with specially high rejection among lower income and working class 'new' Conservatives – precisely the group Mrs Thatcher was thought to have won over for good. But in January 1986 the debate was in its early days and there was little public debate.

When the tabloid press did begin to feature the story, the government's blunder was announced by the headlines before a word of analysis or

BLUNDERS OF PRINCIPLE

Demonstrators in the London Poll Tax riots of April 1990. The vast unpopularity of the tax, which apart from anything else added one per cent to the inflation rate, was the root cause of the Tories' decision to ditch Thatcher as leader in November 1990.

reportage was written. Given the demands of journalese the staid, long winded 'community charge' had no chance against the punchy, attention-grabbing 'Poll Tax'. The fact that, for once, journalistic criteria coincided with the truth meant that, in time, even government advocates would find themselves using the hated term. For if the Thatcher cabinet had forgotten their history or chosen to ignore it, long before the first poll tax demands dropped through the nation's letter boxes in 1988, the Peasants' Revolt, its origins and causes, had joined the Battle of Hastings as the second episode of English medieval history familiar to electors.

For two years, however, Tory voters supposed Margaret Thatcher and her team knew best, and most ratepayers assumed any system would be better than the rates. In March 1987 the Tory local government conference, held at Wembley, gave the plans an enthusiastic reception. The fact that later that year students erupted in protests at the news of a proposed 20 per cent charge on them did little to dent complacency among ratepayers. More ominous was the decision to reduce the transition period down to four years. This, combined with treasury's refusal to meet the full demands of environment ministers for subsidies to ease the burdens on poorer citizens, would be classified by Tory advocates of the poll tax as 'fatal mistakes'. Even so, public debate in England remained muted and the hostile reactions to the tax in Scotland, where it was introduced a year earlier, met with the glassy-eyed indifference typifying the southerners' response to most news from north of the border.

The Abolition of Domestic Rates (etc) Scotland Bill received its second reading in the House of Commons on 9 December 1986 without a single voice of dissent from the Tory benches. Any expression of doubt was met with the assurance that the poll tax bill was 'utterly vital' for the Party's electoral chances in Scotland. In the event, the Conservatives lost more than half their Scottish seats, down from 21 to 10, in the general election of June 1987. How this squared with the enthusiastic poll-tax advocacy of men like Secretary of State for Scotland Malcolm Rifkind is not clear, but it must be admitted in their defence that the issue of the poll tax had hardly been raised throughout the campaign. The Scottish Nationalists attacked it to some effect, but largely as yet another Sassenach outrage imposed from London upon the oppressed Celts. It was not for them to point out that the same outrage was soon to be committed in England.

There, on urgings from campaign managers and spin doctors, Labour's local-government spokesmen were, in fact, barred from using their election material attacking the levy by Neil Kinnock and his colleagues. The Tory press regularly ran stories on 'loony left' councils allegedly wasting rate payers' money on 'politically correct', but electorally damaging, policies. There was enough fire behind the smoke to make local government finance an area in which the Labour leadership felt themselves to be vulnerable.

To be party to muffling democratic debate on the issue may have been reprehensible in some rarefied context of constitutional probity, but it was hardly a blunder in the world of practical politics. In England and Wales the question of the poll tax was still a hypothetical one and the basic factors little understood by the general public. If asked, the average voter would have dismissed as absurd the idea that Margaret Thatcher could contemplate, let alone enact, anything so evidently unfair and plain barmy. On the couple of occasions on which Labour spokesmen did raise the issue, it provoked little media or public response. Even so, when the Tories were returned with a landslide majority of 100 seats, with a manifesto commitment to bring in a poll tax, their electoral mandate was incontestable.

As if to 'make assurance double sure', in July 1987, to plaudits from an audience of Tory backbenchers, Mrs Thatcher pledged the poll tax as the 'flagship of the Thatcher fleet'. That, to contort the metaphor, the flagship was to scupper the admiral, should not obscure some remarkable facts surrounding the 'community charge'. Launched by a Prime Minister who had initially been sceptical; conceived by some of the most brilliant brains available to the political enterprise; adopted virtually without dissent in cabinet; allowed to go uncontested at election by the official opposition; and implemented following a landslide mandate endorsement by the electorate, this policy passed through the Mother of Parliaments, whose sovereignty Britain so vigorously vaunts against the incompetence and oppressions of Brussels, virtually unscathed.

The Local Government Finance bill began its progress through the Commons on 16 December 1987. The Upper House would achieve just two insignificant modifications. In the Commons not a vote was lost. The result was that a radical new tax was imposed on the country with uniform levels unrelated to income and without any initial phase-in period. Provisions of ever-increasing complexity and cost had to be introduced for special cases but hundreds of thousands of people fell outside their scope. And there were many cases of genuine or perceived hardship.

The consequences fully matched the precedents of 1381. True, neither the Chancellor of the Exchequer nor the head of government was actually decapitated but poll tax riots in London, Edinburgh and a dozen other towns and cities flared across the world's television screens. It was Christmas for agitators, but the bulk of the protest was from ordinary citizens. Non-registration and evasion were rife. Ever more complex arrangements for special cases, safety nets and exemptions were introduced, so that even the ministers in charge lost track. In his 1990 budget John Major, the new Chancellor of the Exchequer, changed the benefit system to help a small class of moderately poor people – but forgot to allow resources for Scotland. Muddle and blunder was now so much part of the poll tax pattern that it hardly dented his reputation. And in any case, the £4 million which had to be found overnight was a fleabite in the estimated £27.5 billion that the introduction, transfer costs and dismantling, of the tax cost the national exchequer. It has been plausibly argued that without the poll tax, income tax for 1994–5 could have been 4p in the pound less than it actually was.

And yet, of course, the decision to enact a poll tax was an egregious blunder not only in terms of equity and social justice, public policy and public finance but, worse still for a politician, in terms of politics. For, as Michael Heseltine observed: 'Responsibility for the rates is confused in the legacy of history. Responsibility for the poll tax will be targeted precisely and unavoidably at the government who introduced that tax. That tax will be known as the Tory tax.' In fact, it would better be known as Thatcher's tax for it was her downfall.

But politically that was the limit of the damage. The poll tax was abolished and legislation for the new council tax rushed onto the statute books in time for the election of April 1992. Not only was this won by the Conservatives but a raft of ministers most actively involved in the worst botch-up since the war, William Waldegrave, John Gummer, Malcolm Rifkind and John Major to name a few, were voted back. They had ditched Margaret Thatcher and the poll tax – the four most unpopular words in Britain's political lexicon – and this, apparently, was enough for the British electorate. If, 600 years from now, some future British government (supposing such a thing still to exist) should attempt another rerun of the poll tax disaster, it is to be hoped that the then head of government will not link his or her fortunes so firmly to the policy as did Margaret Thatcher. For that was her real blunder.

The Principle of the Manifesto

There can be no more fitting tailpiece to this chapter of principled blunders than the salutary tale of a minister who believed in the manifesto on which his party had won an election and spoke out of turn by saying so.

In August 1995 the French Prime Minister Alain Juppé sacked his economics and finance minister Alain Madelin. The dismissal of this political heavyweight, then ranking third in the Gaullist camp behind Juppé and President Chirac himself, threatened to destabilize what Juppé called the 'aeropolane of government'. While Juppé may have seen himself in the rather dashing role of an airline pilot, but an incandescent Madelin offered another insight into the workings of the three-month-old government. 'I was thrown out like some damned servant,' he told friends.

A young 40-year-old, with lustrous black hair, the broken nose of a boxer and a habitually wary look behind the humorous eyes, Alain Madelin was always something of an outsider among the high fliers of French political life. He graduated, with a degree in business studies, from a university and not from the élite school of administration ENA (École Nationale d'Administration). From the outset of the 1995 presidential campaign, although he had been for two years industry minister under Balladur, he boldly supported the candidacy of Jacques Chirac. By contrast, the upper echelons of the Gaullist party, who like the rest of the political establishment did not consider Chirac himself to be quite the thing, were either hedging their bets or swinging behind the late runner Edouard Balladur when he finally declared his candidacy. But Chirac won and Madelin was an automatic choice for a top government post.

During the campaign he had vigorously aligned himself with candidate Chirac's manifesto pledge to radical reform of French finances and advocated cutbacks in state spending – above all social security payments and pensions. Appointed minister of economics and finance in the new Chirac–Juppé administration, Madelin was determined to put the campaign rhetoric into action. After all, ex-Premier Balladur's failure to stand up to union pressure to maintain state benefits had earned him criticism from Chirac and the Gaullist right wing. Chirac's victory in the presidential race seemed to confer electoral endorsement. Accordingly, when, in late August, about a month before he was due to present his first budget, Madelin made a speech reiterating that if the economy were to be salvaged there would have to be incentive cuts in taxation and housekeeping cuts in state benefits, he may have counted on presidential support. It was a blunder. Prime Minister Juppé, claiming that his outspoken colleague was in fact undermining the government's reforming intentions, sacked him without more ado, but apparently with the consent of President Chirac. Press reaction was immediate. Barely 100 days old, the government had U-turned on its prime policy commitment and returned to the Balladurian economics of union appeasement.

But union pressure was not the only force at work in the fall of Alain Madelin. He had made enemies as the industry ministry in the Balladur government, by proposing to run down the system of state subsidies to industry. This had alarmed the senior civil servants whose jobs were on the line and

... to obey a majority ... demands a suppleness of character and conviction that I do not possess.

OTTO VON BISMARCK,
GERMAN CHANCELLOR
1871-90

most of whom were from the ENA élite. Excluded from their power games, Madelin lost the full-hearted support of his department staff which is essential for a successful minister. The freemasonry of the ENA extends throughout the top ranks of France's governmental machine, so that when he moved to the finance ministry, he found his planned economies sabotaged as officials in other departments helped his cabinet colleagues resist his plans for reductions in their budgets.

Exclusion from the charmed circle of the ENA weakened his effectiveness as a minister. But Madelin made enemies not only among top civil servants but even among his fellow deputies in the national assembly. His radical economic proposals would have reduced or simply put an end to pension rights and other benefits for officials and generous state retirement subsidies for deputies. In addition to all this, so the rumour went, Prime Minister Juppé, who would have blocked his ministerial appointment had that been possible, had been gunning for his talented young colleague from the outset. The finance minister's challenging remarks gave him his opening. On the morning after the sacking, one headline read: 'In politics words can kill. M. Madelin has killed himself with his own words.' A former Balladur minister (Simone Veil) commented: 'He's a nutter who talks too much.'

But while his colleague may have blundered, Juppé showed scant political finesse in the way he exploited the situation. With typical British understatement, Howard Archer of London's NatWest group commented: 'It might have been handled a bit more tactfully.' France's budget deficit was worrying international finance markets and following the news of the dismissal, the franc fell sharply, though later recovered. The problems of the budget remained, leaving Premier Juppé exposed. Madelin blundered in speaking out on a matter of great political sensitivity at a time when, with the election won, President Chirac was softening his campaigning rhetoric and trimming his sails to the public mood. According to the sacked minister, Premier Juppé held exactly the same views as he did on the question of state benefits but 'didn't have the balls to say so'. Fuming at the method of his dismissal, Madelin was reported as vowing revenge. 'I shall never forget it. Juppé will pay for it one day.'

Few predictions can have been more comprehensively fulfilled. Before the end of the year M. Juppé and his government were buffeted by a tempest of strikes and social protest unparallelled since 1986. It may be doubted whether their sufferings were in retribution for the fate meted out to M. Madelin, but it can hardly be doubted that he was delighted by their fate. For all concerned, the lesson was obvious – principle costs in politics.

CHAPTER 4: BLUNDERING ESTABLISHMENTS

The establishment is, in theory at least, that part of the body politic that cannot be shifted, that element to which others are subordinate and before which they should doff their metaphorical hats. Of course, half the entertainment of history derives from the hat-doffers and the hat-doffees failing to play their allotted roles. Sometimes it seems they forget which is which and, indeed, sometimes it is difficult to be sure which is which. Especially at the beginning of a political evolution. In the early 17th century the monarchy was clearly the establishment in England; by the end of that century it clearly was not. Instead, a strange creature called the king in Parliament occupied the position. Halfway between the two, the Civil War had played midwife to a new political arrangement. And at the start of that conflict, both king and Parliament blundered.

Bad Bargaining

On 25 August 1642, a mere three days after he had set up his standard at Nottingham Castle in defiance of Parliament, King Charles I of England, with the unanimous advice of his entourage, decided to sue for peace. The King, we are told, 'broke out into tears', but he agreed. Royalist forces at nearby Coventry had been routed and Parliament's army heavily outnumbered the demoralized troops rallied beneath the royal standard. Their opponents rejected the royal offer. Perhaps they overestimated the King's strength and saw the peace feelers as a delaying tactic while new supporters came in. At all events, instead of marching straight on Nottingham, the parliamentary army turned aside some miles to the south to await reinforcements themselves. Their rejection of the royal peace overture made sense. Wary suspicion was a safe rule of thumb when dealing with this king who, in 17 years on the throne, had established an impressive record for shifty unreliability. But Parliament's response to the next offer was a blunder. Charles offered to call off his war preparations in exchange for an amnesty for his supporters. Instead of the simple rejection which was all that was needed, Parliament replied that it would cover the expenses of its war effort by confiscating the estates of the King's supporters. According to Edward Hyde, later Earl of Clarendon and the first great historian of England's Civil War, this declaration changed the situation entirely. The prospect of civil war appalled many in England, including lukewarm royalists who would have been happy to keep a low profile on their estates until the great men on both sides had sorted out their differences.

BLUNDERING ESTABLISHMENTS

King Charles I of England and his cavaliers, as envisaged by a 19th-century artist, raise the royal standard at Nottingham Castle in 1642.

It was at this point, according to Clarendon, that they became convinced that their only hope lay in fighting. If Parliament intended to intimidate hesitating royalists into joining its cause, it had miscalculated badly. Maintaining a discreet neutrality was one thing, openly declaring war on one's king was, for any royalist worth the name, quite another. Given the parliamentary declaration, self-interest as well as principle now meant fighting. Recruits swelled the little royal army round Nottingham. Many of the rankers profited, immediately robbing the largely parliamentary citizenry and selling off the loot in front of the castle. When, on 13 September, Charles led his army out of Nottingham, the town was virtually stripped of arms and cash. He, too, had hardened the hearts of his opponents. Nottingham refortified itself in the coming months and held for Parliament throughout the years of Civil War that followed.

Whether these could have been averted by better parliamentary bargaining may be doubted. The conflict between king and Parliament had been in the making for years. In the immediate term Parliament blundered – in the long term the issues had to be fought to the finish. When on that chill January morning in 1649 Charles walked to his death at the hands of the axeman, he made a brave and stately figure, but the prelude to the drama was a script of blunders written largely by himself.

Parliament, George III and John Wilkes: A Failed Royal Feud

On 23 April 1763 the most famous pamphlet in the history of British politics appeared on the streets of London. This was No. 45 of *The North Briton*, edited by Charles Churchill and written by John Wilkes, MP for Aylesbury, under the patronage of senior politicians opposed to the government of King George III. Its target was the Peace of Paris recently concluded with France. It claimed that the French had bought peace with bribes, that British ministers were 'the tools of despotism and corruption' and that the real power behind the government was the discredited Scottish royal favourite and former prime minister Lord Bute. The new prime minister, George Grenville, with the full support of King George, was determined to silence the insolent pamphleteer.

Launched the previous year as the work of a supposed over-enthusiastic Scottish (North British) supporter of Bute's ministry, the periodical satirized the government, and so the King himself, with ever-increasing freedom. Shortly before the appearance of No. 45, while on a trip to Paris where his daughter lived, Wilkes was asked by Madame de Pompadour: 'How far does the liberty of the press extend in England?' 'I do not know,' he replied. 'I am trying to find out.'

In fact, he was beginning to believe that the court dare not touch him. In an attack on financial corruption in the ministry, he had come near to calling the King an imbecile and also made the indirect but unmistakable innuendo of an affair between Lord Bute and the King's mother. Nothing had happened.

Energetic and generous-hearted but famously ugly with a fierce squint, John Wilkes was a moderately prosperous country gentleman, unhappily married but a promiscuous lover. He was a renowned wit and fascinating talker who boasted he could talk away his face with any woman in just 20 minutes. But his tongue, like his pen, could make enemies. His repartee to Lord Sandwich became famous overnight. 'Wilkes,' said Sandwich, 'you will die of a pox or on the gallows.' 'That depends, my lord, on whether I embrace your principles or your mistress.' Later, Sandwich was to prove a vindictive supporter of government manoeuvres against Wilkes.

At the time of No. 45, Wilkes was in his late forties. He had long been associated with the Hell Fire Club of libertines, founded by Sir Francis Dashwood of High Wycombe, had been a sheriff of his county as well as MP and, as a colonel in the Buckinghamshire militia, took a boyish delight in wearing the red coat of its uniform. An eccentric and a firebrand he was still, in 1763, without a real focus for his energies. That the cry of 'Wilkes and Liberty' coupled with the mystic number 45 became synonymous with resistance to the arbitrary power of the Crown was due almost entirely to the decision of Grenville's ministry to bring him to book for the offending pamphlet. Thanks to their blundering incompetence, he became a popular hero. Further miscalculations by Parliament, then even more corrupt than it is today, only increased his reputation as a champion of liberty against oppressive government.

On 30 April, acting on a general warrant which Wilkes's lawyers would later claim was illegal, officers of Lord Halifax, Secretary of State, arrested him and after various delays took him to the Tower of London where he was held for the next six days. During this time a number of prominent politicians and society leaders visited him to show their support. The public was intrigued.

Wilkes was now headline news. Accordingly, when the case of his arrest and its legality came up for hearing in the Court of Common Pleas on 6 May, the courtroom was packed. Speaking in his own defence, Wilkes said that his case would decide 'whether English liberty shall be a reality or a shadow'. The judge ruled that the warrant was valid and that the Secretary of State was within his rights to commit him to prison – but he also ruled that Wilkes should go free because of the privilege he enjoyed as a Member of Parliament.

The fact that he was freed on such a technicality did not worry his supporters in the body of the court who welcomed any reverse for the King's ministry. A deafening yell of delight burst from the packed audience and was carried on by the swaying crowd outside where was heard for the first time the cry of 'Wilkes and Liberty'. In the midst of all this uproar and turmoil, the Attorney-General and Solicitor-General, with the inefficiency characteristic of the government, arrived demanding to be heard with additional arguments on the question of privilege; they were informed that the case was over.

Wilkes's release was celebrated all over London and with particular enthusiasm among the working classes, at that time denied the vote. A club meeting at the Rose and Crown pub, Wapping, took a solemn oath to make an annual commemoration. Only when the oath had been duly sworn did they realize they had made a small, yet significant, blunder. On 19 May they wrote to Wilkes asking for his help. The letter, which is still among his papers, explains that they had sworn to celebrate by getting drunk every year upon his birthday – but had not thought to find out when it was. They begged he would supply the information, otherwise 'we must either get drunk every day for twelve months or be perjured and damned'.

Such popular support was of little practical use as yet. The government, confident in the support of placemen and sinecure holders, pressed for the expulsion of Wilkes from the House of Commons for the publicaton of the *North Briton* No. 45. On 20 January 1764 they won their motion with an overwhelming majority. The fact that the case of the offending publication had still to be tried, or that Wilkes was unable to defend himself, being at that time absent in Paris, made no difference to a House of Commons which knew which side its bread was buttered. In an earlier division, a member who had dared to vote in favour of Wilkes was the following day dismissed from his government post.

In February 1764 the case against Wilkes and the *North Briton* was heard. Convinced that to return to England would mean immediate arrest and no real chance to defend himself, he remained in France. On 1 November sentence of outlawry was passed on him for failing to appear at the Court of the King's Bench. According to the Annual Register, it 'completed the ruin of

John Wilkes (1737–97), polemicist against the government of George III and campaigner for English liberties. He was also a great womanizer and boasted he needed no more than 20 minutes to talk round his notorious ugliness.

that unfortunate gentleman'. The government does not seem to have been so sure. In desultory contacts over the next three years it made offers of a secret pension to be paid to him, if he would make no attempt to return. Generous, extravagant and always in debt, Wilkes certainly needed the money but he could not accept the deal. He was determined to vindicate himself and early in February 1768, despite the terms of the outlawry which meant that he was liable to instant arrest, returned to England to stand for Parliament in the forthcoming general election.

On 28 March he was returned as a member for the County of Middlesex. For two days London was in the hands of the Wilkesites. Every carriage had Wilkes and Liberty or 'No. 45' forcibly engraved or painted on it. The Austrian ambassador, doyen of London's diplomatic corps, was taken from his carriage, up-ended by his ankles and had '45' chalked on the soles of his shoes.

Wilkes was on a campaign of calculated defiance which exposed the government to hostility and contempt. On 20 April, the first day of the Easter Law Term, he presented himself at the Court of King's Bench to surrender as an outlaw. Justice Lord Mansfield, fearful of the consequences for public order if he were to have Wilkes incarcerated, made the astonishing ruling that since the person at the bar had not been arrested in due form by the Attorney-General or his officers, the court could not perceive him. Wilkes was not in fact before the court at all!

The Wilkesites were delighted. Their hero, in obedience to the ruling, walked free. Then, after a week of riotous and well-publicized high living, he sent for an officer to have himself arrested. He then had his lawyer write to the Attorney-General to inform him that the arrest which should have been made by him had in fact been arranged by the prisoner. He was, at last, sentenced – to serve a term in the King's Bench prison in St George's Fields.

Now the chapter of government humiliations, all stemming from the blundering decision to persecute Wilkes five years before, took a new turn. The prison coach was hijacked. The police officers were ejected, the horses taken out of the shafts and the outlaw hero hauled up and down the city streets in triumph by a cheering, jeering, halooing crowd. From time to time, Wilkes leant out to protest that this was all very irregular as he was, after all, the King's prisoner. At last the 'escort' pulled up outside a tavern and in due course the prisoner slipped out, in disguise, and in a hired private carriage made his way to the prison where he had to knock up the turnkey to secure admission.

In the following weeks, while he was waiting for his appeal against the outlawry to be heard, Wilkes's prison was besieged nightly by immense crowds. The government increased the guard, the officers were given wide powers and on 10 May, when a detachment of Scots was on duty – soldiers with no love of the English – matters got out of hand. A volley fired at point blank range killed six and wounded 18 other demonstrators; pursuing a figure they took to be the ring leader, the troops broke into an outhouse and shot dead the labourer working there. A coroner's jury found the soldiers guilty of murder. A packed Grand Jury subsequently quashed the case. The blunder of the 'Massacre of St George's Fields' was compounded by the blatant distortion of justice. Killing Wilkesites was clearly all right by the authorities.

At last, with the government's reputation in London now threateningly low, the appeal against the outlawry came on for hearing. Wilkes was in great danger. An outlaw was without rights, theoretically he could be killed on sight by any citizen. And in reality Wilkes faced the possibility of perpetual imprisonment, subject to the pleasure of a hostile monarch. Lord Mansfield, either because of fears for his personal safety as some claimed, or because he judged the public mood a real threat to the establishment, ruled that the outlawry was void because of a small technical error in the wording of the original writ. London and many another city blazed with fireworks and celebratory illuminations.

But if Wilkes was not outlaw then he was subject to the verdict in the original case of libel and No. 45. For this he was sentenced to 22 months imprisonment. It was to prove the most active and devastatingly effective period of his life.

The King's Bench prison of those days would better be described as a gated pedestrian precinct. Inmates were confined, but the well-to-do lived in considerable comfort, having a small street of shops, coffee house and a tavern to serve their requirements. Thanks to a cascade of contributions, Wilkes lived in a comfortable suite of rooms where the service was excellent. Twenty guineas and a hamper of wine arrived from one group of well-wishers as a 'token of indignation and abhorrence of the government'. Salmon came from Plymouth and Newcastle; butts of ale, bottles of burgundy and claret, fish, baskets of game, collared brawn and hams and even 'a patriotic leg' of pork, arrived from towns all over England and, most generous of all and for the government most ominous, 45 hogsheads of tobacco came from the colony of Maryland.

No restrictions were placed on his visitors, women flocked to entertain the hero, men to admire and conference with him on his political campaigns. He was able to publish pamphlets, organize the election of a Wilkesite MP and himself win election as alderman of the City of London. A sentence of close on two years might seem stern, but the conditions under which it was served make it look uncommonly like yet another government blunder.

But now the House of Commons began a campaign that would boost Wilkes's cause still further. In February 1769, they voted to expel him by a majority of 82. King George was delighted: more dispassionate commentators saw trouble ahead. The City of London was incensed and the electors of Middlesex likewise. At the new election, set for 16 February, no opposition candidate presented himself and Wilkes was returned unopposed to fireworks and musical parades all over London. The next day the House of Commons not only voted to expel him again but declared that he 'was incapable of being elected a member'.

The ban was clearly not on the grounds of personal character or morals, even if, by the standards supposed to govern British MPs in the 1990s, they were a disgrace. If those standards had been applied in the 1770s it is doubtful whether it would have been possible to carry on the government of the country at all. No, to contemporaries it was obvious that Wilkes was expelled because he was the last determined popular opponent to the King's growing power.

On 16 March the electors of Middlesex convened once more to elect a representative; once more John Wilkes was returned unopposed to general laughter and delight; once more the Commons declared the election null and ordered another. On 13 April Wilkes was again returned, this time with 1143 votes to 296 cast for his nearest rival, the sinister Colonel Luttrell, already a Member of the House for the pocket borough of Bosinney. As licentious as Wilkes but brutal, too, he was the official candidate. The government, and through them the King, had entered the contest direct. Or so it seemed to many intelligent observers.

Of course the Commons declared the proceedings null, but now they went a step further and actually seated Luttrell as member, on the grounds that Wilkes having been declared ineligible to stand, votes cast for him had been 'thrown away'. That great parliamentarian Edmund Burke quoting the phrasing of contemporary playbills described it as 'the fifth act of a tragicomedy acted by His Majesty's servants, at the desire of several persons of quality, for the benefit of Mr Wilkes and at the expense of the constitution'.

The Wilkesites now began a campaign unprecedented in the history of British political institutions to buttress London's stand with the support of electors in the provinces – public meetings were organized all over the country to collect signatures on petitions of protest against the conduct of the government. Historians have identified this as the beginning of the idea of popular control in government.

Returns came in from Yorkshire, Bristol, Somerset, Newcastle, Liverpool, Gloucester and many other counties. So successful was the campaign that the King sent out calls to Lord-Lieutenants and other officials to secure counter-petitions – these came in easily enough from Scotland, but in England it was much more difficult. In Exeter a nobleman trying to organize a counter-petition was driven off with cries of 'Wilkes and Liberty'. The general effect of the royal intervention was to increase the turmoil and decrease popular respect for the King's government.

The balance was heavily pro-Wilkes with a total of 60,000 signatures. The King's speech on the reassembling of Parliament took no account of this astonishing expression of opinion but dealt instead with the diseases of horned cattle. The establishment argued that the landed gentry and the majority of gentlemen with large fortunes had not signed the petitions and that, if even a majority of such small freeholders had signed the petitions voluntarily, they were to be considered as a rabble, an ignorant multitude, incapable of judging.

It was commonly held that the Wilkesite resistance had had an immediate effect in America. On 6 June 1768 45 Sons of Liberty, convened at the Whig Tavern, Boston, Massachusetts, sent a glowing testimonial of support to 'Wilkes Illustrious Patriot'. In 1769 the South Carolina Assembly voted him SC£10,000, equivalent to £1500 sterling. On 23 March 1770 a meeting of the freeholders of Boston ordered that Wilkes be sent an account 'of the massacre in this town on the fifth inst.', when four demonstrators were shot down by royal troops. The terminology seemed a little awry, but maybe the Bostonians had in mind the six killed in St George's Fields, London.

Such affrays, hardly worthy of notice on a police file in continental Europe, were exceptional in the British tradition and the officials and officers who ordered them only blundered in misplaced allegiance to the government's cause.

Wilkes went on against all opposition to be voted Lord Mayor of London and preside over a notably liberal term of office. But the unusual image of the City as bastion of popular liberties would not last and Wilkes himself was driven from radical politics by an explosion as unforseeable as it was disgusting. In 1780 the London mob, incited by the crazy scion of a Scottish noble family with a grudge against the government, exploded in the Gordon riots.

Crowds which had once shouted 'Wilkes and Liberty' now shouted 'No Popery'. For nights Catholic businesses and mansions burned. Only Wilkes and the King kept their nerve. With royal approval he called out the militia – 257 rioters were shot down. Here was a massacre indeed, but the riot was ended. So, too, was Wilkes's political crusade.

How to make Martyrs – Establishment Recipe

In the spring of 1916 leaders of the Irish Volunteers were seeking German arms and assistance in their struggle for independence from the British Crown. In Germany itself Sir Roger Casement, the Ulster Protestant diplomat and convert to the struggle for an independent united Ireland and who had made approaches for German help, was also trying to recruit an Irish legion among prisoners of war in the German camps. He failed in his immediate objectives but, thanks to a combination of bungle, legalism and judicial hostility by the British authorities, he and the Volunteers' leaders were to swell the ranks of Irish martyrs – and create a myth of national 'blood sacrifice' that continues to resonate through Irish political discourse to this day.

Casement's failure to raise recruits among the Irish prisoners should not have surprised him. After all, these men were not conscripts. Like millions of English, Welsh and Scottish soldiers, they had volunteered to join the colours in the war against Germany. To many of them, Casement's proposals must have seemed a betrayal of their comrades who had died in the trenches. At this time, among ordinary Irish citizens, Kaiser Wilhelm II was much more the enemy than his English cousin King George V.

Meanwhile, in Dublin plans went forward among the militant organizers for a rising on Easter Sunday to be led by the Irish Volunteers with German support. It was doomed. On Good Friday a German submarine broke surface off the Irish coast and its pinnace scudded over the dawn waters to land a lone tall figure on the Kerry shore. Courageously risking capture and its consequences, Sir Roger Casement had returned to Ireland to warn the rebels to abandon their plans. There would be no support from Germany. He was arrested within hours and never delivered the message.

In fact, the plan had already begun to unravel in Dublin as the Volunteers' Chief of Staff Eoin MacNeill cancelled the plans for mobilization. In consequence, that Sunday passed off uneventfully. But the next day, 24 April, the Irish capital echoed to the sound of gunfire. In defiance of MacNeill's orders, a large force of patriot rebels, led by the schoolteacher and visionary Nationalist Padraig Pearse, had seized the General Post Office and proclaimed the Irish Republic.

Unsupported by any sympathy movement in the country at large, the rebel force held out for four days. When they surrendered, the Post Office and other buildings were in ruins and 450 lay dead, including 100 British soldiers. Remarkable as it may seem, the Easter Rising did not at first receive wide support among Irish public opinion – to many it appeared a treacherous conspiracy in the face of the enemy. After all, hundreds of thousands of

It is worse than a crime, it is a blunder.

ANTOINE BOULAY DE LA MEURTHE, FRENCH POLITICIAN, COMMENTING ON THE JUDICIAL MURDER OF THE DUC D'ENGHIEN, 1804

British troops inspect the ruins of Dublin's GPO building, following the Easter Rising of 1916. The Rising had little support from public opinion in Ireland which tended to solidarity with the British government in the First World War against Germany. Little support, that is, until the military authorities executed the leaders of the Rising – Padraig Pearse, Thomas Clarke, Sean MacDiarmada, Thomas MacDonagh, Eamonn Ceannt, James Connolly and Joseph Plunkett – who instantly became martyrs.

Irish fathers, sons and brothers had gone to fight and die alongside their British brothers-in-arms. Time enough to win the victory at home when the Kaiser had been beaten. London seemed to be offered a miraculous opportunity to resolve the Irish Question amicably, or at least make strides along the road to Home Rule along which they had been feeling their way for years now. Tragically, the government missed the opening.

For 14 fateful days, affairs in Dublin were under the direction of the military commander General Maxwell, a chain-smoking martinet. On his orders, the seven men who had signed the rebel declaration of independence were shot, as were all but one of the Volunteer commandants. Overnight the public mood reversed. From being disloyal mischief-makers, the dead men became martyrs. Through these blundering acts of reprisal and revenge, the London government lost Catholic goodwill, not only among the working classes but also among the prosperous middle class, many of whom had a vested interest in the status quo. Many Protestants, too, were appalled. Whether in wartime rebels who openly declared against king and country could have been allowed to live, is another question. But summary execution by military fiat was something else again. And, in any case, no political will was exerted to evaluate the situation.

The general's blunder was compounded by the fact that, if ruthlessness was to be order of the day, he was not ruthless enough. The survivor among the Volunteer commandants was one Eamon de Valera; born in the US of a Spanish father and an Irish mother, he was officially stateless and hence could not be condemned for treason to the British Crown. He survived to preside over Ireland's break with London and in due course to become president.

Possibly he was spared on orders from London, following representations from the US ambassador. Sir Roger Casement was less fortunate. He was to be tried and convicted, after appeal, of high treason and hanged on 3 August in London's Pentonville Prison – 'the bravest man it was ever my unhappy lot to execute,' said the official hangman. Whatever the legal technicalities of the case, it had been open to the government to recommend mercy. F. E. Smith, the prosecuting counsel and a committed Ulster Unionist, had some years before sought German help and arms for the Unionist struggle against government moves towards Home Rule for a united Ireland and if the Unionists could claim to be fighting to maintain the United Kingdom, they were, equally, fighting to subvert the policy of the King's government – surely itself a treasonable venture. But when Casement's defence attempted to draw the parallel, he was cut short by the presiding Lord Chief Justice. After sentence had been passed, Casement, who all along denied the competence of an English court to try an Irishman, delivered a speech of such eloquence that it would be described years later by another Ulster Unionist as 'the finest document in patriotic literature'.

For 50 years Casement's body lay in Pentonville jail. Then, on 23 February 1965, Britain's Prime Minister Harold Wilson overrode the regulations, and the remains were returned to Ireland to receive a state funeral at Glasnevin. There, President de Valera delivered the funeral oration, head bare, in homage to the dead. He was at the time a sick man. His doctors had urged him not to attend the ceremony but if he must, at least to keep his head covered. 'Casement deserves better than that,' was his reply.

In 1916 there had been an outcry from Irish Americans and a swell of sympathy among opinion in other neutral countries against the execution. The then prime minister, Herbert Asquith, would have preferred to recommend mercy, but hesitated, among other things it was said, because it would seem to show favour to the Protestant knight Casement, above the Catholic commoners who were supposedly his followers and who had been executed in the immediate aftermath of the Rising. In fact, Asquith and his cabinet took the best part of four sessions to come to the conclusion not to recommend the King to exercise the royal prerogative of mercy. In the words of Asquith's biographer, Roy Jenkins, 'There can be few other examples of a Cabinet devoting [so much time] to considering an individual sentence – and then arriving at the wrong decision.'

When it came to the crunch, the politicians proved no wiser in judging the right rather than the legalistic action in the Irish situation than had the Chief of Staff in Dublin when he ordered the executions of the other martyrs-to-be.

A Trick Too Far by the Welsh Wizard

While it would be absurd to describe David Lloyd George as an establishment figure, as prime minister of Great Britain and Ireland he certainly

BLUNDERING ESTABLISHMENTS

The 'Welsh Wizard' in person. David Lloyd George (1863–1945), prime minister of Britain (1916–22), at Cannes, south of France, in January 1922. It was said that he did not mind which way he was going, so long as he was in the driving seat.

headed the establishment. And, as if to establish his credentials, he blundered in Ireland with the best of them.

In March–April 1918 a massive German offensive on the Western Front pushed the British lines back 40 miles. In May–June the French were driven to within 40 miles of Paris. Alarm and despondency on the Home Front and outcries against the 'slackers' who were not in the armed forces prompted Britain's prime minister, Lloyd George, nicknamed the 'Welsh Wizard', to raise the call-up age to 50. In fact none of the new draft was sent to the front, but the gesture pleased public opinion – except for one aspect. Unfortunately, the population on the British mainland classed their Irish fellow citizens as 'slackers', because conscription, in force in Britain since 1916, did not apply to Ireland.

Backbench MPs demanded the system be standardized throughout the United Kingdom.

Informed opinion, even amongst extreme Protestant Unionists, opposed the idea. Ireland had contributed thousands upon thousands of volunteers to the war effort and, still more to the point, compulsion would intensify resistance to British rule on the island and require more troops to enforce than would be brought in.

It was now that a convention of experts which for months had been working to find a solution to the Irish problem formally announced that it was winding up its deliberations, being unable to find any formula that would meet the objections of Ulster to any form of Home Rule. As usual, Irish opinion in America got agitated. With what he considered an adroit policy move, Lloyd George sought to placate the Irish Americans, Ulster Unionists and British home front discontent, by linking the two issues. Compulsion was formally extended to Ireland but was actually to be enforced only when she received Home Rule, within the United Kingdom.

It is difficult to believe that even Lloyd George, that prince of fixers, could have supposed that such a transparent sleight of hand would deceive anyone. It outraged Irish opinion. The Nationalist MPs left the House of Commons in a body and joined forces with Sinn Féin. A national strike on 23 April, England's national day, closed down the whole of Ireland outside Belfast – even the pubs. Worse yet for Westminster, the Irish Roman Catholic hierarchy, which until then had intervened surprisingly little in the political arena, denounced conscription as 'an oppressive law which the Irish have the right to resist by every means consonant with the laws of God'. The American-born Eamon de Valera, wily veteran of the Easter Rising, now became Sinn Féin President and the acknowledged leader of the Irish nationalist cause.

In response to the General Strike, Lloyd George claimed evidence for a 'German plot'. Reprisals included the imprisonment of Sinn Féin leaders in England and the introduction of a military-based regime in Ireland. To mollify Ulster opinion, all talk of Home Rule was dropped – so, too, was all talk of conscription. But this came too late to have any effect. It had never been put into force, it had never been intended to be put into force. But the mere idea had transformed the Irish context. Henceforward no Home Rule formula involving devolution within the Union had any chance of being entertained by any strand of Nationalist opinion. Delight in his own machinations had led Lloyd George into a blunder that finished forever the dream Liberal governments had been working towards for forty years since the time of Gladstone. Ludendorff's great Spring Offensive may not have won the war for Germany but, in the words of the historian A. J. P. Taylor, its aftermath 'caused the British Empire to lose Ireland'.

Chicken Blunder

Blunders by the establishment can be tragic and momentous in their consequences. Equally, they can be hilarious, especially when the members fall out among themselves. Periodically, the British Parliamentary Boundaries

BLUNDERING ESTABLISHMENTS

Commission redraws constituency boundaries to reflect population movements. This may impact on the political balance in constituencies, making previously safe seats marginal as voters of different political views move in or out of an area. Hoping to ensure success at the next election, an MP may leave such a marginal constituency and seek adoption as candidate in one where his party's majority seems more secure. Sometimes, however, the 'chicken run' can lead to the exit. In 1983 the Tory MP for Aberdeen South abandoned the constituency for the better prospect of Roxburgh and Berwickshire. He lost – but the Tory who took over from him in Aberdeen won there.

But for real clowning few can outdo Mussolini, whose career ended when he blundered into the very establishment he himself had founded.

King Vittorio Emmanuele III of Italy (left) and Benito Mussolini, Italian dictator, at the army manoeuvres in the Abruzzi, 1938. The photographer has caught an angle which flatters the diminutive figure of the King. In fact, Mussolini's underestimation of the King's importance would be an important factor in his own downfall.

A Forgotten Establishment

To describe any course of action as a blunder presupposes that there was some other course open to the decision-maker which would have been preferable, even if not ideal. But just as a chess player may find himself in a position where he has to move, even though any move is to his disadvantage, so a politician, after a series of poor policy decisions, may find himself confronting a situation where a choice has to be made from a number of options all of which are bad.

Thus a blunder becomes unavoidable. He can only hope to choose, in the immortal words of British Tory minister Steve Norris, when commenting on the re-election of John Major as Tory leader, the 'least worst' option.

There are those who would say that the entire career of Benito Mussolini, the Italian dictator, was, for Italy, a worst option and chronic blunder. That would be unjust, if only because he came closer than anyone this century to eradicating the Mafia. However, it was true that many Italians endured appalling injustices and suffering at the hands of his fascist thug regime, and that the last three years of his rule as 'Duce' followed a trail of increasingly hazardous policy decisions.

For years effective dictator of his country, he ignored the fact that, in constitutional theory at least, he was subordinate to the King and that the King could command the loyalty of an establishment which, though submissive, remained a potential power in national affairs.

The beginning of the downward slope for Mussolini, though few would have supposed so at the time, was his decision to enter the Second World War on Germany's side in 1940, following the fall of France. With only Great Britain holding out against the Nazi power, the end of the conflict seemed very near and the time ripe to join the winning side. Italy was hardly prepared for a long war, but such a war did not seem to be in prospect. A few weeks, months at most, as comrade-in-arms of his friend and admirer Adolf Hitler would surely guarantee Italy a handsome share in the spoils of war. There must have been hopes of recovering Nice and other territories annexed by France in the 19th century.

As months dragged into years, this dream world of the future dissolved into a nightmare of a present where Mussolini faced a choice between extricating Italy from the war or seeing his Fascist regime of 20 years' standing ousted by a counter-coup. The Anglo-American invasion of Sicily on 10 June 1943 threatened to roll up the Italian mainland, just as allied triumphs in North Africa the previous year had overrun Italy's province of Libya. National humiliation threatened and, as the man whose war-mongering had opened up the prospect, Mussolini was of little further use to his country, unless he could exert his special influence with the Führer to release Italy to make the best terms it could with the advancing allies. If he failed he was, unless he played his hand with exceptional skill, almost certainly doomed to fall. This much he knew. What he did not know was that for some months past a conspiracy had been building against him with the connivance of King Vittorio Emmanuele III.

This was the King whose failure to authorize martial law 20 years earlier had opened the way to the Fascists' 'March on Rome' and Mussolini's coming to power. There were those who said this had not been the result of any royal miscalculation and who considered the King a willing partner to the dictator. Over those 20 years the little man with the big moustache had, as constitutional monarch, received Il Duce in audience each Monday and Thursday, and Mussolini saw no reason to fear a threat from the palace. Maybe he should have suspected, for, in the words of a Fascist malcontent: 'So long as the situation is handled under the aegis of the dynasty, its solution will have a legal character and the troops will obey their orders.' In other words, only the

I could not help being charmed ... by Signore Mussolini's gentle and simple bearing and by his calm detached poise ...

WINSTON CHURCHILL WRITING IN *THE TIMES*, 21 JANUARY 1927.

King had the authority to overthrow the dictator, so the dictator should perhaps have paid more attention to the King. For his part, Vittorio Emmanuele knew that he would get no second chance if he blundered.

His opportunity occurred in July 1943. On the 19th, Duce and Führer met at a hastily arranged rendezvous in a secluded villa at Feltre, near Treviso in Northern Italy. The one to beg permission to leave the field of battle, the other to insist that German forces already in the peninsula be reinforced and the fighting there intensified. In short, Mussolini won not a single concession from his friend and ally across the Alps. He returned to Rome, aware that he had precious few friends there, but unaware just how few.

It is difficult to see what course of action could have saved him: it is almost certain that the one he did choose would end in disaster. Pressured by party leaders, he convened a special meeting of the Fascist Grand Council, the official cabinet of the régime, for the evening of 24 July. *Ipso facto* he submitted his authority to their deliberations. Insofar as one could talk of constitutional procedures in Mussolini's Italy, it was a constitutional blunder. Yet he had good enough reason to be confident that nothing serious would eventuate. In the heyday of his power this periodic assemblage of henchmen had generally been content to listen to their leader's policy pronouncements. As Il Duce himself amiably boasted, there was 'never, I repeat never, any question of voting'.

This time things were different. The argument went raggedly back and forth into the small hours of Sunday 25 July when Count Dino Grandi, a 'moderate', proposed a motion critical of Il Duce. It was passed. Even now Mussolini appeared to be unconcerned about the immediate future. His only concession to the unusual situation was to request a special audience of the King that same day, i.e. a day ahead of his regular Monday morning audience. But the King now triggered the royal conspiracy and gave orders that Il Duce be arrested after the audience. Evidently expecting trouble from the dictator, the King ordered a courtier 'to stand by the door of the drawing room where we shall talk and to intervene if need arise'.

In the event, the need did not arise. Mussolini, arriving punctually, like one of his trains, began his report. But the King interrupted him. In a few disjointed sentences – with characteristic lapses into the Piedmontese dialect – he demanded the dictator's resignation. Il Duce saw that the game was up. He knew his King well enough to realize that, if he dared make such a demand, he already had the backing to enforce it. Mussolini resigned.

Perhaps, reclining in the limousine as he was driven away under escort, he reflected that his principal blunder years ago, when at the height of his power, was not to have disposed of the monarchy once and for all. At all events, a new government under Marshall Badoglio was installed that evening, and many a dazed fascist was left to come to terms with the fact that a forced blunder by Il Duce himself had been followed by an act of suicide by the party leadership. For the council was not to be allowed the luxury of finding a new Duce to present for the approval of the King. The King had at last taken sides. The Fascist system in Italy had blundered to collapse in the course of a single day without a shot being fired in its defence.

CHAPTER 5: PARTY MATTERS AND PARTY LEADERS

A Leader's Reputation in Question

In a democracy the ambitious politician who aims to lead his country must first lead his party. At least this is usually the way. But there are various ways to the top and once there, one is not always guaranteed of holding on to the position. On the other hand, there are some men who have achieved supreme power almost by chance as it were. No fewer than nine US vice-presidents succeeded to the presidency by the death of their predecessor. Some proved outstanding chief executives and none more so than Theodore Roosevelt. His rise to the vice-presidency resulted from a blunder by party managers anxious to neutralize his dynamic humanitarianism. But that same humanitarianism had its weaknesses which led him into a blunder that was to impact heavily on his reputation.

Not all political blunders have immediate consequences, some may have a delayed impact, such was the case with Roosevelt's and his handling of the 'Brownesville Affray' of 1906.

A sickly child, 'Teddy' Roosevelt grew into a tough, adventurous young man. In his twenties he travelled the big game trails of Africa, coming back with many hundreds of trophies. He next made national headlines with his exploits in the Spanish–American war and, having made his reputation, went into politics. A staunch Republican, in those days a progressive party, he won elected office in the New York state administration. He proved as courageous among the capitalist predators that ruled there as he had in the jungles and bush of the game trails. The slum landlords were just one group who were hard hit by his reforming zeal.

But New York's Republican Party bosses decided that he was taking his idealist campaign on behalf of the underdog too far. In 1900 they arranged his selection as vice-presidential candidate under William McKinley, then running for a second term in office. He was duly returned to the White House and Roosevelt gratifyingly neutralized – for just nine months. For McKinley fell to an assassin's bullet in 1901, and the champion of fair dealing followed him as president and took over the government of the whole nation, not just New York state. Now he could go after the real big game, the robber barons who ran the coal, steel and rail cartels and monopolies. While he did not break their power entirely, he did enough to make his selection as vice-president one of the worst day's work a party's fixers ever did for themselves.

Unfortunately, it would seem that Roosevelt, like most of his white

Party loyalty lowers the greatest of men to the petty level of the masses.

Jean de la Bruyère,
French satirist,
1688

Theodore Roosevelt (1858–1919), US president (1901–08), at the Chevy Chase Club, Washington, 1902. He cleared many a political hurdle but blundered over his handling of the 'Brownesville Affray'.

compatriots, had a blind spot when it came to questions of colour – the result was a decision which has badly stained his reputation.

In the summer of 1906 American public opinion was horrified by newspaper reports of an incident at Brownesville. It was said that, on the night of 13–14 August, a body of troops had run amok, terrorizing the community, killing a bartender and wounding a lieutenant of police. What exactly happened that night was never properly established to the satisfaction of detached observers. Certainly, the investigation immediately ordered by the President did not provide the answers.

It was an internal inquiry, conducted by the Army, and proceeded on the supposition that since those implicated included three black companies, the culprits for the 'Affray' would be found among their number. Twelve black troopers were fingered and the inquiry set about finding evidence that would condemn them. Unfortunately, nothing conclusive could be found against the twelve or indeed against any of the black soldiers.

However, there was a public outcry and 'something had to be done'. Roosevelt, always happy to please popular opinion, ordered that, as no individuals could be charged on the evidence, all 170 men of the three companies implicated be discharged from the service without honour. Six of them had in fact been awarded the Medal of Honor and all must surely have been bitter to be victims of such naked racial prejudice.

In fact, doubts were even expressed in the legislature where Senator Joseph B. Foraker contested the presidential decision and exposed the flimsy nature of the evidence on which it was based. What must have seemed a straightforward enough piece of populist policy on the hoof began to look a little less inspired. In March 1909, 14 of the men were declared eligible to re-enlist. The reputations of the others were only finally vindicated in 1972.

Roosevelt's initial behaviour was surely unjust; it was also, in terms of his subsequent reputation, a mistake. However, whether he himself came to regard it as such is not clear; he was not a man given greatly to self-doubt. It may be significant that the episode finds no mention in his autobiography.

The Man who Guessed Wrong and the Man who Did Right

In November 1905 two speeches within a week of one another seemed to signal a split in the Liberal ranks on the subject of Irish Home Rule. At Stirling on 23 November, Sir Henry Campbell-Bannerman, the Party leader, urged what he called a 'step-by-step policy'; at Bodmin on the 25th, Lord Rosebery attacked the policy, declaring 'emphatically and explicitly and once and for all' that he could not 'serve under that banner'. As a former Liberal prime minister, he naturally carried weight. But two other leading Liberals, Herbert Asquith and Sir Edward Grey had, unknown to Rosebery, privately approved the Campbell-Bannerman line. Himself under pressure from dissidents in his own party on Tariff Reform and other topics, the Unionist Conservative prime minister, Arthur Balfour, resigned on 4 December in what he believed would prove a shrewd tactical stroke. He did not dissolve Parliament, thinking that the Liberals, if called to form a government, would in fact be split by their rivalries over Home Rule and other matters and that in the ensuing general election the Unionists would reunite and come through victoriously. It was a transparent manoeuvre and many supporters of Campbell-Bannerman urged him to refuse the premiership. But he argued that if the Liberals held back, the country would never again believe in them as a serious party. He accepted the King's invitation and formed an administration. One of the most talented of the 20th century, it included among the 'new men' Lloyd George as President of the Board of

Trade and Winston Churchill, a recent defector from the Conservative party, as an under-secretary at the colonial office.

In the general election the following month, the Liberals routed the Unionists, returning to power with 377 members and an overall majority of 84. Other parties included 83 Irish Nationalists led by John Redmond and – the sensation of the election – no fewer than 53 Labour members. The Unionists managed only 157 seats and this group was split into factions. Outright Balfour supporters numbered just 32. The former leader had surely blundered.

The Slow Demise of the Liberal Party

On 7 May 1918 an extraordinary letter appeared in *The Times*. It was from Major General Sir Frederick Maurice and it accused the Prime Minister, David Lloyd George, in effect, of having lied to the House of Commons earlier that year about the strength of the British Army in France. Since the German Spring Offensive had come near to defeating the Franco-British forces in northern France before the full force of American reinforcements could be brought to bear, the charge that British troops were in fact below strength when the Prime Minister had assured the Commons that they were above strength, implied a serious indictment. Sir Frederick had been sacked as Director of Military Operations at the War Office the previous month and, inevitably, it would be suggested that he was out for revenge. Whatever the general's motives, his action in making public criticism of his superiors was a startling breach of military discipline.

But the charges, if they could be brought home, would have a devastating effect on Lloyd George, who had displaced Herbert Asquith as Liberal leader and prime minister back in 1916. This had opened a split in the Liberal Party between the Asquithians, or 'Squiffites', and Lloyd George's own supporters who joined him in a coalition with the Conservatives of Bonar Law. After the war Lloyd George would claim that the 'Maurice Debate' was part of an Asquithian plot 'to blow up the government'. If so, it was a strategic blunder of historic proportions for the Liberal Party.

The general had been careful not to use the word 'liar', preferring instead to list the claims that had been made by the Prime Minister, following each one with the phrase 'that is not correct'. The letter ended with a call for parliamentary 'investigation into the statements I have made'. Despite Lloyd George's accusations of plotting, Asquith had no knowledge of the letter before it was sent. However, the moment it appeared, urged by supporters, he moved quickly, putting a question that afternoon to Bonar Law, the Conservative Leader of the House. Momentarily wrong-footed, Law offered an inquiry by two judges. Instead of accepting at once, Asquith demanded a debate before any decision be taken. Supplementary questions led to a proposal by another Liberal member that a select committee of the House of Commons be set up. Law responded with an offer that if he accepted the judicial enquiry, Asquith himself could nominate the judges. Again, Asquith demurred and insisted on a full debate before any inquiry was set up.

Henry Herbert Asquith (1852–1928), the Liberal statesman and prime minister (1908–16), was renowned for his patrician good looks as well as his political sophistication. His fall from power, outmanoeuvred by Lloyd George, intitiated the final decline of the Liberal Party.

The debate was duly held on 9 May on the motion that the House set up a select committee into the allegations. Asquith's short speech did not command conviction. Many members thought that the charges, though serious, were old history – after all, the German armies were still advancing towards Paris. When Asquith posed the rhetorical question 'What is the alternative to a committee?' he was answered by a miners' union MP, who was loudly cheered, 'To get on with the war!'

Replying to the debate, Lloyd George, in a compelling 90-minute speech, escaped from the offer of the judicial inquiry, smeared Asquith with the accusation of politicking and plotting to bring down the government in time of war and utterly discredited Maurice's allegations by revealing to a stunned House that the figures in question had in fact been supplied by the department of military operations of which Maurice himself had been head at the time. Four years later Maurice was to allege that the Prime Minister had received a correction of the figures which he had suppressed. The details were never fully established and were, in any case, irrelevant by then.

At the time, Asquith, unable to counter his opponent's rhetoric, could have withdrawn his motion. He did not do so. Close on a hundred Liberal MPs went into the lobbies with him but the motion was defeated by 295 to 108 votes – a resounding vindication for the Prime Minister. Moreover, the country observed that the official opposition had divided the house against the government (the only time this happened during the war). As Asquith and his followers went home gloomily, some may have sensed that the Liberal Party, already weakened by splits, had to all intents and purposes committed suicide as a major force in British politics.

Looking back, we can identify three serious blunders committed by Asquith and his followers. First, had he accepted the government's initial offer of a judicial inquiry, Lloyd George would surely have been embarrassed during the course of the inquiry, supposing that Maurice's accusations had any foundation in fact, and if he did not believe that, then Asquith should not have taken up the issue in the first place. Secondly, once Lloyd George had exploded the charge in debate, it would have been wise to withdraw the motion. Thirdly, they should have recalled the words of the brilliant F. E. Smith, later Lord Birkenhead: 'The man who enters into real and fierce controversy with Mr Lloyd George must think clearly, think deeply and think ahead. Otherwise he will think too late.'

PR, the Missed Opportunities

One of the longest-running debates in British politics is over the rights and wrongs of proportional representation, generally called PR. In most other European countries, elections are decided on some form of alternative vote or second-round system. In Germany, the continent's most successful postwar economy and arguably most democratic state, government is chosen and conducted on the basis of a constitution devised after the war by a panel including British constitutional experts to guard against a return of dictatorship. It is therefore perhaps somewhat ironic that Britain herself continues to bumble along on a first-past-the-post system that has been called 'the least fair, most arbitrary and least democratic of all methods of election in the democratic world.'

The result is essentially a two-party structure which has, for advantage, the exclusion of extremist groups, whether of right or left; there have only ever been two communist MPs in the House of Commons and not a single representative of the right-wing National Front party. On the other hand, the moderate Liberal Party, which regularly attracts the support of four to six million voters, is excluded from any say in government. Not surprisingly, the Liberals are the strongest advocates of the introduction of some form of proportional voting. Rather more surprising is the fact that on two out of the three occasions when there seemed some prospect of radical change in the electoral formula, they were thwarted by Liberal politicians.

The first instance happened in 1917 and was the outcome of overweening

Proportional representation, I think, is fundamentally counter-democratic.

NEIL KINNOCK, LEADER OF THE BRITISH LABOUR PARTY, 1983

confidence. The Prime Minister, David Lloyd George, possibly the most brilliant and certainly the most unpredictable man ever to occupy Number 10 Downing Street, was a Liberal who had recently come to power as head of the war cabinet in a 'palace revolution', which had ousted Liberal Party leader Herbert Asquith from the premiership. Truth to tell, Lloyd George was loyal to only one party and that with a membership of just one, but he was a master operator in the two-party Liberal–Conservative system which then ruled the British political scene (Labour, barely ten years old, had fewer than fifty members). The Liberals were divided and fatally weakened by his manoeuvring. No matter, he would recruit backing among the Conservatives. So when, in 1917, a Speaker's Conference came out in favour of a form of proportional representation and the proposal was voted through by the House of Lords, Lloyd George blocked the idea as a threat to the two-party environment in which he was so adept. He continued as Prime Minister until 1922 when the Conservatives withdrew their support. Defeated in the subsequent election, he returned to Parliament as leader of a rump Liberal party in 1926. It would never again hold office. Lloyd George's rejection of PR in 1917 had been automatic, almost casual. It was a blunder of structural importance and the Liberal Party has been kicking its collective self ever since.

The second opportunity when Liberals might conceivably have exerted leverage to change the voting system came in February 1974. Following a disastrous miscalculation in election timing, Edward Heath, the Tory prime minister, had lost himself a quite respectable parliamentary working majority. Nevertheless, the Tories held 297 seats to Labour's 301 and there was a chance that if the handful of Liberals, led by Jeremy Thorpe, joined the Tories, a majority coalition could be cobbled together with the other minority parties such as the Scottish and Welsh Nationalists. Accordingly, Heath invited the Liberal leader for talks to Number 10 Downing Street. (Since Labour, although the largest single party, did not have an overall majority either, Heath, as outgoing Prime Minister, had the right to attempt to form a government.) Thorpe accepted the invitation enthusiastically. Critics said that he should first have strengthened his negotiating position by consulting with other centrist politicians. But since, as soon became clear, the majority of the little parliamentary Liberal Party was opposed to supporting a Tory government, it is doubtful that this would have made any difference to the outcome. In fact, Heath offered him a cabinet post and a Speaker's Conference on electoral reform. Thorpe refused both and, to outsiders at least, it seemed the Liberals had blundered and lost their most promising chance in years of winning electoral justice for themselves and the millions who vote for them.

On the third occasion on which Westminster came near to adopting PR, its failure had nothing to do with any individual blunder. In February 1931 Ramsay MacDonald's government introduced a bill for a single transferable vote. It passed the Commons on second reading with a majority of 65, only to be thrown out by the Lords. The only blunderer here was the British constitution which left the decisive vote on a question of constitutional fundamentals to a non-elected chamber.

The Leader who Made a Mistake

Opinion on Margaret Thatcher's premiership used to be divided between those who believed she never made mistakes and those who believed she never made anything else. Her detractors in the second camp supposed, as the evidence of her speeches in office certainly seemed to warrant, that she was a fully committed member of the first camp. After her fall in 1990, evidence emerged that, controversially perhaps, she did entertain the thought that she might, on occasion, have been fallible. Indeed, she described one decision as her worst mistake, which clearly indicates she thought there were others, though these remained unnamed.

The blunder to which Baroness Thatcher confessed, though with the characteristic proviso that she was forced into it by others, was the decision to take Britain into Europe's Exchange Rate Mechanism (ERM). Since the decision was actually implemented by John Major, then Chancellor of the Exchequer, and since its consequences led to a sensational collapse in the value of the pound sterling, it might be thought that it would have impacted, in some way, on his career also. In fact, he succeeded Thatcher in the premiership and was awarded an election victory in his own right by the British electorate – which can only lead one to reflect yet again on what, if anything, can properly be classed as a political blunder.

The debate on British policy with regard to European monetary integration rumbled through most of the 1980s, and if it did not occupy the forefront of Tory policy-making, that was because the Prime Minister and her principal adviser, Sir Alan Walters, dismissed it out of hand. But many senior ministers, pro-European in other matters, were strongly in favour. Of these Nigel Lawson, Chancellor of the Exchequer, and Geoffrey Howe, Foreign Secretary, became the leaders.

On 25 June 1989 they confronted Margaret Thatcher in her study in Number 10 Downing Street, as she was preparing for her flight to Madrid for the European Council of Ministers, with the threat of their certain resignations if a positive commitment to join the ERM were not made publicly and soon. They were serious and she felt pressured into consent. Later that same day, she startled the heads of government assembled in the Spanish capital with the announcement that Britain would, after all, join as soon as certain conditions were met.

The basic 'Madrid conditions' were a drop in Britain's inflation rate to the European average, a strong British economy and the liberalization of capital movements by certain other European countries. Within three months, first Howe and then Lawson were sacked, each to be succeeded in turn by John Major, rumoured to be Mrs Thatcher's choice as her successor.

On becoming chancellor Major, who had voiced his support for the ERM years before, a fact which his patroness had apparently forgotten, set about the implementation of the policy agreed by her under pressure from the two men she had so recently dismissed. Thorough in everything, Margaret Thatcher even blundered with aplomb. But now she and her administration were under stress. Her 'flagship' policy of a poll tax produced rioting

> *The Chancellor's position is unassailable.*
>
> PRIME MINISTER MARGARET THATCHER ENDORSING HER CHANCELLOR, NIGEL LAWSON, SHORTLY BEFORE MAKING HIS POSITION UNTENABLE, 1990.

unmatched since London's Gordon riots of the 18th century (see p. 62). Both the Tory Party's and Thatcher's popularity ratings were plunging on the opinion polls. The pound was under consequent threat.

Not so the recently appointed foreign secretary, Douglas Hurd or Chancellor Major. They knew that the imperious iron lady was effectively shackled by her revenge on their predecessors. The Prime Minister could hardly dismiss four senior cabinet members within twelve months and retain her reputation. Convinced of the advantages of ERM membership, Major accordingly announced in his budget speech of March 1990 that Britain's membership was a question of 'when' not of 'if'. The move was actually made in October and the Prime Minister could only concur. But if she agreed under duress, she found room for one more blunder all her own, making the proviso that there be a 1 per cent cut in interest rates. Given that inflation was already running at 10 per cent, the proviso was not a wise one.

So, despite the 'Madrid conditions' she herself had promulgated, Britain joined the ERM with a way above average inflation rate, in the throes of a protracted recession, and, just for good measure, with the pound at the absurdly high rate of 2.95 to the Deutschmark. About all that can be said in mitigation of this catalogue of errors by a governing party which prided itself on sound money management and a Prime Minister who vaunted the economics of the handbag as the guiding principle of national finance, is that she, at least, had been driven from office by her colleagues before the year was out.

Her replacement by the Chancellor who had implemented the policy is explicable only on political and not on rational criteria. It is supposed that

All friends! Margaret Thatcher at the Conservative Party election briefing, June 1987. On her right is Nigel Lawson, her chancellor. Lawson had already registered dismay at the poll tax, the Party's flagship policy for the election but the root cause of Thatcher's ousting as Party leader in November 1990.

Major was perceived as a nonentity whose accession to the leadership would cause least offence in a party desperate to maintain unity. Moreover, since defeat in the approaching election seemed certain, an interim leader who could easily be dumped thereafter was ideal. To the dismay of more thoughtful Tories, he was in fact returned to office. The economic shambles consequent on their purchase of power over the past 12 years should, by well-established precedent, have been left for the Labour Party to clear up, while attracting the harsh press that went with the job. Instead, a Conservative government had to clear up after itself.

Economic policy at the beginning of Major's administration was determined by the requirements of ERM membership. The result was the longest recession in post-war history. The economy shrank by 2.5 per cent in 1991; the official unemployment figures rose to 2.7 million, and this despite the fact that the calculation criteria had been altered almost annually to yield more favourable results over the Tories' eleven years in office. Interest rates were still running at 10 per cent, 48,000 businesses failed, 75,000 homes were repossessed, some 250,000 people were more than six months in arrears on their mortgage repayments (all this under a party which boasted it was building a property-owning democracy), and social security spending was at a record high. Government revenue, meantime, had fallen some £20 billion in four years. The situation was bleak and the outlook, to informed observers, worse.

Prime Minister Major and Chancellor Norman Lamont, loyally parroted by government spokesmen, assured the country on a regular basis that despite the barren economic landscape, 'green shoots' would be soon appearing. Major even let it be known that he expected the pound to replace the Deutschmark as Europe's strongest currency. Thanks to the speculation of the Hungarian multi-billionaire George Soros and the misconceived financial management of its affairs by the chief ministers of the Crown, the pound sterling tumbled humiliatingly out of the basket of European currencies, losing more than 10 per cent in the process.

A number of people had blundered sensationally, but few of them appearing to be suffering for it. John Major was Prime Minister and Thatcher, a baroness by her own creation, was rumoured to command a speaking fee of up to £50,000. Fortunately, perhaps, her advice was now largely heeded only by American luncheon clubs.

The Leader who Lacked the Common Touch

Through the winter of 1994–5 French political life bubbled in mock speculation as to whether Edouard Balladur, prime ministerial appointee of President François Mitterrand, would or would not stand as a candidate in the elections to be held in April and May to decide Mitterrand's successor. Everyone knew that he would and most people thought he would win. However, they underestimated the importance of the 'common touch'. In the land which prides itself as the home of the Rights of Man and the model for democracy, the political élite does not value this quality. The idea of the

THE LEADER WHO LACKED THE COMMON TOUCH

son of a circus entertainer clamouring for votes while perched on a fruit crate masquerading as a soap box – for thus, some have claimed, did Britain's John Major snatch an eleventh-hour victory in the 1992 election – would be dismissed out of hand by French political commentators.

The Balladur candidacy was given added spice by the fact that, whatever its outcome might be, it would be a classic act of political betrayal. Two years before, he and his Gaullist party colleague Jacques Chirac, Mayor of Paris, former prime minister and two-time loser in previous presidential elections, had agreed that Balladur should accept appointment as Mitterrand's prime minister and in return Chirac should have a free run at the presidency (see also pp. 26–27). But it soon became obvious that Balladur was going to renege on the deal. While Chirac declared his candidacy in October and went on the electoral stump, Balladur – pear-shaped, dough-faced and would-be patrician in manner – parried questions about his plans with pious disclaimers that, as prime minister, he was too busy with the actual business of government to decide on his presidential intentions at this point. He would announce his decision in February. None doubted that – in the best interests of France, of course – it would be positive.

Meanwhile, Balladur appeared from time to time on the country's television screens, seated behind a solemn desk in the PM's official residence, the Matignon Palace, spelling out policies which would one day reduce unemployment and revitalize the economy. In lively contrast to these statesmanlike disquisitions, Jacques Chirac would be seen pressing the flesh in market

Edouard Balladur, France's Prime Minister, campaigning for president, April 1995 – obliged to 'meet the people' but preferably without eye contact.

81

towns and factories, emerging from cow sheds surrounded by farming folk, knocking back tots of dubious home-distilled calvados or farmhouse brandy in smoky vaulted cellars. The smile was always present as he made friends and influenced people with, it was rumoured, deals about favours to come, should he win in May.

Terrible things were said about the man in the bars frequented by the commercial and professional élite of France's provincial towns and in the smarter *arrondissements* of the capital. For, although Chirac, like any serious contender for the upper reaches of government, was a graduate of one of the *grandes écoles*, the nurseries of the élite that governs modern France, he was not out of the top drawer socially, not 'a man of family'. It was claimed, though one hopes without justification, that his table manners were not quite up to par, and even that he was in politics because he wanted power. Outside the stuffy world of French class and privilege, besides which England's variety seems garish and almost jolly, Monsieur Jacques Chirac looked extraordinarily like a serious politician running for office. What is more, he seemed to relish the company of his fellow-citizens, to actually *enjoy* meeting people.

No such charge could be brought against Balladur. In February he duly announced his candidature. Nobody was surprised, and few people were impressed. He quickly dropped into third place behind the Socialist Lionel Jospin who had started the campaign as a complete no-hoper. Balladur's political managers realized that he, too, would have to hit the campaign trail.

Now it was Balladur's turn to smile, no matter how queasily, as good-natured country folk clustered round his entourage and, as the weeks slipped by and his ratings slipped down, reached out hands to be shaken and children to be patted. This was hardly the company for a London-tailored gentleman-technocrat. But this high flier of the *grandes écoles* could grit his teeth as well as the next man and, as a concession to the rustic theme, appeared in a beautifully cut, if idiosyncratic, Barbour-style garment to bolster his image as *homme du peuple*. On one occasion the would-be president was even glimpsed sporting green wellies. But always the cashmere muffler, tucked neatly round the well-fed double chin, gave the game away. This person was not for personal contact.

The more desperate his position became, the more Balladur had to go out and meet the people, and the more he went out and met the people, the more obvious it became that he could not stand them. The 'grand seigneur' inclination of the little body and the pudgy hand extended droopingly on its well-sleeved arm, signalled not the outreach of *bonhomie* but the body language of deep embarrassment. Tactically, Balladur made his first blunder when he delayed his declaration in the belief that Chirac's campaign would run out of steam. But strategically, the campaign was lost before it began.

In the 1990s, even in the land of 'elective monarchy' as French commentators themselves dub the system, he who would run for high office must seem, at least, to be at ease with the *sans culottes*. The mistake of Edouard Balladur was to think that, because a regal president had nominated him prime minister, the citizenry would elect him head of state. His cardinal blunder was to enter the presidential race at all.

Election Blunders Cost a Job

As 1995 drew to its close, it appeared that German politics had found a new dynamic, best termed *Knödelpolitik* (losely translatable as 'dumpling power'). It derived from a resurgence of the fortunes of Helmut Kohl and his right-wing CDU/CSU alliance, after navigating some choppy seas in the election year of 1994. Where French politicians, like Valéry Giscard d'Estaing, published limp sex novels to establish street credibility as cultural icons, Helmut went in for cook books and good solid home cooking at that. Visiting heads of state were regaled with the lugubrious delights of the *Gaststätte* of his home town. Britain's John Major, prime minister of the home of bad cooking, was obliged to murmur 'delicious' over a nicely balanced menu of black pudding, pigs' intestines, beef and potatoes and Apfelstrudel and cream.

For Germany's more sophisticated media, such tastes made Kohl an icon of stodgy, almost un-European traditionalism. But of course, those were precisely the qualities that made Germany the heavyweight in European economics. So, while Kohl's fortunes went through a trough in the public opinion polls in 1993–4 and many commentators favoured the chances of the new and more dynamic leader of the social democratic SPD, the groundswell of German sentiment surged only sluggishly if at all from its natural allegiance to good German *Bürgertum* (bourgeoisie).

Rudolf Scharping, leader of Germany's Social Democratic Party, attacking Chancellor Helmut Kohl's first Bundestag speech following the general election of October 1994. The trouble was that Kohl had won the election, and Scharping's leadership of his Party soon came under threat.

In fact, at the beginning of 1994, German political life was humming in anticipation of the demise of the right-wing coalition in the forthcoming October elections, after more than a decade in government. The SPD were setting the trend under Rudolf Scharping whose lead in the opinion polls was the biggest in years. In March the SPD won an overall majority in the provincial state legislature of Lower Saxony – a major coup. The future seemed to belong to the snappy new left, rather than the stolid old right. But two years later the pendulum had swung and Chancellor Kohl was, for the time being, once more in the ascendancy. How had this happened? How did the CDU/CSU manage to win, even if by a much reduced majority, in the October election?

Most commentators would agree that victory was handed to the right in a sequence of major blunders by the SPD leader, the first being an elementary mistake in economic policy. The cost of integrating the former Communist East into a new united Germany was a central issue of the political debate and the SPD boldly proposed an income tax surcharge. Even in the special circumstances of German reunification, this was a dangerously courageous breach of the golden rule, 'Voters don't like taxes'. When Herr Scharping, in announcing the policy, confused the pay levels at which the new tax would cut in, it was all too easy for his opponents to charge him with economic illiteracy. That April the CDU drew level with the SPD in the opinion polls.

In May Scharping further tarnished his image. The electoral assembly, convened to determine the successor to Richard von Weizsäcker as President of the German Republic, chose Roman Herzog, candidate of the right, in preference to the long-term SPD state premier of Nordrhein-Westphalen and sometime SPD candidate for the federal Chancellorship, Johannes Rau. Scharping voiced some ill-tempered suspicions which did not affect the decision but did earn him a reputation for petulance in defeat. In the Euro-elections of 12 June, the right-wing coalition registered an increase in their share of the vote while the Socialists suffered a drop in support; with the national elections just four months away, this was clearly a damaging setback.

Two weeks later, the Socialists just failed to win an outright majority in elections for the Land parliament of Saxony Anhalt, a province of former East Germany. The scene was set for Scharping's third fateful blunder. The Anhalt CDU proposed a grand coalition with the local SPD, but Scharping vetoed the arrangement. He feared that such collaboration with the right would antagonize left-wing support for the party in the upcoming October national election. Instead the SPD formed a minority administration in alliance with the Greens, which was only able to survive on sufferance of the Party of Democratic Socialism.

It was a strategic miscalculation, as Scharping himself admitted when he avowed he would not repeat the 'Anhalt experiment'. Since the 'Democratic Socialists' were to all intents and purposes the old East German Communist Party under a new name, the SPD suffered a loss of right and centre-right support for seeming to collaborate with old-style communism. The fact that Chancellor Kohl lost more than 100 seats in the October election and emerged with a majority of just ten in the Bundestag lower house of 672 seats, shows how strong sentiment in the country against his government had been. The Socialists' failure was in large part due to their leader's errors of judgement.

SPD fortunes continued a faltering downward trend in 1995, with growing discontent among the rank and file. In September morale sagged still further as two members of the national executive, followed by the shadow economics spokesman and the party's general secretary, all abruptly retired from frontline politics. 'When will Scharping go?', crowed the Christian Democrats, while a national TV network described the situation as the worst crisis in the party's history. Poll ratings revealed a slump in public approval not matched since the 1930s, which was confirmed when, in the state elections of October '95, the Christian Democrats emerged as the largest party in the Berlin state parliament.

It is hardly fanciful to attribute all this directly to the blunders and missed election victory of 1994. Morale, impetus and brio are the fuel of political success. 'Perceptions' is the name of the game. Essential is the ability to seize the opportunity when presented. 'There is a tide in the affairs of men, which, taken at the flood, leads on to fortune. Omitted, all the voyage of their life is bound in shallows, and in miseries.' So said Shakespeare, and who is to say he was wrong. Not Rudolf Scharping, for sure.

At the party conference in November 1995 he launched the party on a new tack, raising probing questions on the previously taboo theme of German politics – the fate of the D-Mark and indeed the whole German post-war political economic consensus with the approach of the European Monetary Union. The change of course smacked of personal political desperation but in view of the fact that some respected German academics were beginning to oppose the EMU and some wealthy German investors were even said to be moving money into Swiss bank accounts, the political calculation had at least some rationale which might benefit the party and its leader.

But that would not be Scharping. In November he was ousted in the party leadership elections by Oskar Lafontaine, though later Scharping was half reinstated as leader of the Bundestag faction. There were signs, too, that the governing CDU was alert to the changing public moods. Insisting on ever tougher criteria for entry to the EMU, it risked antagonizing even friendly European partners and thus making the achievement of monetary union ever more difficult. This, of course, could only please domestic public opinion. Late in 1995 it seemed that short of Helmut Kohl being exposed as a transvestite forger of D-Marks for personal gain, the SPD had missed the tide, thanks to faulty navigation by Scharping the previous year, and that even its new pilot might have difficulty in finding the main channel again.

CHAPTER 6:
ELECTION BLUNDERS

Every country has the government it deserves.

JOSEPH DE MAISTRE,
FRENCH MONARCHIST,
1811

Blundering at election time, the worst sort of error for politicians in a democracy, may range from poor image projection to poor timing and include a gamut of absurdities in between. Very occasionally the actual substance of policies may be a factor and, of course, the failure to offer adequate tax bribes is almost without remedy. In November 1995 Tory Chancellor Kenneth Clarke found himself under attack from members of his own party for a budget which was undramatic and responsible. Grumbled one fellow minister – 'this budget seems geared to rescue the economy, what we want is one to rescue the party'. Clarke's friends countered that, in fact, since the election was not due before summer 1997, he could reserve the bribes for a year and in the meantime pose as a responsible custodian of the nation's finances. This was a risky policy with a majority in single figures, but Mr Clarke was no doubt a man who liked a gamble. That at least suited his somewhat jovial image and in politics few things are as important as that.

Warlord Versus Family Car – Rival Images for Peace

In July 1945 Britain startled the world and herself when the results of the general election were declared. Just two months after the defeat of Nazi Germany, Winston Churchill, prime minister since 1940 and in most people's eyes the architect of victory in the Second World War, was thrown out of office and into opposition. The Conservative Party of which he was leader won only 213 seats to Labour's 393. For, whatever Churchill's qualities as a war leader, his party was remembered from the Depression years of the 1920s and 1930s as the enemy of social justice.

In some industrial towns in that summer election of 1945, workers marched *en masse* from the factories to the polling booths to register their votes for a socialist future. When the results were declared, thousands more celebrated. In Colchester, ancient capital of Roman Britain, the celebrations were on a scale to match those which had welcomed VE-Day in May. Churchill was spared the personal humiliation of losing his own seat but even there a somewhat eccentric Independent opposition candidate was able to recruit some 10,000 votes. This fact gave the politically alert Clementine Churchill intimation of the coming defeat. From the outset of the campaign she had had worries on her husband's account.

Many explanations of the election result were offered at the time and many more have been proposed since. Some reckoned that Churchill had been too generous in allotting portfolios in the wartime National government to Labour men. Attlee was deputy prime minister, with principal responsibility for affairs on the Home Front, while three of his future cabinet appointees held office as Minister of Labour, Home Secretary and President of the Board of Trade. While Winston ran the war, it seemed that Labour were running the Home Front and after victory, the political focus shifted to home affairs. One Tory right-winger grouched: 'We've had a Labour government for five years. Winston hardly touched the Home Front and that's why he's out.' In politics even generosity may prove a blunder.

But there were other reasons. The Tories' record in peacetime; the preponderance of Socialist votes in the armed forces, believing a Socialist government would mean an earlier demob; the determination among the majority of voters that this time they should not be cheated of the fruits of peace as they had been after the 1914–18 War when, promised homes fit for heroes,

During World War II Winston Churchill's broadcasts were an inspiration to an embattled Britain. In the 1945 election his campaigning broadcasts attacking the Socialists as latter-day Gauleiters antagonized many and contributed to his humiliating defeat at the polls.

they had found instead dole queues and wage cuts. But there were less theoretical, more immediate causes. And of these the radio broadcast with which Churchill opened the election campaign on 4 June won overnight notoriety.

For four years a united nation had been happy to follow him in sacrifice and blood against the Nazi German police state, for four years he had led a National coalition government with Labour leader Clement Attlee his loyal and efficient deputy. Now, in a tirade against Socialism, the one-time hero classed his left-wing allies of two months before with the vilest excesses of the regime they had united with him in opposing. The key words, which some reckoned lost the Tories the popular vote before the election was properly under way and which alerted Clementine Churchill to dangers ahead, ran: 'I declare to you from the bottom of my heart that no Socialist government can be established without ... some form of Gestapo.' Years later their daughter recalled that on being shown the draft of the speech, her mother coming to the sentence had said, quite simply, 'Winston, you can't use this.' But he impatiently overruled her.

Attlee handled the situation with the restrained but lethal understatement the English like to suppose is their characteristic response to difficulties. In his radio reply he commented: 'I see that Mr Churchill wishes you to realize that if you vote Conservative you will be voting for the leader of that party, not for the Mr Churchill who led us during the war.' And with a sardonic reference to the right-wing press baron who then dominated the British media he went on: 'That was the voice of Mr Churchill but it was the mind of Lord Beaverbrook.'

By common consent, Churchill's had been an unbelievable blunder. But, if the least forgiveable, it was by no means the only blunder to reveal the Tories as a party out of touch with the mood of the country. It seemed as if they thought that, with the return of peace, the world itself would return to the pattern of life as it had been before the war. The title of their manifesto, 'Mr Churchill's Address to the Electors', was not only stuffy and old-fashioned in style but arrogant in mood, as if suggesting that the Great Man had only to speak to be sure of victory.

It was, to be sure, reasonable for the Conservatives to suppose that Churchill was their greatest asset. When the election was called, even the Labour leaders expected that he would be returned on a wave of gratitude as Lloyd George, hero of the First World War, had been in the election of 1918. After all, he was regularly mobbed by the crowds as he toured the country. Churchill himself told King George VI that he expected to win with a majority of between 30 and 80 seats.

But while people were undoubtedly grateful, they had no intention that gratitude for the past should determine the future. The crowd cheered the hero, but they were to vote for the party of social progress. After all, Labour leaders had served in the wartime cabinets with distinction while their manifesto, 'Let us Face the Future' – changed at the last moment from the more casual 'Let's Face the Future' – sounded workmanlike as well as forward-looking and, above all, like a document put out by people who were inviting cooperation.

This was the tone to appeal to a population who had pulled together

Clement Attlee, successor to Winston Churchill as Britain's prime minister (PM) in 1945 and creator of the Welfare State, was thought by many inside as well as outside the Labour Party as something of a nonentity. He was ennobled and created a Companion of Honour (CH) and awarded the Order of Merit (OM) and wrote the following doggerel in a letter to his son:

Few thought he was even a starter
There were many who thought themselves smarter
But he ended PM, CH and OM,
An Earl and a Knight of the Garter.

WARLORD VERSUS FAMILY CAR – RIVAL IMAGES FOR PEACE

during five years of shared danger. British society was structured on class and inequality, but rested also on a feeling for a common nationhood which the wartime experience had brought to the surface. Time and again the Tory campaign blundered back towards paternalistic attitudes which grated even on Tory supporters. In London's smart Kensington constituency, Conservative posters depicted the candidate in uniform with the simple slogan 'Vote for Captain Duncan'. The campaign manager for his Labour opponent riposted with a poster of his man, also in uniform and also with a simple slogan 'Vote for Corporal Woodford'. The corporal won. In the constituency of Portsmouth North the Tory candidate, Greville Howard, was proclaimed quite simply as 'Churchill's Man' but even in dockyard territory, memories of naval triumphs did not help the war leader appeal against the Labour poster 'Donald Bruce The People's Man'.

The contrast of mood continued throughout the campaign between the unassuming manner of Attlee, and Churchill's style of the great man flanked by his entourage as he delivered a flow of now rather out-dated rhetoric to dutifully staged meetings. Attlee, too, could boast a fine military record, having been decorated for courage under fire in the First World War. However, the press photographs which caught the public imagination during the 1945 election campaign were of him and his driver, Mrs Attlee, snatching a roadside picnic lunch beside the family car. While Churchill's campaign advisers could hardly be blamed for presenting their man in the afterglow of victory, it was surely a blunder. On the other hand, no 1990s image consultant could have bettered the Attlees' working snack as a keynote image for an election about rebuilding the world for ordinary heroes and their families.

During the 1945 election Clement Attlee, leader of Britain's Labour Party, travelling to speaking engagements with his wife at the wheel of their modest family car, came across as a people's candidate, in contrast to the privileged image of his Conservative opponents.

89

The rejection of Winston Churchill by British voters in the election of 1945 – the great war leader overthrown in the moment of his triumph by his own people – will always present a superficial paradox. But Anthony Eden, Churchill's lieutenant and himself later to serve as prime minister, understood why it had happened. In his published memoirs he observed the gratitude accorded Churchill for his wartime role but went on, 'there was not the same enthusiasm for him as PM of the peace'. In his private diary, Eden added: 'Who shall say that the British people were wrong in this?'

The sentiment of common purpose which had seemed to inspire the national effort during the war years lingered on for a time in the immediate post-war period. This, combined with the belief that the Labour Party was more to be trusted to implement reasonable social policies than were the Tories, meant that, despite the austerities of the time, Labour was able to introduce nationalization of the coal industry and the railways, as well as a National Health Service with comparatively little opposition. In the case of the industries, the private sector received decent compensation.

The far-from-revolutionary way in which Britain's Socialists took over the commanding heights of the economy may have disillusioned some of its supporters. But the fear of more to come helped unsettle traditional middle-class sentiment. Despite the fact that they had come to power with one of the largest majorities of the 20th century, there were signs that some in the upper echelons of the party had already lost their appetite for the policy.

Advance Warning

In 1949, with barely a year of its parliamentary life to run, the Attlee government introduced a bill with the proposals which would lead to the nationalization of the iron and steel industry. The government was bound to go to the country by July 1950 at the latest and was wary of the electorate's reactions to the measure. In exchange for agreement by the Tory-dominated House of Lords to withdraw certain ammendments to the Bill, the government agreed not to make any staff appointments to the Iron and Steel Corporation until October 1950, nor to transfer any properties to the Corporation before January 1951.

It was a blunder. The government's evident doubt as to its own policy gave industry the green light for a mass-media propaganda campaign. The steelmakers were of course there, but so were other major industries who feared or purported to fear nationalization plans. Chief among them was Tate & Lyle, the sugar monopolists who employed a public relations organization called Aims of Industry. A stylized cartoon sugar-lump figure called 'Mr Cube' appeared on two million sugar packages decrying the whole idea of nationalization. The insurance industry also set up anti-nationalization committees the length and breadth of the land.

The government duly called the election for February 1950, and just scraped back into office, its 1945 majority of 146 reduced to five seats. There were of course various causes, not the least the fact that, given the need to pay for Britain's war effort, the five years of Labour had of necessity been five years of austerity and continued rationing. But there can be little doubt that middle-class apprehensions in the suburbs caused thousands to switch their votes, and these fears had been mightily boosted by the anti-nationalization campaign.

Although officially dissociating itself from what it chose to describe as a purely private campaign, the Tory party, of course, benefited hugely from a tide of propaganda which cost it not a penny but whose press coverage alone has been reckoned as worth some £200,000 in the values of the day. And the Labour government had largely its own uncertain, almost timid, handling of a flagship policy to thank. The planned nationalization of the iron and steel industry duly went ahead, but the impetus of Labour as a governing party was spent. When Prime Minister Attlee went to the country for a second time in October 1951, he was defeated by the Tories under the 77-year-old Winston Churchill who returned with a majority of 17 seats.

Promises, Promises

In the British general election of October 1959 the Labour Party, led by Hugh Gaitskell, principled but hardly guileful, was opposed by the Tories under Harold Macmillan, known as Super-Mac for his superman-like abilities in political management. A Tory PR campaign, masterminded by Lord Hailsham and estimated to have cost some £500,000, had been preparing the ground over the past two years, while the give-away budget of April 1959 – including reductions in income tax and the price of beer, together with favourable investment allowances – had primed the electorate with suitable inducements. The chancellor's formula in fact fuelled the overheating in the economy which would have to be corrected in 1960 – but that was in the future. For now people reckoned good times had arrived thanks to the Tories and even credited them as the party of sound economic stewardship.

When, therefore, Gaitskell promised to increase the state pension and build more hospitals while holding the rate of income tax steady, and followed this up three days later by promising to remove purchase tax from a range of essential goods, he blundered grievously. The Conservative accusation, that the Socialists were attempting to bribe the electorate, was not only breathtakingly cynical, it was also unanswerable. To point out that the Tory chancellor had already handsomely bribed the electorate some six months previously, not only branded the electors as open to corruption, it also reminded those who might enjoy the experience who their benefactors were.

The main topic of debate in the New Zealand election of 1957 was the introduction of PAYE income tax. Both the Labour and the National Party were committed to the new system, the only difference between them on this subject was the size of the rebate to be offered to tax payers at the changeover. It quickly became the determining issue in the campaign. The Labour Party went to the polls with a simple slogan: 'Do you want £100 or not?' The National Party offered only £75 – it was a blunder. Labour's Walter Nash was returned as prime minister for the next four years.

A politician is a man who understands government and it takes a politician to run a government. A statesman is a politician who's been dead ten or fifteen years.

HARRY TRUMAN

Industrial Discontent

On 7 February 1974 Ted Heath, Tory prime minister with an overall majority of 18 seats in the House of Commons and some 14 months of his electoral mandate still to run, announced a general election for the 28th of that month. The condition in which the country found itself was bizarre. Energy supplies, hit by an embargo by Arab oil producers in the wake of the 1973 Arab-Israeli war, were further limited by a miners' overtime ban and rail union disruption of transport to power stations. In November the previous year, the government had imposed a State of Emergency. Heating was restricted, floodlights and advertising displays on the nations' buildings went dark, panic queues formed at filling stations. As the crisis lengthened, industry was put on a three-day week, domestic power supplies were rationed, and television was limited by curfew closedowns.

Just how one of the world's richest economies could be reduced to such straits was never fully clear. The government naturally blamed the unions; others blamed the government, supposing it was for them to manage the country's affairs so as to obviate, or at least circumvent, such difficulties. On 9 January the respected rail union chief, Sidney Green, made an offer which many thought could have resolved the dispute: if the government would give an assurance that it would make possible a settlement between the miners and the National Coal Board, the other unions would not use this as a lever in their own pay negotiations. The government minister facing him across the table rejected the proposal out of hand and, as Heath did not reverse this decision, the chance was missed.

This surely was a major blunder. Even if he doubted the union leaders' ability to hold the line – negotiators would have had to be saint-like not to use the miners' special case as a bargaining counter – Heath would have been ideally placed in the event of such a union let-down to lay the blame squarely on their shoulders. But either because he disdained such politicking or because he failed to see the opportunity or because he could not go on television to recommend a deal that he did not personally believe – Heath refused the deal.

When on 17 January 1974 Lord Carrington, newly appointed minister of energy, predicted forthcoming large relaxations in the power regime, and the possibility of easing to a four-day week, the Labour opposition were not the only people to wonder about the prospect of an upcoming election. For their part, balloted miners voted for all-out strike action.

Strikes, the threat of strikes and a feeling among the middle classes that the trades unions represented hostile forces, combined with the traditional wolf-crying of the right-wing press to provoke paranoid fears that the government of the country was threatened with collapse.

Never having known the periodic blood-letting of revolution and repression, characteristic of the dealings between government and governed in continental countries during the 19th and first half of the 20th centuries, British society and its insular opinion-formers have no antennae for what lawlessness, anarchy and red revolution really might be like. In France such violence is called 'the democracy of the streets'. It is, of course, possible that the French are right and that an occasional bout of murder and mayhem tones up the system of the body politic, but in Britain the aim is to restrain such expressions of the will of the people. Thus, when, despite the historic tradition of politically responsible activity in British working life, discontent does break out into severe industrial unrest, the establishment is liable to panic reactions in the fear that anarchy will usurp the political process and the country become ungovernable.

This was the spectre that haunted Ted Heath that winter of 1973–4. Ten years later it seemed to be actively encouraged by Margaret Thatcher, bent on destroying organized labour which she dubbed 'the enemy within'. But, where Thatcher regarded government as civil war conducted by other means and aimed to divide the country against itself and so rule, Heath, a person of principle and basic decency, hoped to win people over by argument.

Douglas Hurd recorded a visit he made on New Year's Day 1974 to a constituency preparing for a crucial by-election where he watched the Prime Minister's encounter with party workers. 'He could have worked that audience to a pitch of fiery loyalty and whipped them up against the miners .... It did not occur to him to do so. [He wanted them] to understand the complexities of the issue ... [and] ... saw it as his duty to educate and inform, not to inflame one part of the country against another.'

Of course, it may be said that the deployment of reason in the political arena is itself a blunder, but Ted Heath had other problems. As was later diagnosed, he was suffering from a thyroid deficiency which causes lethargy; he and his advisers were terminally exhausted and behind all was the irrational fear and distrust of the unions.

For the government then the two great questions of early '74 were: could the unions be brought to cooperate with government in the struggle against inflation and, if not, when should the general election, due by June 1975 at the latest, be called? Heath himself had no doubt as to what would be the issue in that election. 'The challenge is to the will of parliament and a democratically elected government,' he said in a speech on 12 February. In headline journalese this became 'Who rules the country?' – a not unreasonable summary of the issue apparently to be decided by the electorate.

Reduced to its fundamentals, the appeal was an ultimatum. But, like all ultimatums, it only worked if the other party to the debate shared the premise. By no means all the voters did. To some it did seem the issue, to others it seemed extraordinary for a prime minister with an overall working majority of 18 and more than a year of his existing electoral mandate still to run, to pose such a question. Better, perhaps, to announce that there was no alternative to paying the miners now, but that the government would be going to the country in the summer with specific proposals to ensure that the trades unions would 'not again hold the country to ransom'. This would have seemed statesmanlike and could have been successful. A tactically more cynical manoeuvre and one suggested by Machiavellian advisers might have stood a still better chance of success. They argued that if an election had to be held in 1974, better earlier than later; better, in fact, before 15 February,

ELECTION BLUNDERS

Do you realize the responsibility I carry? I'm the only person standing between Nixon and the White House.

JOHN FITZGERALD KENNEDY, 1960

when an updated electoral register which favoured Labour came into force.

So, the first general election of 1974 was fought on an issue and at the time of Prime Minister Heath's choosing. It has been argued that he blundered in both particulars. At all events, he lost his majority. When the results were declared, Labour was found to be four seats ahead with 301 against Conservatives 297, the balance of the 635 seats being held by the minor parties. As the incumbent of Number 10 Downing Street, it was open to Mr Heath to try to form a majority government. He approached the Liberal leader, Jeremy Thorpe, but, aided by some blunders of Liberal judgement, the approach failed (see p. 77). Three days later he resigned.

On 11 March the Queen opened the new Parliament with a minority Labour government under Harold Wilson in power. By dint of skilful manoeuvring with minor-party support, it lasted 184 days. The shortest parliament since 1681 maybe, it gave time enough for a further shift of opinion in the country against the Tories. So that, when Wilson held the year's second general election in October, they emerged with just 277 seats as against Labour's 319.

American Errors

In the American presidential election of 1960, Richard Nixon agreed to a series of television debates with John F. Kennedy, the Democratic candidate. It was a serious blunder. As incumbent vice-president, Nixon was a national figure; whereas Kennedy was merely a senator. The debates gave him exposure which Nixon could have denied him. In the public's view he now ranked on terms of equal importance with the Vice-President. In the presidential election, Kennedy won a majority of 118,550 in a total popular vote of 68,337,642.

Succeeding the assassinated President John F. Kennedy, Vice-President Johnson soon won popularity by pushing through a raft of social reforms that Kennedy had only talked about. In the elections of 1964 he won 61.2 per cent of the popular vote – the largest percentage gained by any president – trouncing the Republican contender Senator Barry Goldwater by 496 to 52 in the electoral college. Three years later, Johnson was one of the best-hated men in America and publicly withdrew from the forthcoming presidential race of 1968. His blunder? In one word, Vietnam. The fact that his commitment of US military might in Southeast Asia was a logical continuation of Kennedy's policy and was backed by a resolution of Congress (the Tongkin Resolution), was irrelevant. The nation hated the conflict and the President who in their eyes had led them into it.

A French Mandate Misinterpreted

For Parisians, May 1968 is famously the modern month of the barricades. Having missed the exhilaration of the sixties in the Anglo-Saxon world – flower power, Woodstock and the 1967 'summer of love' – the French had a political explosion in their traditional manner with rioting students and two million workers on strike. They were protesting against high defence spending at the expense of education and social services. Equally mindful of tradition, President Charles de Gaulle prepared for war on the population and won secret assurances of support from the armed forces. In June he won a resounding victory at the polls, by ensuring that his opponents on the left were blamed for barricades they did not put up and for strike pickets they did not command. A year later he was out of office through a combination of arrogance and political ineptitude.

The issue was one of proposed constitutional changes, put to a referendum in April 1969. Seeking to consolidate what he supposed was his ascendancy, de Gaulle announced that he would resign were the proposals rejected. But relief at deliverance from social turmoil the year before had changed to discontent with the old man's authoritarian ways. As if accepting the resignation threat as an invitation to give the 78-year-old general his marching orders, the voters returned a 'Yes' vote of just 47 per cent, that is 4 per cent less than was required. True to his word, the general left office.

I have come to the conclusion that politics are too serious a matter to be left to the politicians.

CHARLES DE GAULLE, 1970

The count in progress in the Interior Ministry, Paris, after the referendum called by General de Gaulle for April 1969. The vote went against him by 52.87 per cent to 47.13 per cent and he resigned in May.

Blunders of Presentation

Since the advent of the televison age in the 1950s, the small screen has ruled decisions about presentation and made a candidate's appearance all important. Famously, Richard Nixon was handicapped by his refusal to accept TV make-up which, because of his fast-growing beard stubble, gave him the dark-jowled and shifty look of an old-style movie villain. 'Would you buy a second-hand car from this man?' was a favourite jibe by his opponents.

However, it is a mistake to suppose that questions of image only began with the advent of television electioneering. When in 1856 Britain's 72-year-old prime minister, Lord Palmerston, was cited in a paternity case, it was the Conservative opposition who wanted the matter played down. Nicknamed 'Pam' he may have been – and the last major British political figure to continue the 18th-century fashion for male make-up – but in an age when manhood meant macho, that accusation would be worth more than one member in the House come the next election.

Alec Douglas-Home, a British aristocrat of the old school, really did not care about presentation. Having renounced a noble title so as to be able to enter the House of Commons and thus become prime minister, he unwisely admitted to his ignorance of economics and joked that he always counted with matchsticks. This may have seemed engagingly modest – it was in fact terminally stupid. In the election of October 1964, Home's opponent was Labour's Harold Wilson, one of the most brilliant electoral campaigners of the 20th century, a consummate TV politician and a trained economist who, at the age of 31, had been the youngest man to achieve cabinet rank since Pitt. Storming the country as the champion of a 'white heat of technological revolution' that was to transform Britain's economy, Wilson derided his opponents to good effect as outmoded backwoodsmen, led by a millionaire hereditary landowner who proposed to muddle the country through with matchstick mathematics. On the morning of 16 October 1964, after 13 years in power, the Conservatives found themselves in opposition.

A Burnt-out Hero

On Monday 7 August 1995 the Polish daily *Gazeta Wybocza* carried a report which further tarnished the once bright image of President Lech Walesa. Apparently the soldiers of at least four companies of the élite corps charged with defence of the government and the presidency, stationed on the Vistula and directly subordinate to the ministry of the interior, had been 'vigorously encouraged' to append their signatures to forms supporting the candidature of the President, then seeking re-election in the autumn.

The allegation caused a furore. Artur Smolko, the opposition deputy of the non-communist left who raised the issue, demanded a parliamentary commission of investigation be set up. Interior Minister Andrzej Milcanowski decided it might be wiser to set up a government-led inquiry. For there could be no doubt that some such manoeuvre had been tried. The claim made by the President's office, that the signatures had been given in a spontaneous gesture, was less than convincing when it was realized that they had been demanded on the presentation of the troops' pay slips. Printed forms, carrying the wording 'I support the candidature of Lech Walesa for the presidential election,' had to be signed if the soldier expected to be paid on time. Any who refused had his pay stopped for several days.

It was said that two years before, Mr Walesa had attempted to transform the corps into a national guard directly dependent on the presidency. Maybe failure on that occasion prompted an alternative approach, either by the President or by a loyal official. But whoever did initiate the unsubtle move had obviously forgotten that, whatever may have been the convention in pre-revolutionary communist Poland, the revolution initiated by Walesa himself had increased the possibilities that official malpractice would be found out. Someone would have to pay for the blunder though not, one could be sure, the President himself and, with equal probability, not the minister of the interior.

An intriguing pendant to the story came some three weeks later, when it was reported from Warsaw that Walesa had suspended Mieczyslaw Wachowski from his duties as chief of cabinet and minister of state. No reason was given for the dismissal of a man who, until that moment, had been reckoned to be the President's closest colleague.

During the exhilarating and often dangerous days of the 1980s, when Walesa as trade union leader of Solidarity in the Gdansk shipyards had graduated from local industrial to national politics to seize the attention of the world and finally to force the overthrow of the Communist regime, Wachowski had been his chauffeur and loyal friend. Just the kind of admirer, rumbled the rumour mill in '95, with the necessary access to the bureaucracy of state to contrive, either with or without presidential connivance, 'spontaneous gestures of support' among troops directly subordinate to the ministry of the interior.

To the outside world it seemed hard to believe that the hero, who had broken the power of Polish Communism and then gone on to become the first elected president of a newly democratic Poland, could have felt it necessary to generate support artificially. In fact, during the later years of his presidential term, Walesa seems to have haemorrhaged credibility. Even friends and supporters complained of his sudden rages, boorish vulgarities, his arrogance and his preference for undistinguished former cronies in the councils of state of whom Wachowski was just one example.

Lech Walesa paid the penalty for his slump in style and his lapse into complacency in the presidential elections of November 1995. In a straight contest, despite the support of the Catholic Church and the spiritual blackmail its priests were able to wield, he was defeated by a margin of some four percentage points by Aleksander Kwasniewski, a coming man in the last days of Poland's Communist regime, when Walesa himself was being hounded as a revolutionary. He suffered the last indignity of being not only defeated by the leader of the refurbished Communist party but of being praised as a hero and then being offered a position in his government, having refused to attend the presidential inauguration.

CHAPTER 7:
FOLLIES OF PRIDE AND OVERCONFIDENCE

By definition, blunders are the result of miscalculation and the most frequent miscalculation is of one's own capacities or resources. Such errors can follow a careful assessment of a situation, the possibility of failure being recognized but rejected on balance as the least likely outcome in the given circumstances. If these be blunders, they are certainly pardonable – action of any kind being virtually inseparable from failure from time to time. On the other hand, many a political disaster has been precipitated by crass arrogance, what the ancient Greeks might have called *hubris* – an overweening conviction that one enjoys special immunity from the fate which afflicts other mortals.

Since the Greeks used the word, it is not surprising, perhaps, that one of the most momentous examples should come from Athens herself, whose culpable overconfidence in her military strength led to humiliating defeat in her long drawn-out war with Sparta, her great rival.

Blunders in the Home of Politics

The word 'politics' itself is, of course, of Greek origin, deriving from the word *polis* ('a city'). Politics was the activity of the citizens (*polites*) in governing themselves. There were in fact many forms of political organization among the Greek states and Athens, for a time the most powerful city of all, was governed by decisions of an assembly of all the citizens, the *demos* or people. However, this democracy was very different from anything we would recognize as such today. Women were of course excluded, but so were the majority of the men who lived in Athens and its surrounding district of Attica. A large proportion were slaves who sweated and died in the silver mines, laboured in industrial production such as shield manufacture, or worked as household servants. Perhaps the best model of an Athenian-type democracy in the modern world was apartheid South Africa, where the vote was reserved to white and coloured citizens, a small minority of the population.

However, there was an important difference between 20th-century South Africa and ancient Athens during the period of her greatness – Athens had an empire. Its origins went back to the early decades of the 5th century BC when she had led the alliance of the cities of Greece against invasion from imperial Persia, with such famous victories as Marathon and Salamis. The

He knows nothing: and he thinks he knows everything. That points clearly to a political career.

GEORGE BERNARD SHAW, 1907

alliance had its treasury on the island of Delos and was hence known as the Delian League. Victory was followed by counterattack on Persian-occupied territory and many Greek islands and cities in the Aegean Sea and in western Anatolia were liberated. They were duly enrolled in the League.

Soon the treasury was moved to Athens and what had been voluntary contributions became tribute money. Athens claimed the right to compensation for her sacrifices during the war and much of the glory of the Acropolis, admired by tourists today, was built on the proceeds of this. The League members were kept in line by the military superiority of the 'mother of democracy' who came to look upon her allies as possessions and the League as an empire. By degrees, however, her extortions provoked a backlash. Eventually the other chief power of the Greek world, Sparta, was persuaded to head the opposition to Athens, and war broke out.

The essentially tiger-and-shark contest between land-based Sparta and the sea-power of Athens ended in a draw in 421 BC, with the balance a little in Sparta's favour. Sparta's power base remained intact and she had won new allies, among them some Greek colonies in Sicily. Athens had lost prestige as a land-power. Resentment was as great as ever in her empire, while leadership at home was divided.

In these conditions, the best political practice would no doubt have been to come to terms with the new realities, keep on good terms with Sparta and abandon any plans of imperial expansion. Second choice was to resume war to crush the Spartan alliance once and for all before attempting to resume imperial expansion. This had been the advice of Athens's great war leader, Pericles, who had said: 'I am more afraid of the mistakes of the Athenians than the plans of their enemies.' But Pericles was now dead and the cut-throat, self-seeking rivalries of Athenian politicians guaranteed the mistakes he had feared.

In the event, Athens blundered into the worst possible policy. She managed to dissipate and divide her forces in a campaign in Sicily, which ended by provoking a second war with Sparta. This time Athens would lose.

The focus of the politicking was Alcibiades, one of history's most vibrant and controversial figures. A dynamic 35-year-old, he favoured war with Sparta, expansion of the empire and tight control of the subject states. The conventional wisdom billed him as an irreligious, flamingly ambitious tearaway. The citizenry at large was dazzled when it was not puzzled. Dramatically good-looking, brilliant, brave and a master orator, he was the ideal demagogue and, in 415 BC, highly popular, having been elected one of the city's generals the year before and having persuaded the assembly to follow his advice on the question of the island of Melos.

A traditional colony of Sparta, this little island kept neutral in the war between the great two rivals, refusing troops to Sparta but sending gifts. Athens demanded the islanders enter the empire. They refused and appealed to international justice. Athens sent an expedition of 38 ships and 3000 troops. In her view, international justice was reserved for states of equal power; the weaker brethren had to take their chance. That winter the people of Melos put up a heroic resistance but finally, after months of siege, they capitulated and threw themselves on the mercy of the Athenian people. A

> *All political lives, unless they are cut off in mid-stream at a happy juncture, end in failure.*
>
> Enoch Powell,
> British Conservative Politician, 1977

debate, famous in the annals of *Realpolitik*, was accordingly held in the assembly of Athens and the policy urged by Alcibiades democratically voted through. Every adult male of the island population was slaughtered, its women and children were sold into slavery, and Melos itself occupied by 500 Athenians.

Very much the man of the moment, the popular general scored his next success in the debate over whether or not to send an expedition to Sicily, where Sparta's ally Syracuse was having trouble with a minor city friendly to Athens. The opposition urged against getting involved. Sicily was far away, it was no threat to Athens and an expedition would weaken Athenian financial and military resources. Alcibiades argued that here was an ideal pretext for a major expedition which, by conquering Syracuse, would assure Athenian control of all Sicily, which would become a power-base for domination of the entire Greek world. The Assembly agreed.

The decision to support this unimportant colony was bad enough. The blunder was compounded when Nicias, the general who had argued most strongly against the expedition, was elected as a member of the high command, along with Alcibiades. More absurd yet, just before the expedition, the largest to sail the Mediterranean since the Persian wars, set out, Alcibiades was charged with acts of impiety. Perhaps this was a last-ditch attempt to halt the enterprise while the general stood trial. If so the move failed. Alcibiades was refused the chance to clear his name and sailed under a cloud of suspicion and in great bitterness. In a world which believed in omens and auguries, it is difficult to conceive a better formula for sapping the morale of a fighting force.

One theory holds that his political enemies planned to delay the trial until, with his friends and supporters in the army safely committed to the Sicilian campaign, the general could be brought back to trial and certain condemnation and death. Incredible as it may seem, he was actually arrested on active service and embarked on a state galley for Athens. But a stormy petrel is not so easily snared and the brilliant Athenian escaped his escort and sought sanctuary in, of all places, Sparta. There he deployed his oratorical skills to persuade his country's great enemy to go to war against her. In part thanks to his military intelligence and strategic advice, the campaign ended in complete victory for Sparta and her allies.

Defeat in Syracuse spelt disaster for Athens. Her military capacity was drastically reduced, her treasure depleted and the dream of an expanded empire effectively at an end. A sequence of blunders born of the political world which made her the most fascinating of the Greek cities was to be her downfall. The Syracusan expedition brought Sparta back into all-out war. Proud but erratic, Athens was fighting now for her life and to maintain her empire, source of so much of her wealth. That she went down to defeat was in large measure her own doing.

Lionheart Caged by his Own Folly

Richard I the Lionheart, king of England, was once famously described by

Sir Steven Runciman as a superb soldier but a bad husband, a bad son and a bad king – he was not much of a politician either. When in the summer of 1191 he arrived at the Syrian port of Acre, besieged by the crusaders assembling to recover Jerusalem (lost to Islam in 1187), his royal status, coupled with his unparalleled military genius, made him the effective commander of the cosmopolitan expedition. Unfortunately, whatever his skills on the battlefield, he soon revealed severe shortcomings in the art of man-management.

Some months before, the aged Frederick I Barbarossa, ruler of the German lands and as emperor recognized as the head of Christendom, had died while leading a large, well-equipped expedition *en route* for Acre. When his death was reported to Saladin, the conquerer of Jerusalem, that great man hailed it as an intervention of Allah on behalf of Islam. The imperial forces had lost a fine soldier and Christendom a great leader. Finally, a shattering blow had been dealt to the Germans' morale. Some contingents returned home, a few pressed on to join the defence of Acre under siege from the Saracens.

One of these contingents was that of the arrogant and touchy Leopold of Austria who, in the absence of his emperor, saw no reason to take orders from the Frenchman who called himself King of England. Duke Leopold's standard, planted on his orders next to King Richard's on the ramparts, was a rallying symbol for others in the small German force. Richard of England saw it as a challenge to his authority as commander-in-chief. On his orders, the banner was wrenched out of its socle and hurled down into the moat.

A flame-haired, deep-chested and athletic six-footer, Richard was reputedly descended from Melusine, the Devil's daughter. Like all his family, he was dangerously hot-tempered. That day he made himself an enemy for life. The immediate result was the departure of the Austrian contingent from the crusading army. For Richard personally, as for his kingdom of England, the long-term consequences were still more serious.

Richard sailed from Palestine in October 1192. Thanks to him, the Crusade had recovered much territory for the Kingdom of Jerusalem but the city itself remained to Islam. Generous in victory, Saladin allowed any Christian soldiers who wished to visit the Holy Places and thus complete their pilgrimage, for many the real motivation of their long trek from home. King Richard did not join them. If he could not fulfil his vow to reconquer the city for Christendom, he was not worthy to enter its gates.

His journey back to his lands of Normandy and England was fraught with problems. With winter approaching, the sea journey would be hazardous as well as slow. Overland, the route lay either through France or the territories of the German empire. The first, the quicker, was out of the question. King Philip of France, after brief participation in the crusade, had returned to more practical politics at home. His objective was to drive the English king from his hereditary possession of Normandy and by collaborating with his brother, Prince John, make all possible trouble for him in England. When a storm wrecked his ship on the coast of the Adriatic, Richard decided to risk the German route.

Leopold's seething resentment and his determination to get even with the king of England were public knowledge. Richard and his entourage took to the road disguised as monks. They made good progress through the alpine passes, but this party of cowled figures, one immensely tall and deferred to by his companions, alerted a Tyrolean innkeeper. The man sent word to Duke Leopold and the King was seized and incarcerated. The duke's revenge was the sweeter when the new emperor Henry VI bought up the ransom rights in his captive.

Christendom was now entertained to the spectacle of the recent hero of the wars against the infidel being held as a trading good by the Holy Roman Emperor. The haggle stretched over months, Prince John and Philip of France manoeuvring to delay Richard's release. The price was finally fixed at 150,000 silver marks and a ceremony of homage in which the King rendered his kingdom to the emperor and received it back at his hands as an imperial fief.

The first massive instalment of the ransom was found. Richard's mother, the beautiful, imperious 70-year-old Eleanor of Aquitaine went with the bullion convoy to Cologne and returned to London with her son. The imperial knights who provided the honour escort, astounded by the wealth of the city, swore that had their master been better informed, the price would have been double.

As it was, in terms of humiliation suffered, time and treasure lost and deepening political turmoil at home, King Richard had paid dearly for the blundering arrogance which had antagonized Leopold of Austria on the windswept ramparts of Acre.

There was a footnote to the blunder a little more than two centuries later, when Henry V of England was preparing to receive the Emperor Sigismund on a state visit. As the imperial barge approached the beach at Dover, Humphrey Duke of Gloucester, the King's brother, cantered through the breakers, sword drawn, to demand formal renunciation of all authority the emperor might claim to exercise in England by virtue of the act of homage performed by his predecessor.

The Cocksure Medic

Born in 1737, the son of a Protestant pastor, John Frederick Struensee rose rapidly in his own chosen profession of medicine to become court physician to King Christian VII of Denmark. From there, he rose still further to become principal minister of the royal government. But only for a year. His blunder, as we shall see, was overconfidence in his position as the Queen's favourite.

As royal physician, Struensee had a demanding job since Christian VII, sexually profligate if not over-virile, early contracted syphilis. A masochist before the term was coined, he found stimulation in being beaten by his groom of the bedchamber, Count Holck, and was also mentally unstable to a clinical degree. In fact, he was certified insane before the age of 30, Denmark being ruled by regency governments until his death in·1808.

Christian's childhood was a catalogue of horrors, from a drunken father in the grip of *delirium tremens*, to a tutor who often thrashed the young prince senseless. But in the view of Cabanès, a French observer at the Danish court, the King's madness was also hastened by his practice of *manuélisation*. The Victorians, it appears, were not the first to suppose that masturbation rotted a man's moral and physical properties. Christian's indulgence also ruined his family life, since 'even the presence of his domestics did not prevent him from relieving himself in this manner'.

The unhappy wife of this rather disgusting little man was Caroline Matilda, sister of King George III of England. Somewhat above middle height, her hair a startling blonde and 'her complexion the finest imaginable', she had been bustled off to Copenhagen in the cause of dynastic politics at the age of 15. In the next few years she grew up into striking womanhood with 'a bosom such as few men could look on without emotion, or women, without envy; and she displayed more of its naked charms than *strict* modesty could approve; and far more than the Danes had witnessed in preceding queens'. Even so she had to vie for the King's attention, not only with the flagellant favourite Count Holck but also with a string of common prostitutes to whom it was Christian's engaging practice to detail his wife's performance in the royal marriage bed.

Despite these distractions and the malevolent manoeuvres of his stepmother, Christian managed to give his wife not only syphilis but a son. Juliana Maria, Queen Dowager and second wife of Christian's father was, when Caroline Matilda arrived at the Danish court, manoeuvring to wrest control of the country. Her idiot stepson was clearly unfit to govern and she hoped to supplant him with her own son by the former King. She was reportedly dismayed at the blow to her plans when Queen Caroline was safely delivered of her boy.

The father, by way of celebration, went on a riotous progress through Holland, Great Britain, France and Germany, accompanied not by the Queen but by the ever-present Holck and also by his court physician, Struensee. Tall, black-haired and handsome, the 31-year-old seems to have been one of the few people in the entourage who treated Christian with consideration and respect. He displaced Holck as favourite and soon after the return to Denmark was put in charge of the Queen's health. He cleared her of the syphilis and soon Count and Queen were regular companions in the hunting field and ballroom. Christian, having ennobled Struensee and appointed him prime minister, was held under what amounted to house arrest in his own palace while his court physician ruled the country by day and the Queen by night.

The lovers were not over security-conscious in their affair; society was scandalized by gossip and rumour; the able Count Bernsdorff was dismissed as chief minister. But the new head of government did much that today would seem enlightened. Reforms included a large measure of liberty for the press; lifting the immunity from arrest for debt enjoyed by the aristocracy; abolition of numerous revenued sinecure appointments; foundation of charity schools; abolition of the death penalty for robbery; and a regulation 'for the diminution of law suits in the courts of justice'.

In barely a year Struensee had radicalized government in Denmark – and

FOLLIES OF PRIDE AND OVERCONFIDENCE

Count Johann Friedrich Struensee (1731–72), the Danish courtier and reforming chief minister whose love affair with the Queen led to his being horribly executed for treason.

made himself an army of enemies. Had he been content with a backstairs intrigue with the Queen and left the running of the country to those who knew best, namely the lawyers and (usually indebted) noblemen; had he perhaps persuaded Caroline to come to terms with the Queen Dowager; had he, in short, shown some repect for the rules of the political game, he might have had a chance. An adventurer at heart, he can hardly be blamed for following his adventure to its dramatic conclusion in the royal bed. Most medical men would agree, there is a certain cachet in having a crowned queen as one's mistress. Struensee's crucial blunder was, once having achieved power, to try and use it openly for the country's good.

In January 1772 Juliana Maria browbeat her witless stepson into signing a warrant for the arrest of Caroline Matilda, Struensee and his colleague

Brandt. They were duly taken in the small hours of the 17th. Caroline's attempt to reach her husband and have him reverse the arrests was thwarted. On the morning of 28 April Struensee and Brandt, after months of torture, were publicly dismembered and beheaded. There had been a strong move of public opinion for the Queen, too, to go to the scaffold. However, thanks to the intervention of her brother, the powerful king of England, she was divorced before being exiled to Celle in Hanover. There she died three years later, aged just 24, of a contagious disease contracted from one of her servants. However, there were those who recalled that she had been implicated in secret schemes to restore her to the throne only weeks earlier.

Lord Randolph Churchill – the Man who was Dispensable

In 1906 Winston Churchill published his biography of his father, Lord Randolph Churchill, who had resigned as chancellor of the exchequer exactly 20 years before, to the stunned disbelief of the Victorian chattering classes. The given reason, the Chancellor's objection to what he considered excessive proposals for spending on the Navy, seemed so improbable that the resignation had to be part of some crassly miscalculated political manoeuvre. Perhaps to destabilize the government and replace the Marquis of Salisbury as prime minister? But instead, Lord Salisbury seized the chance to rid himself of a colleague whom he neither liked nor trusted. Lord Randolph, who died in 1895, never again held office.

The impact on his 12-year-old son, Winston, was lasting. The book, *Lord Randolph Churchill*, aimed to justify his father's reputation but also, perhaps, his own political career. Enemies had accused them both of adventurism. In Winston's eyes they were both heirs of Disraeli's reforming Toryism, but his father had been exploited by clever reactionaries. Struggling for power, they had paid lip-service to his ideas of 'Tory Democracy'; once in power, they had taken the first opportunity to jettison him.

For us Lord Randolph's fall has a special resonance as a formative event in the career of a titan of 20th-century history. For his contemporaries, the resignation letter to Prime Minister Salisbury, delivered by hand to Hatfield House at 1.30 a.m., as the Marquis and Lady Salisbury were farewelling guests after a Christmas season ball, was quite simply the most breathtaking political folly of the 19th century. 'With that letter,' wrote his wife, 'he resigned all that he had worked for for years, and, if he had but known it, signed his own political death warrant.'

The Tories had swept to power in July 1886, ousting Gladstone's Liberal government thanks in large measure to the corruscating rhetoric of Lord Randolph, the one orator in that era of political oratory who could match Gladstone. Thus, at the age of just 37, the firebrand of the Conservative Party got his reward, being appointed Leader of the House of Commons as well as Chancellor of the Exchequer. Informing Queen Victoria of the appointment, Salisbury said he 'feared it was unavoidable'. The Queen, who knew that Lord Randolph was in bad health, though not that his complaint was advanced syphilis, was worried that he was 'so mad and odd'.

The minister excited both admiration and loathing, but no one denied his brilliant talents and political standing in party and country. His mother, dowager duchess of Marlborough, welcomed his success with 'bright ecstasy and joy'; his wife, the beautiful Brooklyn heiress Jennie Jerome, whose ambition was the premiership for her husband, reckoned they were on their way, and many friends hoped to rise with the new star. Lord Randolph himself forecast that he would hold the job just six months: 'And after that ?' asked a friend. 'Westminster Abbey,' came the reply.

He assumed he would be dead and, typically, had no doubt as to where he should be buried. In fact, he was out of the government in less than six months and his career in public life finished for good. In a sense this political demise, though not due to syphilis, was the result of a disease – the disease of overweening pride.

In a society which loved social 'lions', Lord Randolph was a dinner-party star: his conversation brilliant, his gaiety and good humour infectious, his arrogance and his rudeness legendary. If seated next to company he found tedious, Lord Randolph was apt to decamp, knife and fork in hand, to another place at the table. In his dealings with his political colleagues, arrogance came as second nature. Prime Minister Salisbury sighed that conducting cabinet business was like conducting an orchestra in which the first fiddle played one tune while everybody else, including the conductor, wished to play another. But Lord Randolph had to be humoured.

He had his problems, it is true. Not least, it must be said, with the sheaves of decimal statistics that flowed across his desk: 'I never could make out what those damned dots meant!' More serious were his growing isolation within cabinet on economic policy and his rudeness to other members of the government, even friends, on the floor of the House of Commons. One who tried to silence Randolph with an icy stare was rounded on with, 'Don't think you are going to unnerve me with that poached egg look!' Small wonder that before the session was far advanced, he felt 'entirely alone and solitary'. This self-contrived isolation had about it an element of the farcical when Lord Curzon, that 'very superior person' and a byword for snobbishness, complained: 'I used to know Lord Randolph well, and to be on familiar terms with him. But, since he became a swell, I find that the barest civility is all one can expect.'

Nevertheless, that autumn, the world outside Westminster supposed that the great minister was now launched on a career that could only end in Number 10 Downing Street. He confided to a friend: 'There is only one place, that is P.M. I like to be boss.' *The Times* 'did not think there is much chance of turning out Randolph for a long time to come'. His friends urged him to bide his time. His enemies in cabinet were content to play a waiting game too, convinced that he would hang himself, given the rope. Their strategy was to avoid all rows with him and let him 'hammer away' until he put himself 'entirely and flagrantly in the wrong by some act of Party disloyalty which everybody can understand and nobody can deny'.

It happened much sooner than they dared hope. Rich in charisma, that quality so much vaunted in modern political life, Lord Randolph was short on patience and quite innocent of any sense of political strategy. He chafed that he had 'no influence at all ... whether on foreign policy or home policy or expenditure', though this was surely his fault. He believed the ship of state was 'proceeding headlong for a smash'. In consequence, his reputation was in danger. Where a shrewder politician would have worked to see that the Prime Minister and other colleagues were clearly identified as the figures on the bridge, his thoughts turned to jumping ship.

His perception of politics seems to have been entirely blinkered by self-esteem. If the government crashed, he, Randolph Churchill, would suffer a loss of reputation because he, Randolph Churchill, would surely be held responsible. Even Winston alleged that his father 'rated his own power and subsequent responsibility too high'.

An artist's impression of the House of Commons, in September 1886: Lord Randolph Churchill for the Tories at the dispatch box and Mr Gladstone for the Liberals, recently defeated in a general election, slumped on the Opposition front bench.

> *There is a difference between Lord Randolph Churchill and the Mahdi [the fanatical religious leader who defeated the British forces under General Gordon in the Sudan in 1885]. The latter is sane but pretends to be half mad, whilst the former occupies precisely the opposite position.*
>
> LORD SALISBURY, TORY PRIME MINISTER FROM WHOSE CABINET LORD RANDOLPH RESIGNED IN 1886

He began the week that was to decide his political fate as a guest of the Queen at Windsor Castle. He and another cabinet minister travelled down together and there, in the privacy of a reserved first-class compartment on the Great Western Railway, Lord Randolph announced his intention to resign to his thunderstruck colleague. He wrote his letter of resignation from Windsor but told the Queen nothing of his intentions. Nor had he informed his wife, who was making last-minute arrangements for a great reception they were to hold. Three days later, during a visit to the theatre, he astounded her by saying: 'Don't worry about that, it may never come off.' His resignation letter was already on its way to Hatfield. On leaving the theatre, apparently to go to his club, he went instead to Editor William Dawson at *The Times*, to give him the letter for publication. The play that night was *The School for Scandal*.

If he hoped for support in return for the scoop, he was to be disappointed. The next morning the paper carried the letter with a scathing attack on its author for driving a wedge into the Tory Party at a most critical moment. At Hatfield the house guests had included Lord Randolph's mother: another wrote to a friend, 'picture yourself the bomb that exploded this morning, the duchess wept large tears of fury and mortification and was conveyed to London speechless'.

The Queen, who had been coming to admire his skill and judgement, now fumed at 'the want of respect shown to me and his colleagues ... Lord Randolph dined at my table on Monday evening and talked to me about the Session about to commence. And that very night at the Castle he wrote to Lord Salisbury, resigning his office! It is unprecedented!'

Why did he do it? Lord Beresford said that there must be a woman in the case. 'Liver? Madness?' were Salisbury's suggestions, though the motivation hardly interested him. Asked about when he might ask Lord Randolph back into the cabinet, he replied: 'Did you ever know a man having got rid of a boil on the back of his neck, who wanted another?' Lord Randolph commented to his wife: 'Quite a surprise for you.'

If he hoped to bring Salisbury down, he had failed. 'He has not the stuff of a leader in him,' wrote one journalist. Far from rallying supporters, he was shunned. The government shook for a week, but it did not crack. G. J. Goschen accepted Salisbury's offer of the Chancellorship. 'I forgot Goschen,' commented Randolph, suggesting that calculation of some kind had played a role in his action. The old policies continued, no crash ensued which might have damaged his reputation. But then by now it had vaporized.

His meteoric career in politics from 1880 to 1886 comprised effectively six years in opposition and six months in office. His gifts were essentially critical and destructive in kind and thus ideal for opposition politics. It seems he lacked the will, if not the abililty, to harness his talents to more constructive purposes. Nevertheless, after his death, one bemused old Tory, who found he had lived into an age when democracy of a kind seemed to have arrived, acknowledged that somehow 'he made the people believe in us'.

He committed political suicide by an impulsive resignation. The decision came, apparently from nowhere. In the words of one editorial writer:

'Lord Randolph ... played the frog in the fable, blowing himself up to look like a bull ... to find that he is received simply as a frog.' He himself once said: 'We live in an age of advertisement.' One of the first politicians to recognize that truth, he was, perhaps, deceived into his blunder by his own image.

An Un-American Mistake – Joe McCarthy and the Army

In February 1950 America was stunned by a speech made in Wheeling, West Virginia by the 42-year-old Republican Senator from Wisconsin, Joseph Raymond 'Joe' McCarthy. He claimed to have names of 205 Communists in the US State Department and held a document aloft as proof. The Department wired for the document so the charge could be investigated. It was never produced and a six-hour debate on the floor of the Senate failed to extract one concrete piece of evidence implicating any of the now '81' cases McCarthy claimed to have knowledge of. In four years in which he terrorized American public life with accusations of Communist subversives, he never offered proof capable of rational debate. He quickly learnt that he did not need to.

These were the years of the Cold War against the Soviet Union and its satellites. The idea that the ideological enemy might have a fifth column in the govenment and among opinion-formers seemed horribly plausible once it had been suggested. For four years Joe McCarthy's unsubstantiated accusations destroyed reputations by the hundred in national and local politics, in the stage and film industry and in many other professions. To be mentioned meant being entered on a black list and losing all chance of employment.

From his desk in the Senate chamber, McCarthy came near to hypnotizing his fellow legislators and the media. Bludgeoning opposition with repeated 'points of order', sometimes the Senator brandished documents, sometimes he made knowing references to 'the files', sometimes he spoke of mystery witnesses. Not once did he produce concrete evidence. But each day brought new charges, nevertheless. For journalists always want stories and Joe McCarthy produced them to order.

One morning, out of the blue, he told a couple of newspaper men that he meant to subpoena President Truman. Of course he never did so. But the story was printed. He was, after all, a Senator and surely would not fabricate lies. But that was precisely his game. It was fun. It brought him fame. And the multiple untruth can never be disproved.

The 1953 Republican Congress made him chairman of a permanent Senate investigation sub-committee, known as the 'Un-American Activities Committee'. Nothing could have been more un-American than the activities of the Committee itself. Sneer, slur, slander and innuendo were the tools of investigation it employed. Abetted by a public and political class frozen like rabbits mesmerized by a stoat, McCarthy terrorized citizens and government officials alike – until, that is, he blundered into his own downfall.

I think it is a shoddy, unusual thing to do to use the floor of the Senate to attack your opponent without any proof whatever.

SENATOR JOSEPH (JOE) MCCARTHY, 1956

Between 1951 and 1954 the Senator had used his position and his chairmanship of the so-called Un-American Activities committee to destroy the careers of thousands of Americans in government service and the communications industry by innuendo and unproven accusations of supposedly treasonable activities.

US Senator Joe McCarthy, hand raised, emphasizes a point during a huddle with collaborators in one of his notorious anti-communist witch-hunt hearings, September 1953.

In April 1954 he accused the Army Department of trying to conceal evidence of espionage activities allegedly uncovered at Fort Monmouth, NJ. Career officers were mocked and traduced on the witness stand, just as if they were senators or liberals or ordinary citizens, the committee's customary victims. But the army counterattacked and it did so in kind – with a smear. It so happened that a former consultant to the committee was now doing service as a private in the army. Charges were brought that McCarthy and his aides had sought by the use of improper means to obtain preferential treatment for their erstwhile colleague.

The televised hearings of the Fort Monmouth 'investigation' lasted until August 1954. Night after night an audience of some 20,000,000 watched as the white knight of true Americanism exposed himself for a hectoring bully and moral defective. However, when the hearings were officially suspended they were never to be resumed. McCarthy was cleared, but his power and his spell were broken.

In December, to his own considerable astonishment, he himself came under investigation by a Senate committee, on a motion of censure. Chairman Senator Watkins would brook no bluster. If the famous Wisconsin war cry, 'Point of Order', rent the air, it was silenced by a gavel like a headsman's axe. Once McCarthy complained that such behaviour was 'the most unheard of thing I ever heard of!' It probably was. Certainly, after the committee ended its hearings with a vote of condemnation, he was never again heard with respect or interest. At last legislators found the courage to ignore the witch-hunter when they met him in the corridors of the Congress building. Joe, it is said, was hurt and puzzled. 'Don't people realize it was all just politics ... nothing personal,' he complained.

Most mistakes come from failing to match action or intention to reality; blunders are simply heightened results of the condition. Few people this side of madness can have had a more tenuous awareness of reality in the domain of human relations than had Senator Joseph McCarthy.

A Shadow without Substance

In October 1995 the British prison service was thrown into disarray by Home Secretary Michael Howard's enforcing the resignation of the Director-General of the service, Derek Lewis. The sacking followed within hours of the publication of a report which revealed startling failures in discipline, in judgement and in staff morale, which in turn had produced a number of sensational breakouts. One of these had led to the dismissal of a prison governor under controversial circumstances.

The minister's often-stated view was that while he was responsible for policy, it was the Director-General and his team who were responsible for day-to-day operational matters. With such a damning report in his hands, he said, he had no option but to dismiss the Director-General. Lewis claimed that, in fact, Howard broke his own rules and meddled in operational matters on a daily basis – specifically that the decision to sack the prison governor had been his. He implied that the report had been skewed to produce justification for the minister who wanted his head. And he observed that during his two-year term in office there had, in fact, been many improvements for which the minister took the credit while distancing himself from the failures. Since this merely described what had become standard procedure for any government minister who could get away with it and since, under the ingenious Howard regime, the minister, as the Chief Inspector of Prisons had already observed, was 'not responsible for anything at all', the point seemed hardly worth making. But the ex-director's sense of grievance was so strong that he was to initiate legal action against the minister for wrongful dismissal.

The case went back over a period of months. Answering the subtle question of whether or not Howard had put pressure on Lewis to make operational decisions against his better judgement, seemed to depend on establishing intricate timetables of events and the exact words used in long-past confidential conversations. It was, in short, a political quagmire of the kind in which the plausible Howard was a proven and sure-footed operator. Holding the ministerial portfolio charged with guardianship of the integrity and credibility of the nation's legal and judicial system, he had, indeed, established some kind of record by having decisions and actions of his indicted no fewer than five times by the courts and yet remaining in office. This was the man that the Labour opposition seems to have thought could be finally brought down by a debate in the House of Commons. On Thursday 19 October, at very short notice, they changed the motion for debate from the one they had listed for that day to 'This House has no Confidence in the conduct of the prison service'. It was to turn out to be a strategic blunder of considerable proportions.

There were numerous difficulties. First, Director-General Lewis had asserted before a parliamentary select committee that the decision to suspend the governor had been his, and he had repeated the admission in a television interview. Secondly, the intricacies of the case would not make for easy parliamentary debating tactics. Thirdly, the Tories had just completed an annual Conference at which Howard had won a large rank-and-file ovation for harsh 'law and order' policy initiatives. Fourthly, although close analysis (of a kind which is not the *métier* of Britain's legislature) might weaken its impact, as it stood, the report on which the minister had based his action and which had astounded public opinion with its revelations, offered convincing grounds for a minister to decide a new director was needed.

As the debate in the House proceeded that Thursday afternoon, another and crucial weakness in Labour's offensive was revealed. Their spokesman on home affairs, Jack Straw, was easily outpointed in debate by the Home Secretary. To start with, he could provide no answer to the simple question: Would he have dismissed the Director-General? In the words of one political commentator: 'From that moment he was finished.' Others spoke of a 'rambling' performance; at one point he seemed to lose the thread of his argument to the evident embarrassment of his front-bench colleagues; at another, the Deputy Speaker had to order the Tory hecklers to give him a chance to be heard, the ultimate humiliation in that bear-pit known as the Commons debating chamber. Eventually, Labour leader Tony Blair intervened to take over the floundering attack and thus diminished still further the standing of one of his own front-bench team. It is not disclosed who in that team urged the switch of debate to the prison issue. It was reported, however, that when it was over, Blair refused to speak to his home affairs spokesman.

By the end of the business it was difficult to dispute the triumphant Tory yell: 'It's a massacre.' Their man was home and dry and had, in the process, routed the Opposition. Howard was to exploit his position to the full by removing Judge Stephen Tumim, inspector of prisons, the one man left prepared to voice opposition to the retrogressive government policies. In the parliamentary debate itself nothing had been clarified, no contribution made to the crying need for reforms in the prison service and its administration, no boost given to the morale of the men and women working in that beleaguered service. But none of these matters had been on the afternoon's programme. The question at issue was not the fitness of the minister to discharge duties once thought to include responsibility for the prisons. The question was simply the man's political survival.

In passing, the role of Howard's policy initiatives in debilitating the day-to-day running of the prison service was hardly noticed. To take just one example. One prison, the site of a sensational break-out, had been refused funding for a state-of-the-art fence alarm system in the interest of ministerial cost-cutting measures. Howard's claims not to have intervened in operational decisions was derided by one prison governor: 'He's been messing everywhere.' By the end of the Lewis affair and the debate which sealed the Home Secretary's triumph, the job of Director-General was reclassified by one worker in the field as 'the post of Michael Howard's whipping boy'.

But such parliamentary occasions have a logic all their own. When the vote was declared, Labour's discomfiture was complete. The government, with a paper-thin overall majority of seven in a full House, came home in this debate with a majority of 49. As a result of an ill-considered and ill-conducted debate, Labour, surfing into the new parliamentary session on high opinion poll ratings, had opened it with a thudding failure. They had not only left in place a minister they had hoped to dislodge, a minister whose populist law-and-order policies had powerful voter appeal with a general election in prospect, but had strengthened his reputation as a parliamentary performer and given his party an unlooked-for surge of confidence. Blunders do not come much better.

Well perhaps they do. Barely a fortnight after his crucifixion by his Tory opposite number in the Commons, Jack Straw suffered a side thrust from one of his own colleagues in the shadow cabinet. In a television programme on Sunday 29 October, Labour MP Claire Short found time to restate her well-known views on a matter central to Straw's brief, that consideration should be given to the decriminalization of soft drugs. While they remained in the criminal domain they were liable to be supplied by the same dealers as handled hard drugs, so the transition from the one to the other was easy.

Two factors transformed a thoughtful and persuasive contribution to a serious debate into the kind of blundering misjudgement beloved of political opponents. The first was that, earlier that year, Labour campaigners in a by-election had remorselessly pilloried a rival candidate as 'soft on drugs', simply for advocating an inquiry into the topic. The second, and far more important, factor was that Ms Short held the shadow cabinet portfolio of transport. Within hours, Straw rushed on to the air to put the record straight. Short was, he said, speaking purely on her own account. There was no question of legalizing soft drugs as Labour policy. It was too late of course. On the same radio programme, Michael Howard was able to score an easy political bull's-eye with the accusation that 'New Labour', like Old Labour, was hopelessly split on major policy issues, and that Short's comment had slipped the mask on the face of the Party's new image.

The fact that senior members of the police and other law enforcement agencies were moving to the position expressed by Short had no bearing on the politics of the matter. For the run-in period to an election campaign, it is a rule-of-thumb to follow convention and allow one's home affairs spokes-person to set the line on drugs and persuade the transport expert to confine him or herself to railways and such matters. Within 24 hours Labour leader Tony Blair read the riot act to his shadow cabinet colleagues to follow party policy whatever their private views. For some observers the whole incident confirmed the conviction that Labour was determined to unravel the skein of success fate seemed anxious to hand them for the up-coming elections. The impression was strengthened some weeks later, when shadow Secretary for Education, Harriet Harman, revealed that her sons were attending a school which practised selection in its admissions policy. Since the Party's education policy was opposed to selection, it seemed a blunder, to outsiders, that Harman had not offered to resign her position nor had been asked to do so.

CHAPTER 8: PROBLEMS OF LEADERSHIP

For a politician, the chief problem of leadership is getting oneself elected leader of one's party. After that, leadership of the country is a reasonable expectation if one has, of course, chosen the correct party in the first place. In America, however, the choice of a second-in-command can also be critical. A good vice-president is, essentially, one who does not make waves; such candidates are not always easy to come by.

Choose your Partner Carefully

The choice of vice-president can make or break an American politician's chance of winning the presidency and, in at least one case, impacted on his position even when safely elected. During the Democratic primaries of 1972, Senator George McGovern of South Dakota won large support among students and minority groups on a platform of party and national reform. The momentum continued through the National Convention and he emerged an easy winner of the party's presidential nomination with Senator Thomas Eagleton of Missouri as his vice-presidential running mate. Only when the Convention was over did it emerge, to stunned reaction among Democratic Party managers, that Eagleton had been three times hospitalized for mental depression in the previous decade. Many among McGovern's supporters thought that to drop him from the ticket on these grounds would be an act of prejudicial discrimination. Many others thought that such a clinical record, though perhaps a fit subject for sympathy, was no qualification for a potential successor to the most powerful man in the Western world. Reluctantly, McGovern asked Eagleton to resign the vice-presidential nomination and R. Sargent Shriver Jr., a former head of the Peace Corps, was chosen in his place. It made no difference, the Democratic team was destined to be beaten out of sight by Republican victory in 49 of the 50 states in the Union.

Vice-Presidents can mean Vice

The news that McGovern and Shriver had been in electoral combat with a couple of criminals – a president who connived at burglary and a vice-president guilty of tax evasion and corruption – came too late to affect the issue. Incumbents President Nixon and Vice-President Agnew roared back into office with a share of the popular vote which fell only half a point behind Lyndon Johnson's 1964 record of 61.2 per cent.

The campaign was marked by rapidly flagging morale in the Democratic camp, and by a campaign of dirty tricks, excessive even by American standards. The nadir was reached with the break-in to the Democratic Party national headquarters in Washington's Watergate Complex. The most notorious blunder in the Sargasso Sea of US presidential campaigning history, Watergate receives separate billing in Chapter 2 (see p. 23). Here we note that under any other president but Nixon, the selection of Spiro T. Agnew would have been deemed an act of criminal misjudgement. Even for 'Tricky Dicky' Nixon it proved a blunder.

Agnew's role in the campaign had been that of bully boy, dishing the dirt while Nixon appeared in the role of statesman. With all the grace of a Nazi Brownshirt Storm Troop leader, Agnew characterized those who dared mobilize opinion against America's war in Vietnam as 'an effete corps of impudent snobs'. The fact that 20 years on, the Vietnam conflict was the one war in America's history whose veterans were shunned and humiliated by national consensus, might seem to vindicate the arguments of the 'impudent snobs'. At the time they were hardly proof against the moralizing whiplash of the Vice-President's rhetoric.

But the Nixon presidency was barely nine months into its second term, when an investigation by the Justice Department produced evidence that during his term as governor of Maryland, Vice-President Agnew had accepted sweeteners to award contracts to engineering firms and others tendering for state commissions. The evidence strengthened the credibility of rumours that Agnew was still accepting bribes during his first term as vice-president. The last straw came when he faced charges that he had evaded federal

President Richard M. Nixon (left), who was to resign office to avoid impeachment, and his vice-president, Spiro T. Agnew, who was to resign in the wake of corruption charges, shake hands in mutual congratulation on winning the nomination for a second term at the Republican Party Convention, July 1972.

income tax during his term as governor. Pleading 'no contest', he resigned the vice-presidency, thus giving a new twist to the old saw: 'When the going gets tough, the tough get going.' He was fined a token $10,000 and sentenced to a three-year probation. He was succeeded as vice-president by Gerald Ford.

Agnew had served Nixon well during the President's first term. His selection as running-mate made sense – a right-wing border-state governor pleased southern white voters. The appointment was a blunder, but not because Agnew was caught law-breaking. It became a blunder because the news of the tax evasion broke just as the media were poised to take the President himself to the cleaners for his own dirty dealings. Agnew resigned in October 1973; Nixon followed just nine months later, after protracted political death throes, in August 1974.

Look after your Friends ...

In the Republican Convention of 1976 Ronald Reagan made the bold decision to campaign for nomination as presidential candidate, even though the president in office, Gerald Ford, was a Republican aiming to run for a second term. Many observers reckoned Reagan would pull off a sensational victory and Ford, indeed, won the convention only by a narrow margin. In fact, he might well have lost, had it not been for a blunder by Reagan and his advisers.

The team entered the contest with the most powerful delegate backing of any challenger in a century but, aware of his reputation as a reactionary, Reagan sought to win moderate votes on the floor of the convention by declaring that if selected, he would ask Senator Richard Schweiker of Pennsylvania (considered the most liberal man in the party) to run as vice-president.

The move backfired badly. Very few moderates were convinced and Reagan's right-wing friends were furious at this flirtation with liberalism. So, instead of being able to devote their energy to building a winning combination, the Reagan campaign team were stretched to the limit, holding on to their core support. Ford came home with a small, but useful, majority.

> *He is used to dealing with estate workers. I cannot see how anyone can say he is out of touch.*
>
> LADY CAROLINE DOUGLAS-HOME.
>
> **From a report in the *Daily Herald* in October 1963, explaining that her father, Alec Douglas-Home, who had just surrendered his title as 14th Earl of Home to become prime minister, was not remote from everyday experience, as he regularly spoke to workers on his several-thousand-acre family estate.**

The Customary Processes

On the evening of Sunday 6 October 1963, the day before the British Tory Party Conference was due to open in the seaside resort of Blackpool, the Earl of Home dined alone with Britain's ailing prime minister, Harold Macmillan. The question for debate was whether the PM should stand down. Home, as always when the topic came up, as it increasingly did, urged him to resign. Macmillan, however, seemed determined to carry on; indeed, on Tuesday he phoned the Queen's private secretary with the news. But, within hours, he was being rushed to hospital for an emergency operation. During much of Wednesday he drafted and redrafted what was to all intents and purposes a letter of resignation, to be read out to the delegates at the conference.

Just after 5 o'clock on the afternoon of Thursday 10 October, Lord Home appeared on the platform of the Winter Gardens. His gaunt death's head of a face and slender figure conjured up for many the idea of a weak but honourable personality anxious as a member of the old aristocracy to do his duty by the country but with no interest in power for its own sake. But Sir Alec Douglas-Home, as he would soon be known, was a politician of long standing. He had been Chamberlain's private secretary at Munich 25 years before, he had held various cabinet posts and when he drove up to Blackpool that day, he believed he had Macmillan's backing.

The rumour was already simmering on the conference floor. Lord Home's apparently aloof, even diffident, emergence into the arc lights was, for those who knew their politics, a moment of tantalizing expectation. Within minutes the Conference was transmogrified, as far as such a thing was possible, into the first cousin of an American presidential nominating convention. Having explained that he came direct from the PM's hospital bed, Lord Home went on to say that he had been asked to read the following letter, 'as soon as I could after arriving at Blackpool'. With a suitable sense of climax, the letter announced that it would for health reasons in fact

Iain Macleod (right) and Lord Home (left) applaud Deputy Prime Minister R. A. Butler after his speech at the Tory Party Conference, Blackpool, October 1963. In fact, it was Home and not Butler who succeeded Harold Macmillan, whose resignation had been announced during the conference, as prime minister.

PROBLEMS OF LEADERSHIP

> *After half a century of democratic advance, the whole process has ground to a halt with a 14th Earl.*
>
> HAROLD WILSON ON ALEC DOUGLAS-HOME, 1963

be impossible for Macmillan to lead the party into the next election and that he hoped it would soon be possible 'for the customary processes of consultation to be carried on within the party about its future leadership ...'.

The customary processes in question were cabal politics at their most secretive. This was to be the last selection of a Tory leader without any form of democratic process. Views were canvassed, opinions were sought, and judgements sounded. In this way, so went the theory, all elements of the party at Westminster and in the country could make their views known and the best choice be made. But it was the role of the party leader himself to assess, from all this diverse information, who was the most likely candidate to command party unity and advise the Queen accordingly. Wisdom was expected from the leadership and reverence from the foot soldiers. But of course it was politics as usual.

Leading candidates were: R. A. Butler, deputy prime minister and to most progressives in the party the heir presumptive; Quintin Hogg, 2nd Viscount Hailsham, former party chairman; and, now it appeared, the 14th Earl of Home. It was said that Macmillan would never allow his great rival, Butler, to succeed and it seems he at first favoured Hailsham. Somewhat disingenuously, Home told his colleagues that he should not be considered as in the running.

Technically speaking, the convention that a prime minister must come from the House of Commons debarred both of the last two men. But (ironically thanks to a successful battle by the Labour peer Anthony Wedgwood Benn, Viscount Stansgate, to disclaim his peerage a few years before) the mechanism existed for them to return themselves to the rank of commoners. They had in fact discussed the prospects for a vacancy in the premiership some time earlier and now, on the way back to the conference hotel that October afternoon, Hailsham reminded Home, somewhat testily one imagines, that they had agreed there was room for only one peer in the contest.

The response was less than non-committal and Hailsham, who was due to address a fringe meeting that evening, decided that he should take his initiative before it was too late. What followed suggested that, while he might have many qualities to fit him for the post of a Tory prime minister, understanding of his own party was not high on the list. When he came to the end of his prepared speech, he announced he had one more thing he wished to say to his audience, namely that, after deep thought, he had decided to disclaim his peerage.

> *As far as the 14th Earl is concerned, I suppose Mr Wilson, when you come to think of it, is the 14th Mr Wilson.*
>
> ALEC DOUGLAS-HOME ON HAROLD WILSON, 1963

Whatever hopes he may have had died on the evening air. He had broken ranks, staked a claim, breached the code – the man was barely a gentleman. Anyway, from that moment on the precipitate viscount was out of the running. The fact that he went ahead and disclaimed his title could make no difference now. He had blundered and he knew it. Home kept his cool, and his title, until he won Macmillan's approval and recommendation to the Queen. Only when he himself had taken soundings and found he could rely on majority support within his party, did he renounce the title and seek and win election in a safe and deferential parliamentary seat to take his place on the government front bench in the House of Commons. The apparently weak and ineffectual hereditary peer, the supposed political innocent had, either by good fortune or by design, outmanoeuvred the newcomer to aristocratic rank. Hailsham's father had been active in politics before being ennobled and he himself had made his name with a book on the subject. But it was he who blundered on the final stretch to the top job.

The Blunder that Broke an Ideology

In seven years of office, from 1945 to 1951, Britain's Labour Party changed the landscape of British society for a generation. In 1964, with the election of Harold Wilson on a wave of enthusiasm for technological change, it seemed it might continue the formula. But inspiration petered out and gradually perceptions shifted so that the Tories were able to portray Labour as a coalition of trouble-making trade unionists and incompetent, mistaken socialist idealists.

When Jim Callaghan lost the 1979 election to Margaret Thatcher, thoughtful observers assumed that with North Sea oil coming on stream to fund the necessary tax bribes, the Tories would be in power for at least two parliamentary terms. The election of Michael Foot as Labour leader to succeed Callaghan in October 1980 commuted that assumption into a cast-iron certainty. The obvious man for the job, runner-up Denis Healey, became deputy leader.

With an enviable record at the ministry of defence and a reputation as a cost-cutting chancellor, a bruiser in debate and a man of charismatic and ebullient good nature, a compelling TV performer, witty and every bit as powerful an intellect as Foot but wise enough to conceal the fact behind a blustering manner, Healey was anathema to left-wing ideologues. He was also disturbingly larger than life for the mediocrities of all political nuances in the parliamentary party which formed the electoral college.

By contrast, Michael Foot had a record as a campaigner for unilateral nuclear disarmament, was passionately devoted to old-fashioned socialism and, if a dazzling parliamentary orator, was a turn-off as a television performer with his donnish appearance and rhetorical mannerisms of speech. Clearly an honourable man, he was immediately identifiable as little better than a pacifist and a 'do-gooder', a type particularly suspect to the British voter of the early 1980s. This was not the figure to contest the public hustings with the glamorous and hectoring apostle of greed and self-interest who now headed the Tories in the person of Margaret Thatcher.

A party which could so sensationally blunder over the question of personnel selection was clearly not fit for government. When the election was duly called in 1983, Labour compounded their error of selection with a campaign strategy which, while it had the advantage of largely keeping him off TV screens, bustled their man round the country in a series of bungled and exhausting meet-the-people whistle-stop appearances all too often embarrassingly free of actual electors. The Labour manifesto, a turgid script of unwanted and tax-hungry social policies with – for additional unpopularity in the aftermath of victory in the Falklands War – a pledge to cancel Britain's new Trident nuclear defence capability, was later dubbed 'the longest suicide

A sartorial blunder
It may well be that the British Labour Party was unelectable at the time of the 1983 election. Their choice of veteran socialist Michael Foot to succeed James Callaghan as leader back in 1980, had ensured their defeat. For Foot, though a brilliant parliamentarian, was an intellectual who embodied in his ill-kempt hair, crumpled dress sense and moral passion everything which the British electorate associated with, and rejected as, 'Lefty' politics. When, as Leader of the Opposition, he turned up at the Cenotaph one Armistice Day, wearing a donkey jacket among the sober suitings of the other dignitaries, he was accused of blundering bad taste. Paradoxically, Queen Elizabeth the Queen Mother, observing the chill of that November morning from her VIP balcony window, thought his choice of top coat eminently practical.

Britain's 'Gang of Four', Bill Rodgers, Shirley Williams, Roy Jenkins and David Owen, take a photo-call behind baskets of cheques and postal orders contributed to their newly founded Social Democratic Party, February 1981.

note in history' by Labour's Gerald Kaufman. But, in truth, the overdose had been taken three years before with the election of the lost leader.

The choice of Foot as leader was one of the chief factors which drove four of the party's leading right-wingers, Shirley Williams, Roy Jenkins, David Owen and Bill Rodgers to the desperate but futile gesture of forming a fourth political party, the Social Democrats. But many of those who remained with Labour were fully aware of the blunder that had been made at the time of the change of leadership. During the parliamentary election campaign, as the dynamic style of Deputy Leader Healey increasingly stole the headlines, their worries became embarrassingly audible. On 27 May 1983 Labour's campaign manager, Jim Mortimer, was quoted to the following astonishing effect: 'At the campaign committee this morning we were all insistent that Michael Foot is the leader of the Labour Party and speaks for the party .... The unanimous view of the campaign committee is that Michael Foot is the leader.'

As the final week of the election dawned, Jill Foot, the leader's wife, made a still more fearful blunder. Under the impression that she was addressing a private group of Labour supporters, she confided that her husband would certainly resign if Labour lost, and then went on to the effect that, even if the Party should win, she did not think he would stay on for long, but would retire so as to give time 'to make room for a younger man'. There was in fact a reporter present and the story, carried in a local paper, was immediately taken up by the nationals. The image of a party running under the leadership of a man who even his wife considered too old for the job could have been crippling, had not Labour's chances collapsed long before.

When the returns were in, Labour had 209 seats to the Tories' 397. Not since 1900 had a Tory premier been re-elected after winning the previous election, while the increase in Tory seats was the largest ever for an outgoing administration. But not only were the results a personal triumph for Margaret Thatcher, owing much, no doubt, to Britain's victory under her in the Falklands campaign against Argentina – the so-called 'Falklands factor', they were also an indictment of the political philosophy of Labour's left wing.

Accustomed to attribute the Party's failure at the polls to a failure to espouse true socialist policies, the left now had to account for a defeat sustained under its chosen leader and one in which the Tories had won crushingly even when, as the statistics showed, the Tory vote had actually fallen. To cap it all, the veteran left-winger Tony Benn, second only to Foot in the vaunted purity of his socialist credentials, lost his seat.

As for the maverick right-wing 'Gang of Four', Owen, Jenkins, Williams and Rodgers, they had blundered so far in their objective of establishing a new dynamic in British politics that they did not contest even this, their first, election as an independent force, joining, instead, in uneasy alliance with the Liberals. All in all, British Conservatives could have been forgiven, in the summer of 1983, for regarding British socialism as a broken and scattered force.

Nor is it clear that such an analysis would have been wrong. In large measure, Labour's catastrophe could be traced to the Party's decision to choose as leader an ideologue rather than a politician. In the following decade, first under Neil Kinnock and then under Tony Blair, the Party's high command devoted its energies to pulping the historic documents of doctrine for reprocessing into manifestos of political acceptability. The left-wing accusation that the Party was not presenting the electorate with the truths of socialist theory became incontestable. But after the collapse of socialist regimes all over Eastern Europe, it was no longer so clear that this theory was valid anyway.

Ladies First

The year 1974 was surely an *annus horribilis* for Edward Heath. In January he was prime minister of a country in the turmoil of industrial unrest; in February he led his party to electoral defeat and was ousted as PM by Harold Wilson who managed to construct a minority administration. In a second election in October the Tories were again defeated at the polls. From 325 in January, their representation in the Commons had slumped to 277 seats, a drop of 48. To achieve this result he had surrendered a working majority of 18 in an election of his own choosing, both as to issue and timing. The fact that Labour, under Wilson and then Callaghan, were able by hook and by crook to remain in power with an overall majority of never more than three for close on five years, rubbed salt in the wound. But by that time the Tories had another leader.

It could hardly be otherwise. Heath had lost two campaigns in eight months, having dictated timing and tactics for the first decisive encounter. What had seemed a blunder in January did not look any better in October.

In the intervening months, Tory critics – and there were many – had held their fire, given the fact that Labour, heading a minority government, was bound to go to the country sooner rather than later. With Labour's victory in October, the barrage started up in earnest and in February 1975 Ted Heath faced a new electorate – his own MPs. The first round was by way of being a vote of confidence and those who considered themselves the Party heavyweights, William Whitelaw and Sir Geoffrey Howe chief among them, held aloof. They preferred at this stage to leave the running to former education minister Margaret Thatcher and stalking-horse candidate Hugh Fraser. It was their collective blunder. Out of 265 votes cast, Ted Heath received just 119 and immediately withdrew. It was clear that he had lost the confidence of the party – it seemed equally clear to many that Margaret Thatcher, with 130 votes, had won it. The heavyweights failed to see it that way and this was their second blunder. In the second round a week later, Thatcher – with 146 of the 271 votes cast – emerged with a clear majority; Whitelaw, the runner-up, received only 76 and Sir Geoffrey 19. Fortune, they say, favours the brave and no-one ever doubted Margaret Thatcher's courage. The ease with which the Tory Party, until this time conventionally mocked for its patronizing attitude to women, elected and then accepted the first woman leader of a major western political party, is in itself noteworthy.

Miscalculation Down Under

In the late 1980s, New Zealand politics seemed, to outside observers, to be changing course as former welfare policy came under increasing challenge from what was called 'New Right' thinking. In 1989 this produced ructions in the Labour government of David Lange, as finance minister Roger Douglas urged radical reshaping of the welfare programme. He publicly accused the Prime Minister of presidential-style leadership, of ignoring the views of cabinet colleagues and of being 'impossible to work with'.

It proved an ill-considered outburst. Douglas was dismissed from office and, if he was relying on his standing within the Party to maintain himself, he had miscalculated. Challenging Premier Lange in a Party leadership contest, the ex-minister was rejected with a vote of 38 to 15. But if they did not want him as leader, it seems the Party valued him as a colleague and a caucus called on Lange to mend fences with his rival.

Now it was the Prime Minister's turn to blunder. Or perhaps he was, as alleged, impossible to work with. At all events, he ignored the request. On 29 June he paid the price of his arrogance when a vote of confidence went against him. As most people expected, Lange continued to battle his corner and many supposed that after a period of winter turbulence he would re-establish his hold. But on 7 August he confounded the analysts and startled the public with the announcement of his resignation from office. And if his critics considered he had only himself and his high-handed conduct of affairs to blame, Lange could at least reflect with satisfaction that he had finally out-manoeuvred Douglas, for he was succeeded in post by his own nominee, Geoffrey Palmer.

Dog Eat Dog

All Britain's major political parties have well-established procedures for electing a new leader. But, whereas both Labour and the Liberal Democrats have recorded ballots so that all may know how any MP placed his vote, the Tories' is a secret ballot. Preening themselves as the world's most sophisticated electorate, they are certainly the world's most untrustworthy. As a senior whip in the 1950s Edward Heath advised one of his juniors 'to remember just one thing: they're all shits'. It seems that he did not remember that advice in 1975 when his leadership was challenged by Margaret Thatcher. Backbenchers queued up to pledge their support. In fact barely 45 per cent of them voted for him on the first ballot and Margaret Thatcher forced him into resignation (see also p. 122).

Every campaign manager in a Tory leadership election buffers his estimates of the likely outcome with a 'lie or fib factor' of at least 15 per cent. In her memoirs, Thatcher recorded that she, like Heath, had been fed over-optimistic reports by her campaign team. The Heath camp's error? They made the mistake of believing the estimates. She discounted the information and continued working on the campaign until the last possible moment. Yet when she confronted the life-and-death challenge to her own leadership 14 years later, she, too, seemed to have forgotten the value of cynicism when dealing with MPs concerned with only one thing: ensuring their own re-election come the next voting day.

In 1990, after eleven years of power, Margaret Thatcher's government looked weary and was moreover saddled with a pack of recent political blunders which seemed certain to end their chances of victory in the forthcoming general election. Chief among these was the poll tax local government levy, pushed through at Thatcher's own high-profile insistence. In November of that year, Thatcher found herself challenged by a raft of serious contenders for the Tory leadership, most formidably Michael Heseltine. But eleven years is a long time in power and she was, after all, the doyenne of Western political leaders. So Margaret Thatcher fell to the number one no-no of all successful endeavours – complacency.

There are those who date the beginning of Margaret Thatcher's fall from the day in the summer of 1989 when she sacked Sir Geoffrey Howe as her foreign secretary, making him Leader of the House of Commons instead. On the first day in his new and less prestigious job, he was given a rousing welcome as he entered the chamber by leading Tory members waving their order papers. It amounted to a public warning from her party that the Iron Lady's contempt for all ideas but her own and her indifference to the feelings of anyone whom she considered too weak to do her harm, could go too far. She paid no heed. Later she created Howe Deputy Prime Minister, but nullified whatever value the promotion might have had by her studied and publicly expressed disregard for the man with the empty title. On 1 November 1990, after enduring months of casual humiliation, Sir Geoffrey resigned. The seemingly undislodgeable Prime Minister was unmoved, even though, behind the scenes, Tory MPs were already being canvassed for the first round of voting in an election for the leadership of their party.

I would not wish to be Prime Minister, dear. I have not enough experience for that job. The only full ministerial position I've held is Minister for Education and Science. Before you could even think of being Prime Minister you'd need to have done a good deal more jobs than that.

ELEMENTARY PRINCIPLES OF GOVERNMENT SPELLED OUT BY MARGARET THATCHER IN AN INTERVIEW ON BRITISH CHILDREN'S TV IN 1973.

Two years later she became leader of her party and in 1979, without further experience, prime minister. Thanks to what became known as the 'Falklands factor', one of Britain's most unpopular prime ministers became one of her most popular. It appeared that a varied c.v. was not as important as a 'short successful war'.

> *She is trying to wear the trousers of Winston Churchill.*
>
> LEONID BREZHNEV ON MARGARET THATCHER, 1979

Labour's Denis Healey once famously remarked that being attacked in debate by Geoffrey Howe was 'like being savaged by a dead sheep'. On 13 November 1990, in a resignation statement of measured but searching hostility to Thatcher, the ovine zombie showed it had teeth with a cutting edge. In a long political career, the former cabinet minister had won wide respect in the party and his resignation could only cause serious damage to his leader: she accepted it without demur. Her failure to realize the importance of the event was sure evidence that she had lost touch with the realities of political life.

Her second mistake was the decision to keep her distance from the actual campaigning. She is reported to have said to one supporter: 'If they don't know me now, they never will.' More to the point, she thought that going out to 'press the flesh' would demean the image of the 'Iron Lady'. These were pretty obvious miscalculations in the art of 'man-management', but at least they were political, not on a par with the overweening character failing revealed by David Owen's reflections on the qualities of leadership. 'The man of character,' he wrote, 'incorporates in his own person the severity inherent in his effort ... a leader of this quality is inevitably aloof, for there is no authority without prestige, nor prestige unless he keep his distance.' It is hardly surprising that Owen's attempt to launch a fourth party on the British political scene, the Social Democrats, ended in humiliating failure.

Thatcher compounded her error of aloofness by leaving for Paris during the closing stages of the first ballot. The event of long standing in her diary was a summit to mark the end of the Cold War. It would have been difficult to cancel but wiser to have returned to London at the earliest possible opportunity to rally support for a second round. Instead, she stayed on because, it was later claimed, she believed it would help her cause to be seen representing Britain on such an historic occasion.

On Monday 19 November the result of the first ballot was announced. Britain's longest-serving prime minister this century, commanding a Commons majority of 80, had failed by four votes to win the majority required to avoid a second round of voting. It was seen to be a sensational rebuff by everybody but Margaret Thatcher. She appeared briefly on the steps of the British Embassy that evening to acknowledge the news before retiring for the night. There was no indication that she would return to London to rally support in the second round. Perhaps the political atmosphere of Paris, where the locals described Mitterrand's tenure of office as *la présidence monarchique*, anaesthetized the sensibilities of one increasingly heard to voice the royal 'we'. Many believed that it was a major blunder to leave London on the day of the election, but that not to return to argue her case was fatal. A change of vote by just two MPs would have saved the Prime Minister's position. Surely she could have charmed or hand-bagged two of her once adoring parliamentarians into supporting her in the second round. But Margaret Thatcher had come to regard the canvassing of support, like listening to other people's opinions, as demeaning.

Probably, however, her biggest blunder in the one area of judgement indispensable for any politician in a democratic society, was the choice of campaign team. George Younger, the campaign director, was preoccupied with his work as a bank chairman, so day-to-day command fell to his number two, Peter Morrison. Unfortunately, he was such a committed Thatcherite that he had trouble communicating with anyone outside the congregation of true believers, with anyone, in short, who was wavering in their support – precisely the type of person with whom communication was essential.

He shared his leader's complacency of victory, until it was too late. Whereas John Major's HQ seems to have been run like a military operations room, with colour-coded charts of supporters papering the walls and an hourly updated computer central register, Morrison was content to keep his master list of firm supporters in the breast pocket of his suit.

A Chairman should Know his Onions

In September 1994 Britain's Prime Minister, John Major, made a resounding attack on the prevalence of yobbish behaviour in British society and the need for a new get-tough law-and-order policy to combat it. Three days later rioting hooligans at a London boxing match caused several casualties among the fans. The incident, which was shown on TV, shocked decent opinion. The following day Jeremy Hanley, only recently appointed as Tory Party chairman, the person with the job of managing the Party's public relations, interviewed on TV, dismissed the mayhem as 'natural exuberance'.

On the day of Hanley's appointment Norman Tebbit, life peer and a former party chairman but familiarly known as 'Rottweiler' Tebbit because of his savaging of the Major government on every possible occasion, opined that 'few people would have named Jerry as one of the party's top brains' and 'we have to wonder whether he was the Prime Minister's first choice for the job'. The boxing match gaffe prompted the right-wing tabloid *Daily Express* to banner-headline 'Tory chief's riot blunder'. Rupert Murdoch's organ, *The Times*, for once perhaps justified in its anti-Major campaign, commented that everybody seemed agreed Hanley was a 'frightfully decent chap' but suggested that chairmanship of the Tory Party required a few additional qualities, 'like being able to remember Tory policies'. The remark seemed to be a fitting culmination to a sequence of howlers which had marked Hanley's brief tenure of office up to that time. It was in fact merely a prelude. As Tory Central Office put out face savers about a new chairman learning on the job, their man freely admitted, again on television, that his earlier comments had certainly thrown into question his ability to handle his job. As this was precisely the charge his critics had been levelling since he first took the job, he might have reflected that honesty, while engaging, and in a politician astounding, is not always the best policy.

Whether this was a blunder, of course, is more difficult to judge. He remained party chairman until July 1995. Cynics said this was to save Major the reputation of being the most stupid man in his party. Following the PM's triumph in the leadership election that month, Hanley received his marching orders. With just two years to the next election the Tories needed a skilled chairman whose other job is to plan the election campaign.

CHAPTER 9: FOOT IN MOUTH

US President Calvin Coolidge was famous for his taciturnity. The story goes that one bubbly dinner-guest told the President she had been bet that she could not get three words out of him all evening, but was silenced by the reply: 'You lose'. On another occasion, when told he had died, another flapper quipped, 'How do they know?' But the President's formula was hard to beat as a recipe for political survival. More careers have been broken and in former times lives lost by the untimely remark or ill-considered admission than by almost any other form of blunder.

The Fatal Admission

For 17 years Mary Queen of Scots, who had also a claim on the throne of her second cousin, Elizabeth I of England, lived under house-arrest in England. Throughout that time she was in contact with her cousin's enemies, encouraging their plans for invasion and using her money to pay their agents. But although the English Privy Council knew of many of these plans, Mary was not in danger of her life so long as she did not put her name to any plan for the assassination of the English Queen.

Maybe Mary sensed that so long as she kept clear of advocating regicide, her royal second cousin would not agree the Privy Council's demands for her death, despite her conspiratorial attempts to subvert the English state. But in July 1586 she broke her golden rule and committed to writing her approval of a plot on Elizabeth's life. With this one blunder she signed her own death warrant.

In fact Mary, such a romantic figure in literature and legend, was a trial to her own people and a menace to the English. Whatever her qualities, political common sense was not among them. She lived the first 19 years of her life at the French court and was, briefly, queen of France. On the death of her husband, King Francis II, in 1561 she returned to her native Scotland, landing in August of that year in a country where her mother, recently dead, had been regent. A woman of beauty and passion, she married Henry Darnley and then James Hepburn, 4th Earl of Bothwell who, so the rumour went, had murdered Darnley with her connivance.

A faction of Scottish noblemen rose against the Queen, took her prisoner to Edinburgh and there forced her to abdicate in favour of her one-year-old son, James VI (later James I of England). A romantic youth helped her escape from the island castle of Lochleven in May 1568, but her attempt to regain her throne was defeated the same month and she fled to England to beg refuge of her cousin Elizabeth I.

A politician is a statesman who approaches every question with an open mouth.

ADLAI STEVENSON (1900–68), US DEMOCRATIC PRESIDENTIAL CANDIDATE IN 1952 AND 1956

THE FATAL ADMISSION

Aged just 26, Mary had certainly had an eventful, if notably unsuccessful, life as a queen. Having failed to navigate the turbulent waters of Scottish politics, she embarked on a course of ingratitude and conspiracy against her kinswoman. It certainly was a remarkable paradox in the Europe of the Wars of Religion, a Catholic queen under house-arrest in the protection of a Protestant one. But Elizabeth – who remembered her own years as a prisoner of her sister Mary I and had a cousin's compunction and a queen's natural reluctance to order the death of another, even one deposed by her own subjects – let Mary live.

Elizabeth's raven-haired, Italianate-looking spy-master Sir Francis Walsingham, meant to change things and he knew his business. Philip of Spain once commented bitterly that his most secret dossiers seemed to be read by Elizabeth of England and leaked to his own courtiers by her agents before he had time to discuss them with his ministers. And Walsingham was determined to find evidence that would send Mary to her death. It was to prove difficult, but his chance came in 1586 when Mary fell into a trap carefully prepared for her.

In July of that year, Walsingham's cipher expert Thomas Philips decoded a letter Mary had written on the 19th to the conspirator Antony Babington. The crucial sentence read as follows: 'When all is ready, the six gentlemen must be set to work, and you will provide that on their design being accomplished, I may be myself rescued from this place.' These rather mysterious but apparently harmless words turned out to be dynamite when read in conjunction with Babington's letter of 12 July in which he lists the three basic requirements to ensure the success of his plan to set Mary on the throne of England and thus restore Catholicism. A harbour must be chosen for the landing of the troops to be sent by Philip of Spain; Mary must of course be rescued from her gaolers; and 'the usurping competitor' had to be 'despatched' by the six noble gentlemen who had pledged themselves to undertake 'that tragical execution'.

By responding positively to his plan, Mary had blundered into her own death warrant. It had been made easy for her by spy-master Walsingham.

Below left: Mary Queen of Scots, who plotted the death of Elizabeth of England. Below right: Sir Francis Walsingham, Elizabeth's secret service chief, who trapped her into a fatal blunder.

Some months before, he had learnt of the existence of new plots against Elizabeth involving Mary and was determined to flush out the truth. First, with the Queen's consent, he had her cousin moved from close confinement to a new place of detention, Chartley Hall. To the disgust of Mary's warder Sir Amyas Paulet, it required 80 wagons to shift the books and personal effects of the Queen and her ladies. At Chartley it was easier for would-be conspirators to gain access to Mary and for Walsingham's own agents to operate more easily.

One of these was the seemingly innocent but sinister Richard Giffard, a renegade Catholic who had won Mary's confidence. He offered to open communication with Antony Babington, a rich young Catholic gentleman who during a tour of the continent had made contact with Mary's agent in Paris, and a Jesuit called Ballard. All had been duped by the turncoat Giffard. He arranged with the brewer who supplied the Hall that letters should be carried in empty beer barrels.

But the brewer also had been turned by Walsingham who thus was able to read the entire correspondence. He let the plot develop until Mary's role was unquestionable and then revealed it to Elizabeth; reluctantly she ordered her cousin's trial. With still greater reluctance she agreed to her execution and with the extremest reluctance she signed the warrant. Mary was beheaded at Fotheringhay Castle, Northamptonshire, in February 1587.

The Catholic courts of Europe, who had been abetting plans for the assassination of Elizabeth during most of her reign, were indignant. Philip of Spain had plotted Elizabeth's death and the Cardinal Secretary of Pope Gregory XIII had assured two enquiring English Catholic nobles that 'whoever sends that guilty woman of England out of the world with the pious intention of doing God service, not only does not sin but gains merit...'. Even Mary's son, the Protestant James VI of Scotland, who had privately assured Elizabeth that he would not act to avenge his mother's death, felt duty-bound to express outrage.

It was the legalistic formalities which shocked. Elizabeth herself, who had agonized so long before signing the warrant, and seems not to have intended that it should be acted on, accused the councillors who did act upon it of having made her an object of hatred and calumny. But if the Queen was loath to authorize the execution, her councillors had no intention of committing it without authorization. In the end the deed was done and Mary Queen of Scots, from being a murderous and incompetent conspirator, passed onto the stage of legend as a wronged romantic victim.

Ministerial Misdemeanours

In the days of her greatness, Britain was habitually ruled by men who today, when a deputy governor of the Bank of England was asked to resign for pleasuring his mistress on the carpet in the governor's office, would be classified as drunks and philanderers. Lloyd George, the prime minister who led the country to victory in the First World War, in addition to scores of more or less casual liaisons, had a full-time affair with his secretary and was reputed, on occasion, to call on her sexual services even in the cabinet room of Number 10 Downing Street.

William Pitt the Younger, prime minister for the first decade of the wars against Napoleon, daily drank a bottle of port before lunch and maintained a steady intake until retiring to bed in the small hours. The great Duke of Wellington, victor at Waterloo, was notorious for his affairs. When threatened with exposure in her memoirs by Harriet Wilson, a renowned lady of the town, he replied with the now proverbial 'Publish and be damned'. Herbert Asquith, prime minister for the first two years of the First World War, was 'a fairly heavy drinker ... occasionally ... a little unsteady (even in the House of Commons)'.

In the Second World War, Winston Churchill was rarely far from a bottle of champagne or whisky. Later in life, in a famous exchange with an opposition woman MP, he allowed himself to lapse into boorishness. Encountering him in the corridors of the House of Commons after a debate, she burst out disgustedly: 'Mr Churchill, you are drunk.' 'And you, Madam,' came the cheap response, 'are ugly. But tomorrow I shall be sober.'

But no one in post-war British politics achieved a reputation for systematic intoxication while on duty, so to speak, to match that of George Brown, Labour's foreign secretary from 1966 to 1968. What is possibly the best known of tipsy politico stories is commonly pinned on him. It comes in various versions, a notable one being set in Peru. Brown, so far as is known never having visited South America during his term in office, the venue is suitably diplomatic.

As the band struck up towards the end of a notably liquid state reception, so goes the yarn, Her Britannic Majesty's Secretary of State for Foreign Affairs was seen to wobble across the ballroom commandeered for the occasion, towards one of the more distinguished guests. Sinking to his knees with upturned tearful eyes and clasping his hands in supplication, he cried out: 'Lovely creature in scarlet; Oh, lovely creature in scarlet, dance with me ...!' The refusal was to the point: 'In the first place you are drunk; in the second place they are playing the National Anthem; and in the third place I am the Cardinal Archbishop.'

A politician is an animal which can sit on the fence and still keep both ears to the ground.

ANON.

An Unwise Minister

Early in 1989 President Daniel arap Moi of Kenya went on a visit to Europe. While he was away, Vice-President Josephat Karanja played an unusually prominent role in the nation's affairs. It was a blunder. Returning home in April, Mr arap Moi made a speech at Nairobi airport in which he stated in the most emphatic terms that no one had been designated as acting president during his absence and also condemned the dangers of gambling. His hearers rightly deduced that Vice-President Karanja was in trouble; in addition to the unwisely active part he had played during the President's absence, he had a large and very profitable share in a Nairobi gambling house.

A member of the dominant Kikuyu tribe and also minister for home affairs, Karanja automatically carried considerable weight in Kenyan politics and a wiser man might have been content to maintain a low profile and bide his time. As it was, he found himself criticized for arrogant behaviour, accused of pushing Kikuyu interests and even charged in parliament with secretly receiving funds from Uganda to destabilize the government. This barrage of accusation was followed by a vote of no confidence, so that early in May Mr Karanja thought it wise to pay the price for his blunder during the President's absence and resign. Reflecting perhaps that he had himself been mistaken in giving so much influence to one man, President arap Moi assigned the vacant portfolios to new ministers. To make assurance double sure, he ordered Karanja's suspension from the ruling KANU party. After barely twelve months in office the unwise minister's downfall was complete.

Unwise Citizens

The theme of this book is the folly, and worse, of politicians. Their blunders may cost them their jobs, their nation its pride or economic health, a family its reputation or happiness. But, as they are never tired of reminding us, politicians are only human and they do not have a monopoly of stupidity. The follies of citizens who step out of line in delicate political environments, especially citizens whose training or education are such that they should know better, are not political blunders perhaps, but they are certainly mistakes. Some readers may find among the following blunders actions of political courage, but just as courage is the last thing a politician in a democracy should cultivate if he wishes to survive in office, so it is the last thing a citizen in many of the world's countries should practise if he wishes to survive at all.

During 1982 three of Ghana's High Court judges were kidnapped and killed. In June 1989 the Ghana Bar Association planned a series of lectures to commemorate them. Before the lectures could be given, its president, Peter Ala Adjetey, and secretary Nutifafa Kuenyehia were arrested.

In May 1991 the Ivory Coast government of President Houphouët-Boigny announced new laws that would guarantee the freedom of the press. One of Africa's poorest countries, Ivory Coast had recently dedicated a multi-billion dollar basilica church, built by order of the President who had himself just won his seventh five-year term of office by the customary landslide margin. Nevertheless, two foolhardy journalists decided they would take the assurances at face value and published articles critical of the leader. In August they were jailed on charges of insulting the President.

In October 1989 students at the University of Zimbabwe erupted in demonstrations following the arrest of the president and the secretary-general of the student's union. No doubt, despite President Robert Mugabe's declared aim to establish a one-party state, the recent formation of the opposition Zimbabwe Unity Movement led them to suppose that democracy was breaking out. They behaved accordingly, shouting slogans against the President and in favour of the new Unity Movement. The government responded as governments usually do in such situations by dispersing the demonstrators. But then the University was closed. Two weeks later it was temporarily reopened so that those students prepared to give an undertaking of good behaviour could take their exams.

Bad Debts – Good Politics

In November 1988 the Belgian government announced its intention to reschedule the repayment of the debts owed to it by Zaïre. There was an outcry from press and parliament, alleging that Zaïre's President Mobutu Sese Seko was a corrupt dictator who appropriated foreign aid to his own use and aggrandisement. The Zaïrean foreign minister bridled at such insulting language and threatened reprisals. Belgian's foreign minister, Leo Tindemans, attempted conciliation. Unfortunately for him, it was at this point that a Belgian judge ordered the expropriation of all Mobutu's assets in Belgium. This seemed a perfectly reasonable ruling to the judge who was presiding in a case in which a Belgian company had lost all its Zaïrean assets to a nationalization takeover ordered by Mobutu back in 1973. Politically it was a gross misjudgement. Mobutu threatened to sever diplomatic relations with Belgium. The court order on his assets was immediately lifted. Clearly, the price of an independent judiciary could come too high.

However, the Belgian government thought it might decline to fund new development projects in Zaïre until progress be made on debt repayment. This, too, was a blunder. Zaïre threatened to halt debt repayments altogether and in January 1989 all its companies operating in Belgium moved their head offices out of the country. The effect was like magic. The Belgian government agreed to cancel the whole of Zaïre's public debt and one-third of its commercial debts with interest-free payments rescheduled over 25 years for the balance. Finally, any interest that was paid would be put in a special fund set aside for new development projects in Zaïre.

Did He know what He was Saying?

In 1918 the women of Britain finally won the right to vote, though only women of 30 and above. Younger than that, it was supposed that their pretty little heads were not quite up to the serious business of politics. The arrival of the 'flapper' with her bobbed hair and short skirts no doubt confirmed men in the wisdom of the age limit and, as the 1920s Charlestoned their way along, they congratulated themselves on having avoided the hazards of the 'flapper vote'. Then, one day in April 1928, an astounded world woke up to find that the government, a Conservative government, had passed a bill which lowered the voting age for women from 30 to 21 with the same straightforward residence qualification as for men.

The effect was to put five million new voters on the register. The general election of May 1929 returned Labour as the largest party with 288, the Conservatives took 260, the Liberals 59 and minor parties the balance. Disgruntled Tories blamed the flapper vote for the second Labour government, though there is no evidence to back this. None of the parties made

The United States will not be a threat to us for decades.

ADOLF HITLER IN A SPEECH OF 12 NOVEMBER 1940.

He was probably right, his blunder was to declare war on the US himself in December 1941.

any special policies to attract the new voters. Maybe they were too stunned by the extension of the suffrage to take account of it, for there was considerable puzzlement on all sides as to how it had come about. A puzzlement which lasted for years afterwards.

On one thing all commentators were agreed. It was the doing of Sir William Joynson-Hicks, Home Secretary in the Conservative government. Ennobled on his retirement from office as Viscount Brentford, he could perhaps be dubbed for his philistine and reactionary views as the original 'Essex man'. Why 'Jix' of all people, as he was derisively called, should have triggered this enlightened measure, was the real question. Most commentators have supposed that he had blundered but how or why was beyond explanation. Writing in 1965, the historian A.J.P. Taylor claimed that the commitment was made in the excitement of a public meeting. Since the speaker was Home Secretary, Prime Minister Baldwin and his government felt they could not wriggle out of the commitment. But Winston Churchill in a newspaper article of 9 August 1931 gave quite a different account.

According to him the startling new policy initiative, originated in an aside during a poorly attended Friday debate on a totally different question 'no one took very seriously'. Interrupted by Lady Astor, the Home Secretary 'quite unexpectedly, and without the slightest consultation with his colleagues, said that the Conservative Party would enfranchise men and women on the same terms "at the next election"... . Never was so great a change in our electorate achieved so incontinently. For good or ill,' concluded Churchill, who had opposed the measure, 'Jix should always be remembered for that.'

The real offence of Joynson-Hicks was that he resisted classification. Reactionary in matters of religion (he blocked proposed changes to the Church of England *Book of Common Prayer*) and in questions of morality, he was also a 'philistine' in his dislike of modern art. However, on social matters his attitudes could prove disconcertingly liberal. He infuriated Tory opinion by refusing to lift restrictions on shop working hours – according to him eight o'clock in the evening was quite late enough for shop assistants to stop work. And where Churchill saw the General Strike of 1926 as an enemy to be destroyed, Joynson Hicks took the moderate line favoured by Prime Minister Baldwin.

For younger Tories, Jix easily headed the list of the 'Old Gang' they wanted to see displaced but then Churchill himself came second. His initiative on women's voting rights seemed to most Conservatives, Churchill among them, an egregious blunder. No one has ever satisfactorily determined what Jix himself actually thought in the matter.

Old-fashioned Talk
When Mikhail Gorbachev returned in triumph from incarceration in his Crimean dacha, following the collapse of a putsch *by hard-line Communists in August 1991, he supposed he was still in charge. But his attempt to bring to order Boris Yeltsin, the man whose defiance of the tanks in Moscow was seen as ensuring the coup's failure, and his clarion calls for reforms in the Communist Party, when most people then wanted to see the end of the Party altogether, proved classic misjudgements of the public mood.*

The Stumbling President

During the 1976 presidential campaign, the incumbent Gerald Ford, running for re-election, made so many foot-in-mouth gaffes that one wit mused as to whether the President could walk and chew gum at the same time. Most notorious of all these fumbled comments was when Ford, for the past two and a half years supposedly central to foreign policy plans, observed that Eastern Europe and notably Poland was not (sic!) under Soviet domination. It was not clear whether he actually believed this. It is doubtful whether he recovered the Polish American vote! And this was an election when every vote counted. In the event, Ford lost to Democrat Jimmy Carter by a mere 1,745,000 votes or 2.2 per cent of the popular vote and by 297 to 241 votes in the electoral college, the closest margin in 60 years.

The Ambassador's Mistake

Following the 1980s overthrow of Argentina's military dictators, who for years had waged a 'dirty war' of killings and torture against the citizenry, the civilian government of President Raul Alfonsin came under great pressure to exact retribution. Convinced that vindictiveness could spark destabilizing violence from the military, the US government urged leniency, a policy it apparently believed had always characterized its own dealings with opponents. Frank Ortiz, US Ambassador in Buenos Aires, concluded his plea to President Alfonsin with, he thought, a rhetorical question.

'Why, Mr President, do you suppose we have never had a military coup in the United States?'

'Oh, that is simple,' came the immediate reply, 'there is no US ambassador in Washington.'

Education Ministers should be Seen and not Heard

John Patten, Britain's education minister from 1992 to 1994, promoted to the cabinet at the comparatively young age of 48, had a troubled, not to say accident-prone term of office. In a government notoriously liable to gaffes, his characterization of a leading educationist as a 'nutter' and a 'madman', while no doubt chiming with traditionalist views on modern theories of education, was hardly the tone for a minister to take in public with a senior member of the educational establishment. Furthermore, the libel writ which followed cost him heavy (some £15,000, it was rumoured) as well as an apology in the High Court. He was dismissed by Prime Minister Major soon afterwards and in the summer of 1995 announced his intention to stand down as an MP at the next election.

A Journalist's Blunder

Summertime, when the living is easy for the citizenry at large, can be hard for journalists. Politicians, their preferred targets, tend to be on holiday neither doing nor saying very much. But August 1995 seemed to be an exception for the British press. As if from nowhere, a squall of criticism blew up among Labour left-wingers that threatened to cloud the golden-boy image of party leader Tony Blair. It was in this context that London's *Evening Standard* printed an article purportedly by Brian Gould, a former member of the shadow cabinet who had subsequently returned to his native New Zealand. Headed 'Tony Blair's total lack of vision' and beginning, rather oddly, 'I was three and a half during the winter of discontent ...', it branded Blair as an unprincipled power-seeker and warned that a party which jettisoned awkward ideological commitments to win electoral favour would face difficulties in office. Commonplace as the analysis was, it carried piquancy if the work of a former colleague of the victim. In fact, the author was the 19-year-old son of Tory Home Secretary Michael Howard and his age at least should have been apparent from the opening sentence. The 'winter of discontent' was the winter of 1978–9, when Gould was in fact 39.

This time it was the press with egg on its face. The paper explained the goof as a mix-up at an office fax machine. Apparently no one thought to check with Mr Gould on the rather extraordinary opening sentence. He had in fact written an article for the *Standard* which it published some days later and which began 'Tony Blair has had a brilliant first year ...'. The newspaper did not, apparently, sack anyone, though it is safe to assume that, had such a blunder been committed by a politician, the press would have been loud in its demands for resignations.

A Commitment Too Far
In October 1978 the politician's golden rule, 'Never make any commitment you can possibly avoid,' was broken in dramatic style by James Callaghan, Britain's Labour prime minister. In his speech to the Labour Party Conference that month, he amazed veteran commentators and politicians by announcing there would be no election that year. It was true that the year had little more than two months to run but it was also true that Callaghan presided over a minority government dependent on the far-from-automatic support of minor parties. His room for manoeuvre was slight indeed: renouncing the option of a snap election reduced it to zero.

Third Party, Fourth Party – Who's Counting?

'I do not believe in a "Third Party". I do not believe it has any future,' remarked British MP Shirley Williams, speaking in 1981. It is not clear what Mrs Williams meant by this remark since for most people there had been a 'third party' in British politics for some 80 years, the role being occupied in 1981 by the Liberal Party. However, it may have been related to the rumours that she and other disaffected Labour MPs, among them Roy Jenkins, David Owen and Bill Rodgers might be thinking of founding a fourth party. Dubbed the 'Gang of Four' in gently derisive allusion to the bloodthirsty Gang of Four who had terrorized Communist China in the declining years of Mao Zedong, they duly launched the new Social Democrats just months after Williams's Delphic comment. It was disbanded in 1991; the Liberal Party – now the Liberal Democrats – remain a presence in the British Parliament.

Lip-Reading

The case of George Herbert Walker Bush, President of the US from 1989 to 1993, should warn all politicians to watch their words. Ronald Reagan's Vice-President, he was battling statistics as well as Democratic contender Michael Dukakis when he entered the 1988 presidential race. Since the triumph of Martin van Buren in 1836, though no fewer than eight vice-presidents had succeeded to the office through the death of the incumbent, not one had come to the White House by direct election. Bush was further hampered by the fact that after eight years of 'Reaganomics', as the outgoing president's fiscal sleight of hand was known, the US could boast the largest budget deficit in her history and status as the world's largest debtor nation.

As most intelligent observers knew, and perhaps even the electors guessed, any honest attempt to face matters would involve higher taxes. Second in command of the spendthrift regime which had produced the problem, Bush was hardly well placed to call for austerity. And he had no knowledge or even supposed expertise in financial management. By contrast, the Democrat's candidate was credited (wrongly, but no matter) with having worked economic miracles while governor of the State of Massachusetts.

Following the golden rule of democratic politics at election time, 'Tell them what they want to hear', President-to-be Bush pledged, 'No new taxes'. He repeated the commitment with almost every speech and, so there could be no mistake as to his intentions, regularly invited his enthusiastic audiences to 'Read my lips'. It escaped notice at the time that the one section of society who actually can read lips are the deaf.

Certainly, the electorate was deaf to reason. Bush romped to victory, taking 40 of the 50 states and 53 per cent of the popular vote. By the spring of 1990 reason was asking for readmittance to the Oval office and, to the anger of leading Republicans, in June of that year President Bush formally renounced his election slogan. His popularity ratings immediately plummeted, a deficit reduction plan was killed by the House of Representatives and the government was almost forced to close down for lack of money while a new budget proposal was drafted. Taxes went up.

Nevertheless, it seemed that Bush had weathered the storm. As the 1992 election approached and the Democrats seemed incapable of selecting a credible candidate, no serious commentator on American affairs doubted he would win a second term. In the event, as poll ratings showed Bill Clinton for the Democrats moving from position of no-hoper towards favourite, memory of Bush's broken pledge loomed high in the political sky.

Now would you join me in a toast to President Figueredo, to the people of Bolivia ... no, that's where I'm going ... to the people of Brazil.

PRESIDENT RONALD REAGAN OF THE UNITED STATES OF AMERICA PROPOSES A TOAST IN BOGOTA, THE CAPITAL OF COLOMBIA, 1982

A Mistake of Protocol

On a visit to the Opera in Dresden, Hitler happened to notice a gold crown over the box assigned to him and was assured by the proud local officials that it had once been the box of the kings of Saxony. They could not know that the Führer's attitude to royalty was a strange mixture of contempt and superstition. On one occasion, dozing off during a business meeting with Goebbels and others, he woke with a start and hissed: 'You must on no account make me Kaiser or king.' Had they known better, the Dresden officials would not have boasted the royal connection. To their dismay, Hitler turned on his heel screaming: 'And you expect me to sit in the box of an abdicated king? Never!!!'

CHAPTER 10:
FAULTS IN FOREIGN FIELDS

Politicians are very like people. For them as for us 'abroad', dignified in their trade by the term foreign affairs, can hold special traumas. 'Discretion is the better part of valour', though a drab injunction, is surely the best watchword for politicians and certainly for diplomats. Private indiscretions, failures in judgement and even failures of memory have a nasty tendency to become public blunders when made by public men.

Early in 1898, when the Spanish imperialist regime in Cuba was under threat from Cuban revolutionaries and American opinion was becoming worked up about the oppression of liberty by the Spanish imperialists, Spain's minister to the United States, Enrique Dupuy de Lome, wrote a letter to a friend in Havana. In it he unwisely confided his frank opinion that America's President McKinley was weak and 'a bidder for the admiration of the crowd'. It was the ambassador's ill-luck that the revolutionaries had friends and agents in the service of the Cuban mails. The letter was seized and sent direct to William Randolph Hearst, famed to a later generation as the Citizen Kane of Orson Welles's film but at this time building his reputation as the controversial press baron. On 9 February Hearst's *New York Journal* carried the letter. It cost Lome his job (he resigned immediately) and Spain her colonies.

American public opinion was incensed by the insult to the head of state. McKinley was spurred to exactly the kind of action that Lome had no doubt feared. On 11 April he sent a message to Congress that, as the Spanish government seemed unable to suppress the rebellious unrest in Cuba, US military intervention was necessary to establish peace on the island. On the 19th, Congress adopted a joint resolution for such intervention and the next day it received the President's signature. With the end of the ensuing war, which spread far beyond the Caribbean, Cuba emerged as an independent republic under US protection, while Spain's colonies of Puerto Rico and the Philippines became outright dependencies of the United States.

Nearly two centuries ago Sweden was deprived of sovereignty over the largest island in the northern hemisphere. The reason? A simple lapse of diplomatic memory. The territory in question, Greenland, had been discovered by Norsemen in the early Middle Ages and became a dependency of Norway. But the settlements were neglected and, when Norway was united with Denmark under the Danish Crown by the Union of Kalmar in 1397, forgotten. When resettlement began in the early 18th century, first by Norwegians and then by Danes, Greenland was still, technically speaking, dependent from that part of the joint Dano-Norwegian Crown which was Norway. To anyone who remembered it, the technicality must have seemed an academic irrelevance.

Minneapolis Journal.]

The Spoiled Child.

WILLIE HEARST: "Guess this is my little boss. I bought him. Guess I can break him if I want to."

And so indeed it was, until 1814. In that year, the international community, sorting out the mess left by Napoleon's wars, decided to punish Denmark for her alliance with France by awarding Norway to the Swedish monarch. The cession was embodied in the Treaty of Kiel, but the draftsmen omitted to specify Norway's dependencies. The oversight could hardly be rectified when Norway duly achieved her independence from Sweden in 1905. Thus Greenland, granted internal autonomy in 1979, remains a Danish dependency to this day.

William Randolph Hearst (1863–1951), the ruthless US press baron whose papers forced as many blunders as they revealed, caricatured in the Minneapolis Journal *as a spoiled and destructive child.*

A Failure of Intelligence

South Africa a hundred years ago was scene of a fateful contest between the British and the Boers. These descendants of Dutch settlers and ancestors of the modern Afrikaaner population had established two independent republics, the Orange Free State and the Transvaal, but felt themselves threatened by the British in Cape Colony, which was dominated by the looming ambitions of the English empire-builder and diamond millionaire Cecil Rhodes. With the discovery of gold in the Transvaal in 1886 and the influx of thousands of prospectors, mostly British, to the burgeoning city of Johannesburg, the Boer republic felt still more under siege.

The government, fearing takeover by the *Uitlanders*, as they called the newly arrived outsiders, denied them citizenship and taxed them heavily. These, in their turn, resented the discriminatory regime. Rhodes had the idea of a 'spontaneous' revolution, to be masterminded in Johannesburg by British agents and diplomats, which would provide the pretext for intervention in support by a strike force led by L. S. Jameson stationed in Britain's Bechuanaland Protectorate on Transvaal's border. Colonial Secretary Joseph Chamberlain was closely involved and drove the concept forward even when Rhodes was having second thoughts.

Despite Chamberlain's urging, the increasingly reluctant conspirators finally faltered in December 1895. However, though the rising he was supposed to be supporting had 'fizzled out', on the 29th Jameson led his band of adventurers into Boer Territory in what was now an act of aggression without even a pretext. This, the notorious Jameson Raid, did immeasurable harm, not to the Transvaal, for the participants were quickly rounded up, but to relations between British and Afrikaaners; it did more than any other single event to precipitate the Second Boer War, one of the most stupid and, so far as its standing in the world was concerned, most damaging wars undertaken by the British Empire.

The idea behind the Raid may have originated with Cecil Rhodes, imperial business entrepreneur extraordinary, the decision to push ahead with it may have been that of the erratic Sir Leander Starr Jameson, adventurer and social lion. But the impulse which drove the plan forward long after it had any chance of success came from Chamberlain, the politician. The greatest political blunder of his career, it soon dragged him and Britain deeper into the South African quagmire.

In 1897 Sir Alfred Milner was sent out as Britain's High Commissioner in South Africa. It has been said that he was 'one of the few men who ever "made a war"', for it is generally recognized that he manoeuvred the Boer leader Paul Kruger into initiating hostilities. Equally, however, Milner made the mistake 'not uncommon among politicians' of imagining that the soldiers would conduct the war as competently as he had brought it about.

In fact, the war was eventually won, but not before Britain's moral standing in world affairs was crippled. This was a time when people still believed that great powers could claim moral virtues and a time also when many in Europe grudgingly conceded that Britain had a right to such a claim.

Milner was committed to redressing the wrongs of the *Uitlanders*, indeed he passionately believed that the only hope for peace and progress in southern Africa lay in the conquest of the two Boer republics and the anglicization of their Afrikaaner people. He urged the Home Government to take up the cause. Chamberlain was responsive. Military preparations ensued, the Boers of the Transvaal issued an ultimatum and on 12 October 1899 crossed into British territory, hoping to overrun all British South Africa before the main force could arrive. The British expected a quick and easy victory, what Milner called 'a slap in the face'. In fact, hostilities opened with a series of dramatic Boer victories which outraged British opinion and delighted the world at large. A few detachments of peasant troopers from a handful of farming communities had forced the imperial lion, which had so long lorded it on the world stage, to turn at bay.

British public opinion was more bitterly divided than at any time since the Civil War in the 17th century. To be 'pro-Boer' was to be more hated than to be pro-German in either of the two world wars. Lord Salisbury, a

Tory of the old school, dismayed at the adventure, lamented that the country would be committed to action 'upon a moral field prepared by Milner and his Jingo supporters'.

The Boers' Liberal supporters in Britain, however, made their mistakes too. True, the Boers were fighting to preserve their independence, but they were fighting as hard for less admirable things – a mean-minded policy of racial exclusion and their right to tyrannize the black population. Their supporters in Britain failed to understand this, tending to accept the Boers' romanticized self-presentation as hardy, good-hearted, independent farming folk.

But if the pro-Boer faction was wrong about the Boers, it was right about the war. At a time when people believed that powerful nations had a moral dimension, the underlying issue at stake was not whether the Boers stood for a moral cause but whether the British Empire stood for one. After three years, the conflict ended as it had to if Britain was determined to fight. The Boers lost the war, but they won the peace. The consequences would reach far into the future.

Although Kruger was disappointed in his hope that European powers, notably Germany, would come in on his side, Britain's role in the conflict was more roundly condemned by enlightened European opinion than that of any other Western belligerent before France's intervention in Algeria or America's in Vietnam. Britain's strategy of destroying farmsteads and denying the Boer guerrillas the support of their communities by rounding up non-combatants in what were termed 'concentration camps', introduced a word to the world's languages which Nazi Germany was to use as a taunt recognized by most Europeans, if by few Englishmen, against

The plotting of the Jameson Raid of 1895 into Boer territory in South Africa was an act of criminal folly by the British ministers involved. It was a blunder which smeared Britain's reputation in Europe. Here a French artist depicts rugged, honest Boer troopers escorting the humiliated Jameson on his way to imprisonment in the Transvaal.

'British methods of barbarism'. The British Empire had lost the moral high ground which it prided itself in occupying, among the *kopjes* of the South African *veldt*.

The Indian Dimension

Between the wars, the most important question of British policy outside the European theatre was its future in India, linked to Great Britain for close on two centuries. 'Ruled' would be too strong a word for most of the period. It was not until 1858 that the government in London took over the direction of Indian affairs from the East India Company and not until 1876 that Queen Victoria assumed the title of Empress of India. Even then immense tracts of the sub-continent were left under the effectively autonomous rule of hereditary princes whose families had for centuries plundered their territories and were content to accord notional paramount status to an 'imperial' power thousands of miles distant, so long as they were permitted to continue doing so.

Thus, when the London Conference convened in 1922 to discuss the future of the subcontinent, the British Raj in the full sense of the word was barely 50 years old. And yet the question before the Conference was essentially the time-table for self-rule. Thanks to the non-violent civil disobedience campaign led by Mohandas Gandhi and a growing sense in Britain that the situation was anomalous, majority opinion in government circles was that something had to be given away.

The question was, were concessions to be made in the near future and with good grace, or were they to be made slowly and grudgingly? Lord Irwin, appointed Viceroy by Stanley Baldwin, favoured the appeasement of Indian nationalist demands and he continued the policy when Baldwin was replaced as prime minister in the election of 1929 by Ramsay MacDonald.

Many Tories who went into opposition were violently critical of the Viceroy and the India Office; chief among these was Winston Churchill who famously described Gandhi as 'that dirty little man in a loin cloth'. Even his friends did not claim that Churchill understood Indian affairs, one of them even wrote 'such knowledge as [he] had of India he had acquired as a young cavalry officer in the reign of Queen Victoria'. His opinions on the subject were antiquated and ill-informed, they were also passionate. Vehemently opposed to any form of Indian independence in a foreseeable future, he resigned his position in the Business Committee when colleagues rejected his views in favour of Baldwin's pro-independence line.

His departure from the Conservative political scene, where he had occupied usually a central and always an important position, was welcomed with ill-concealed delight by lesser, more conventionally ambitious politicians who made sure that he was barred from the Tories' inner sanctum for years to come. To his friends it was a personal tragedy and, increasingly, a national disaster. It seemed to them that the only man of political stature in Britain who saw the threat to world peace posed by the burgeoning power of Nazi Germany had, by one pointless gesture of principle, reduced himself to impotence. The gesture was pointless because, while in opposition, he and his colleagues could hardly hope to determine Indian policy and in any case Britain could not continue indefinitely to rule a land mass some 10,000 miles distant and with a population more than ten times greater than her own. Many people thought that Churchill's views on the question were morally indefensible as well.

By the normal standards of political calculation, this resignation from the Tory shadow cabinet was a blunder of egregious dimensions. But then Churchill was not a politician by normal standards. He had little sense of party – he changed allegiance three times in 20 years – and no sense of the popular mood in normal times. During wartime it was a different matter. In war, too, Churchill made his blunders but they did not unseat him because he had that one quality that ensures all the others – courage.

Blunders in the Name of Principle

In the recurring debate as to who won the Second World War, the fashionable assessment in the mid-1990s tipped towards the Russians rather than the Americans. However, without the decision of the British prime minister, Neville Chamberlain, to draw a line against appeasement on Germany's invasion of Poland, it is unlikely that France would have prosecuted hostilities, and possible that there would have been no war at all in Western Europe. After all, Hitler's admiration for the British Empire and wish to have it as an ally was well known. In September 1939, Soviet Russia was actually a partner with the Nazi government in the Molotov–Ribbentrop pact, while the USA not only remained neutral until December 1941, but did not even then declare war on Germany until Hitler, stupidly, declared war on her. He did this, it appears, to show solidarity with the Japanese – a bizarre and uncharacteristic gesture of principle.

But if Hitler blundered in provoking the US into intervening in Europe, it could be argued that Chamberlain made a major political blunder in terms of Britain's national economic self-interest by declaring war at all. When victory was finally won in May 1945, Britain had sold millions of pounds worth of overseas assets to support her war effort. In August 1945 she applied to America for a grant in aid to cover her dollar gap until her financial position could be recovered. Instead, the best terms she could get was a loan repayable over 50 years, starting in 1951, by which time she was to have settled with her sterling creditors who would then be free to buy in the dollar market and to dismantle her system of imperial preference. In return, America refused to consider reducing her own high tariffs or limit her enormous export surplus.

It was a fine reward for the country which, in the words of the London *Economist*, 'fought earliest [and] fought longest ... In moral terms,' it went on, 'we are creditors; and for that we shall pay $140 million a year for the rest of the 20th century'. But then principles cost. An amusing sidelight on the unexpected ways in which they may do so is provided by the little-known fact that ever since 1945 a £1 surcharge has been levied by the French government on cross-Channel ferry fares from England in compensation for the damage done to French towns by Allied bombing at the time of the invasion of France.

A Dictator Duped by his own Cunning

In June 1947 the foreign ministers of Britain, France and the Soviet Union met to discuss the possibility of a joint reaction to the US proposals for economic aid, to be known as the Marshall Plan, after Secretary of State, General George Catlett Marshall. The American aim was to buttress the war-torn economies of Europe by bridging the Continent's dollar gap and thus avert the danger of Communist takeovers. Innocently, it was explained that the USSR was to be considered a European nation. Had Stalin taken the offer at face value, he could almost certainly have sunk the Marshall plan even before it was launched, as the US Congress would never have voted massive aid to the USSR and Marshall's terms were that the plan should be a joint one including all participants who made the initiative. In fact, the Soviet Union refused cooperation. It was a gross blunder on Stalin's part, for it opened the door for the countries of Western Europe to accept the proffered US aid.

Principles can come Too High

In 1955 General Abdel Nasser, President of Egypt, began receiving military and technical aid from the Soviet Union and its allies. Aiming to counter Communist influence in the area, Secretary of State John Foster Dulles committed the US to a substantial loan towards Egypt's projected Aswan High Dam project on the River Nile. When Nasser continued to accept aid from and maintain friendly relations with the Soviet bloc, America, unable to countenance the idea of a Third-World country pursuing an independent path in the Cold War between the Communist and capitalist powers, withdrew its commitment without notice. The policy reversal, instigated by Secretary Dulles, proved a diplomatic blunder with far-reaching consequences.

US relations with the Arab world froze and Communist stock in the area rose correspondingly. In June 1956, announcing his intention to raise funds for the Dam from other sources, Nasser nationalized the Suez Canal Company, at that time controlled and operated by British interests, the Canal having been built by the French and bought by the British in the 19th century. In October, Egypt was invaded by British and French troops in collusion with Israel. President Eisenhower indicted the action as morally wrong and America, collaborating now with the Soviet Union, prompted action by the General Assembly of the United Nations which forced Anglo-French withdrawal from Egypt.

Almost simultaneously, encouraged by 'Voice of America' broadcasts to the Eastern European countries, the citizens of Budapest in Hungary rose against their Communist dictatorship. For a time, it even seemed that the rising might succeed. But the West was fatally distracted by the Suez crisis so that the Soviet Union was able to send in troops and tanks to crush the revolution.

In the Middle East, moreover, thanks to Suez and America's action against her traditional allies, the Soviets were even able to pose as the champions of the sovereignty of smaller nations and their influence in the region rose still further. America's policy-makers were seriously alarmed. In March 1957 Congress appropriated funds for economic and military assistance to certain Middle Eastern nations and approved the use of American armed forces to resist any Communist aggression. It was the kind of action Hungarian patriots would no doubt have appreciated the previous year and Syria and Egypt, moving yet more firmly into the Communist camp, accused the US of aiming to dominate the region. The battle lines of the Cold War were firmly back in place.

Had America continued with her funding for the Aswan High Dam, she might have found herself competing with the Communist world economically for the favours of a developing country, but the Suez crisis would never have blown up. America would not have sapped her influence in Egypt which took more than a decade to repair nor would she have ruptured friendship with her traditional allies. The indignation of the world community would have been focused on events in Hungary and could have forced Moscow to hold back from the brutalities of her armed intervention.

In November 1956, thanks to the distraction of world attention by the British and French intervention in Egypt aimed at recovering the Suez Canal, Soviet tanks and troops were free to move in and crush the Hungarian rising of that year against the Communist regime.

A Courageous Blunderer

Jimmy Carter, well-meaning, hard working, liberal and fair-minded and, so far as is possible in a politician, honest, is generally reckoned to have been one of the least effective of US presidents. Blunders resulted from his qualities. Although loyalty and courage are demanded of public figures, the politician is generally wise to avoid them. In *Yes, Minister!*, Britain's mordant TV political sitcom of the 1980s, the hapless, craven, but ultimately triumphant minister Jim Hacker was effortlessly diverted from any policy disapproved of by his civil servants with the magic words, 'Most courageous minister'. For Hacker and his manipulative chief adviser Sir Humphrey this was code for 'electorally suicidal'. In his dealings with Iran during the second half of his presidency, President Carter displayed both courage and loyalty with consequences that Sir Humphrey could have foretold and Carter's own Secretary of State, Cyrus R. Vance, actually did.

At the time Iran, then under the regime of Shah Mohammed Reza Pahlavi, was the lynchpin of US policy in southwest Asia – vital for its oil and as a buffer against Soviet expansion in the area. But the Shah's was a repressive and corrupt regime and its pro-Western stance increasingly objectionable to the growing sentiment of Shia Muslim fundamentalism in the country. Early in 1979 bloody revolution drove the Shah into exile, his remaining loyal ministers were ousted or butchered and a rabidly anti-American policy instigated under Ayatollah Ruhollah Khomeini. The immediate consequences for US interests in the region were terminal. In the longer term they impacted gravely on Carter's re-election chances.

The Shah's fall was epic. From being one of the world's most powerful and courted figures he was in danger of becoming a pariah, thanks in part to revelations of the cruelties of his ousted government. A still greater factor was the world's desire to court the new regime and the Muslim world in general. In consequence, the fallen ruler had difficulty finding a government willing to befriend him. His sufferings were compounded by his contracting cancer. When he sought treatment in the US, President Carter made no move to ban the entry of his former ally.

Generous, but surely ill-judged, the gesture infuriated fundamentalist opinion in Teheran and on 4 November 1979 a mob of students seized the US embassy and took 66 hostages. From that point on 'the hostage issue' mounted ever higher in US public opinion as the 1980 presidential elections approached. Anguished by the fate of his fellow citizens, Carter took a number of measures, including the freezing of all Iranian assets in the United States. In April he made the bold decision to authorize a military rescue operation. Secretary of State Vance advised against this course of action, believing the chances of success were remote and risk of extensive loss of life both of hostages and military personnel too high. But inspired perhaps by the triumph of Israel's 'Entebbe raid' on Uganda in 1976, the President held firm to his decision.

The result was a military tragi-comedy. Equipment failed in the desert conditions and, the mission having been aborted, eight US servicemen died when a helicopter collided with a transport plane about to take off as the force withdrew. But it was the President, not the army, who took the blame. Although the Carter administration did finally negotiate the release of the embassy hostages, the agreement was signed on the last day of his presidency, 19 January 1981. Two months before, in November 1980, he had suffered a humiliating defeat at the hands of Ronald Reagan, who won a majority in the electoral college of 489 to 49 and 44 out of the 50 states.

Maybe Secretary of State Vance had a telepathic premonition of disaster from the mists of Persian history. For, by one of those quirks of fate which prompt speculation as to whether planet Earth may not in fact be the plaything of some delinquent infant deity, his first name was that of an ancient Persian prince, Cyrus the Younger, killed in a foolhardy rising against the Persian government at the Battle of Cunaxa in 401 BC.

Money Saved is not always Money Gained

Published in 1985, the Franks Report criticized the Conservative government of Margaret Thatcher for its decision to withdraw Britain's scientific research vessel HMS *Endurance* from the South Atlantic in 1981. It may be thought that this was a classic exercise in hindsight and that Thatcher could not reasonably have been expected to foresee that paying off the ship, Britain's sole presence in those waters, would be taken as an admission of weakness on Britain's part and of a lack of determination to defend its interests. Governing the country on the principle of handbag economics, Thatcher's only interest often seemed to be to save money and this decision would save two million pounds. But it did have other consequences and, interestingly enough, these were foreseen by David Owen, Labour's Foreign Secretary from 1977 to 1979.

In 1977 the then Defence Minister Fred Mulley was keen to cut back on his budget and urged the Foreign Office to do exactly what Thatcher did five years later. Rejecting the idea, Owen wrote, in April that year, '...news that *Endurance* was to be withdrawn would be an indication that the government's withdrawal from the South Atlantic was already under way'. In fact the Labour government, on hearing rumours that Argentina was planning for invasion, ordered a nuclear-powered submarine with a small surface task force into the area, arranging for the Argentines to 'discover' the plans through secret channels. Even so, it was feared that withdrawing *Endurance* would depress the morale of the Falkland Islanders and lay the government open to the charge of preparing for a sell-out to Argentina.

But in 1981, Nicholas Ridley, then Minister of State at the Foreign Office, remarked to the author of this book at a private luncheon that that was exactly what the Thatcher government was planning. At that time Ridley was negotiating the withdrawal of British forces from the then British colony of British Honduras (now Belize) coveted by its larger neighbour, Guatemala, relying on the assurance of the Guatemalan government 'as gentlemen' that they would not subsequently attempt to take over their neighbour. 'We have 13 colonies left,' he observed, unaware of the historical irony that that was the number of Britain's colonies in North America on the eve of the American War of Independence, 'and it is my job to get us out of them. After Honduras, the Falklands are next on the list.' Later, in July of that year, he proposed a lease-back formula in which Argentina would gain sovereignty of the islands and then lease them back for Britain to administer. On coming into office, Margaret Thatcher's first instinct had been to surrender sovereignty altogether. The Royal Navy, in the interests of the handbag, was being pared down drastically. It had been decided to scrap the aircraft-carrier *Hermes* and

> *I have said this before, but I say it again and again and again: your boys are not going to be sent into any foreign wars.*
>
> PRESIDENT FRANKLIN D. ROOSEVELT CAMPAIGNING FOR RE-ELECTION IN OCTOBER 1940
>
> **Following Japan's attack on Pearl Harbor in December 1941 and Hitler's declaration of war on the US the next day, US troops were mobilized for mass intervention worldwide.**

two assault ships and to sell off the mini-carrier *Invincible* to the Australian navy which was preparing to take it over when the Argentines invaded.

In this context, the withdrawal of *Endurance* as a cost-cutting exercise was not as stupid as it seemed to outsiders. Until, that is, Argentina landed troops on the Falklands dependency of South Georgia and then proceeded to move against the Falklands themselves. Now the withdrawal of the research vessel could be seen for the blunder that it was. In the ensuing war, 255 British lives were lost and nearly 800 wounded, large tracts of the islands were made uninhabitable as a result of mine-laying, and, according to the estimate of Lord Hill Norton, Chief of Defence Staff, speaking in the House of Lords on 17 January 1983, it had cost between two and three thousand million pounds to defeat the Argentine aggression. Few objective commentators now doubt that the Falklands War need never have been fought. An unequivocal warning direct from Downing Street to Buenos Aires that Britain would fight to regain the islands would have seen the recall of the task force even on the high seas. This surely was a blunder on a monumental scale. For Mrs Thatcher herself, however, it would prove in retrospect a brilliant, even inspired, chance ensuring, as it did, her tenure of Number 10 Downing Street. For before the war her popularity ratings were among the lowest recorded for any British prime minister, whereas after victory in the Falklands she went on to a massive election win in 1983.

The blunderer proved to be Argentina's President General Galtieri. Had he waited a year, the ships which in fact formed the heart of the successful task force, *Hermes* and *Invincible* and the others, would have been scrapped or in service under the Australian flag. British intervention would have been impossible and the Falklands would have been his by negotiation. Even so, lengthy negotiations through the UN and the good offices of the US, keenly pursued by British Foreign Secretary Francis Pym, seemed to offer a possibility of a peaceful solution to the problem. As it was, following his defeat, Galtieri and his military dictatorship were driven from government and democracy restored to Argentina under President Alfonsin. The end of the terror regime in Argentina was the one undoubted plus of the Falklands conflict. For Britain the 'Falklands' factor', as Mrs Thatcher thereafter loved to call it, ensured the continuance of Tory government for the rest of the decade.

Blinkered by Ideology

The EU's Schengen Agreement to ease frontier controls (signed in Schengen, Luxembourg in November 1993 and coming into being in 1995) was recognized as a political blunder by thinking people almost as soon as it was signed. Britain opposed it from the start on the grounds that any relaxation of frontier checks, at a time when organized crime was developing the drugs trade across the community, was unwise. Spain instituted draconian controls at its frontier with Gibraltar to restrain tobacco smuggling from North Africa and, more importantly, to pressure the colony into seeking political union with Madrid. Little or nothing, however, was done to restrain the activities of Galician fishing boats ferrying drugs of every kind from mob-owned ships anchored just outside Spain's territorial waters, which could then be run across Europe. France wanted a six-month extension to Schengen's three-month trial period and early announced her intention to delay full implementation of the Agreement, concerned about the flow of illegal immigrants across community frontiers.

Even Germany, champion of the Schengen Agreement, soon had doubts. The accession of Sweden to the EU in January 1995 raised the prospect that thousands of Third World and East European refugees, for long allowed easy access to Sweden, would move south through Denmark to tap the welfare provisions of the Bundesrepublik. Thus Germany immediately put pressure on Denmark to strengthen frontier controls with her northern neighbour.

The mistaken political judgement embodied by Schengen had especially hard consequences for a couple of Danish frontier policemen who, in the pursuance of their new duties, tried to arrest a Swedish tourist for refusing to show his passport. The Swede, a man in his late thirties, about to board a ferry travelling from Denmark to Germany, argued quite reasonably that, as a citizen of an EU member state, he was under no obligation to show identification. Rather less reasonably, he sought to reinforce this stand on principle by hitting one officer over the head and sinking his teeth into the arm of the other.

Germany even found herself having difficulties with France, having agreed to give French police unrestricted rights of 'hot pursuit' across the Franco-German frontier and even powers of arrest within German territory. From 1 July 1995 German officers notionally enjoyed rights of pursuit, though not of arrest, in French territory but were wary of testing this out. Luxembourg proposed to resume checks on French travellers, after Paris decided to continue border-controls despite the provisions of Schengen. At the beginning of July, Paris had announced that it would maintain border-controls with its neighbours. President Jacques Chirac had cited what he considered Dutch laxness in controlling the drug trade as a major reason. However, following a terrorist bomb attack in Paris later in July, French border-controls were intensified still further. As a weary Bonn official commented: 'The French like to sign a treaty and then do precisely what they want.'

True though that may be, the record of post-Schengen measures throughout the EU indicates that France is not alone in ignoring the provisions of the accord when it considers national interests are at stake. It would appear that the superficial expression of European unity aimed at by the simple expedient of abolishing border-controls does not outweigh serious considerations prompted by the free movement of illegal substances or unauthorized immigrants.

Border-controls cannot of themselves prevent crime but, on the principle that the wise householder secures doors and windows when going on holiday, even though the determined burglar can break through such barriers, it is surely sensible to multiply rather than reduce obstacles to international crime. As a measure with foreseeable negative consequences pushed through in accordance with unquestionable ideological premises, the Schengen Accord had the hallmarks of a classic political blunder.

A Glorious Blunder

When, in July 1995, he announced his government's intentions to conduct nuclear weapons tests in the South Pacific later that year, President Chirac, Gaullist president of France, may not have anticipated the world-wide protests such an announcement would provoke, but he no doubt had in mind the traditions of '*la gloire*' so notably upheld by General de Gaulle himself. The announcement was obviously going to be contentious in a world which, however mistakenly, believed the prospect of nuclear warfare to be a thing of the past. But the President's statement was notably high profile.

In any other country this would have been a blunder of foreign policy PR. In France, however, 'they do things differently'. Maybe world reaction was anticipated and discounted. Secure in the ascendancy of the Paris–Bonn axis in European affairs and largely indifferent to world opinion, the President relied on technical and defence arguments and on the right of France to exercise her national sovereignty by conducting tests on her own territory, for such is the status claimed for the atoll of Mururoa in French Polynesia where the tests were to be held.

Naturally, Chirac and his advisers expected trouble with Greenpeace. Its patrol ship *Rainbow Warrior II* duly obliged, sailing into the twelve-mile exclusion zone proclaimed by France around Mururoa. The interloping do-gooders were rammed by a French tug, boarded, overpowered with tear gas and forcibly escorted from the area. Their TV and satellite equipment was immobilized and installations demolished with blow torch and jig saw.

So far developments were par for the course. A decade before France had ordered the bombing of *Rainbow Warrior I* in Auckland harbour. A man was killed in the blast. In 1995 Australia and New Zealand protested against the violence of the French navy's action. Dominic Gérard, ambassador to Canberra, refused to apologize while Jacques Le Blanc, ambassador to Wellington, explained that though tear gas might be considered a weapon of war in New Zealand, 'on the French side it is not'. An admission which may be perceived as a cameo political blunder in its own right.

When Australia withdrew her ambassador from Paris for consultations and boycotted the 14 July Bastille Day celebrations it was seen that things might be getting out of hand. Consumers in both Australia and New Zealand boycotted French goods. Some days later Philippe Séguin, President of the French National Assembly, in the best tradition of Gallic neurosis, was to inveigh against 'an Anglo-Saxon plot'. In view of the muted criticism of French action from Washington and the almost total silence of London on the matter this, if not a blunder, was unnecessarily tactless at a time when France needed all the support in the international community it could muster. As the trade boycott against France began to harden – not only in luxury goods but also in defence contracts – Chirac's intransigence began to look somewhat mistaken.

Much more important, and indeed quite serious when seen from Paris, was the strength of reaction in Germany. Two months before, Paris had looked virtuously on as the German Greens led a vehement and successful campaign to force the Anglo-Dutch oil giant Shell to scrap plans to sink an oil rig in the deeps of the Atlantic Ocean. Now these German activists were turning on France. Friedrich Wolf, a German member of the European Parliament, dubbed Chirac 'a neo-Gaullist Rambo raging across Europe'. On 11 July the opening of the Strasbourg summit meeting between Chirac and German Chancellor Helmut Kohl was drowned out by foghorns and air-raid sirens sounded by protesters. French goods were boycotted and demonstrations were held outside the French embassy in Bonn. A German opinion poll revealed that 95 per cent of those canvassed were opposed to the French tests. Chancellor Kohl maintained a calm public face in response to his partner's intentions, describing it as an internal matter for France. However, it was privately reported that he was 'furious' at the decision and the failure of the French President to give him advance warning.

Elsewhere in Europe public opinion, and even official attitudes, hardened against France. In Belgium the President was pilloried as 'Hirochirac' – an allusion to the 50th anniversary of the dropping of the atom bomb on Hiroshima in August 1945. The Dutch led a protest, supported by Sweden, Austria, Ireland, Finland, Denmark and Luxembourg calling on France to abandon the tests. Italy's Green Party was given official permission to stage a demonstration in the Campo dei Fiori, near the French embassy in Rome, to coincide with the celebrations for Bastille Day. When President Chirac rose to address the European Assembly, his voice was almost drowned out by shouts of protest from the assembled Euro MPs, and the television screen was dominated by the protest banners they held aloft. The influential German weekly *Der Spiegel* commented that, 'The arrogant national go-it-alone stance of our neighbour threatens to throw into question everything which has been achieved in Franco-German understanding.'

France's standing in Europe provides the fulcrum for her leverage in world affairs. The Mururoa affair and the mounting pressure of events in Europe threatened foreign policy objectives. Radio interviews following the traditional sabre-rattling parade of military matériel and personnel down the Champs-Élysées on Bastille Day, produced the startling result of young Germans condemning French militarism – 'such a parade could not be held here'.

But Paris seemed to register the international signals. A member of the French Foreign Affairs Institute opined that Chirac's advisers realized they had played the issue wrong. However, he also believed that the President 'could not back down now' for fear of loss of face. On 6 September European Commissioner Jacques Santer was booed by European MEPs for refusing to take a stand on the French tests.

No one of course gave much thought to the peoples of Mururoa. Paris claimed that, as an overseas territory with its own deputy in the National Assembly, the region had had ample opportunity to protest the action. In fact the infant independence movement in Polynesia attempted its own token boycott of the 14 July celebrations in the capital, Papeete. As a sardonic cartoon in France's leading daily *Le Monde* indicated, such gestures were quite irrelevant. It depicted an emollient Chirac facing Kohl across a large terrestrial globe. From the top of the globe, the approximate position of Paris, projected a button and from somewhere near the bottom, where

Wellington, New Zealand, 4 September 1995. Demonstrators outside the French embassy protesting against President Jacques Chirac's announced intention to resume nuclear testing.

Mururoa could be imagined to be, emerged a puff of smoke. 'You see,' the President is saying, 'it's quite safe. You press the button up here and it goes off down there.'

When set against France's atomic objectives, it seems that the global outrage, the demonstrations from Hong Kong to Santiago, Chile, even the hostility of her European partners, were secondary. More serious were reports that some French scientists believed that the tests were not technically necessary. If this was true and if simulated tests would have produced the desired information equally satisfactorily, then Chirac's nuclear *démarche* was a blunder, not just in technical and scientific terms but with consequences for the image of France as an egalitarian and progressive force in world affairs.

On his visit to New York in October 1995 to attend the 50th anniversary of the UN, Chirac went on US television, speaking in English, and told viewers that the scheduled eight tests might be reduced to six. Intended as a conciliatory gesture, this merely fuelled speculation that if the number of tests could be so casually reduced by 25 per cent, how serious were the preliminary studies which had determined the programme in the first place.

But the impact of the tests themselves was probably far less important than comments and reactions by French public figures. Perhaps Stockholm's decision to withdraw France's invitation to the world fireworks championship in Stockholm on 30 July was less than serious, but deputies' contemptuous reactions to world opinion in general did the national image no good. One Gaullist deputy, commenting on Australia's furious reaction, observed that

Australia was a remote country only too glad to be able noisily to draw attention to itself.

To outside observers, it was remarkable that public opinion was not behind official policy. Traditionally, any gesture vaunting France above world opinion has been guaranteed public support on patriotic grounds, but now opinion polls showed 60 per cent of the French opposed to tests. More remarkably still, a number of people felt, in the words of French Green leader Brice Lalonde, 'ashamed of being French'.

Whatever the technical or military advantages gained by the tests, they had done deep damage to France's standing abroad and the self-esteem of her citizens at home. It is perhaps the nature of political blunders that their consequences are not always immediately obvious or directly quantifiable in the way that a defeat in battle is. But it is also true that those consequences can be deep-working in their effects.

CHAPTER 11: BLUNDERS OF MISPLACED TRUST...

Croesus, King of Lydia (d. 547 BC), legendary for his wealth, was worried about the growing power of the Persian empire across the River Halys frontier. He consulted the oracle at Delphi to receive the cryptic advice, 'Should you but cross the River Halys, you will destroy a great realm.' Reading this as an omen of victory, he crossed the river at the head of his army, only to be defeated by Cyrus II of Persia. A great realm was indeed destroyed – his own!

Even the most powerful tend to put their faith in something, whether it be the gods, some other human being or their own mastery of intrigue. Whatever the object of their trust, the effect is to lower the guard, to relax the eternal vigilance which is the *sine qua non* of survival in politics. A few cautionary tales past and present point the moral – never trust anything or anyone.

...in One's Subordinates

On 9 November 1989 there was partying on the Berlin Wall, the monstrous stone-built, armoured barrier that for close on 30 years had divided Germany into two hostile camps. It is hard to recapture the breathless sense of elation that seized the countries of Europe as this emblem of Communist oppression was festooned with singing, waving, laughing people.

That day the border between East and West Germany had been opened by the Berlin authorities, as a safety valve for social pressures that were already blowing the lid off their regime. Hundreds of thousands of East German citizens had swarmed west. In the rest of Europe, the results were compulsive television viewing. By 22 December, when the Brandenburg Gate was symbolically opened, the East German Communist Party had already changed its name. Genuinely free elections had been set for 6 May 1990. The Communist regime in East Germany, long rated among the harshest of the central European Communist dictatorships, was dissolved.

The speed with which the Soviet empire collapsed was not really credible at the time. On 2 October, according to Jacques Attali, then a senior aide at the Elysée palace, that shrewd observer of world affairs, President François Mitterrand, commented: 'People who talk about a future reunification of Germany don't understand anything. The Soviet Union will never let it happen. It would be the end of the Warsaw Pact. Can you imagine that?' On 3 October 1990, a year and a day later, the former East and West German states were reconstituted as a single united Germany, the Soviet

Union itself was already disintegrating while the Warsaw Pact was dissolved in February 1991.

This startling sequence of events remained a conundrum. Some were to suggest that it was the result of blundering by Communist agencies, aiming to displace the old guard of the iron curtain regimes by manipulating popular insurgence in favour of a new, but still Communist, brand of, so to speak, enlightened oppression. If so, the security services of the People's Party, which for 70 years had mismanaged the economies of Russia and Eastern Europe to disaster, seemed to be leaving the world stage with a magisterial display of incompetence which even the greatest absurdities of capitalism barely approach.

Mikhail Gorbachev, the Soviet Union's Communist Party boss since 1985 and Soviet President from 1988 was, so the argument ran, determined to end the Cold War and its concomitant armaments race that was bankrupting the Soviet Union. He worked for, and got, a *rapprochement* with the Western alliance led by US President Reagan, but along with this went commitments to a more open society in the USSR and her East European satellites. The regimes here were sluggish in responding to Moscow's wishes. They saw no obligation to surrender the security of tyranny they thought they enjoyed to help an ailing Soviet state, and they knew, better apparently than Gorbachev himself, the hazards of relaxing discipline on an already fractious population.

The East German government of Erich Honecker was the most recalcitrant. Urged by Gorbachev's KGB, elements in its own secret service, the STASI, we are told, set about destabilizing the regime to open the way for take-over by a leadership able and willing to manage controlled change. And some changes were already in train.

Back in June, Honecker had agreed to issue multiple entry passes for West Germans visiting their relations in the East and revoked the orders requiring border guards to shoot on would-be escapees. The border remained closed and refugees from the East, instead, found refuge in the West German embassy in Berlin. To the amazement of the outside world, nothing was done by the East German authorities to stop them and finally, on 8 August, the embassy itself had to close its doors to any further influx.

But still the German Democratic Republic continued haemorrhaging citizens. With the western border closed, they flooded east, thanks to the puzzling tolerance of Communist Hungary and Czechoslovakia. On 10 September Hungary opened its border with Austria to let through thousands of East Germans and then the Communist German authorities agreed to allow refugee trains from Prague to travel to West Germany, provided they halted in East German territory where the escapees could be stripped of their papers. Apparently, it was thought that being reduced to the condition of stateless citizens would so humiliate them that they would prefer to leave the train and return home. In fact, while the trains waited in the East German transit stations, scores more of refugees, who had failed or not bothered to make the eastward break into Czechoslovakia, swarmed on board.

The situation was degenerating into international bedlam when President Gorbachev of the Soviet Union solemnly arrived in East Berlin to attend the 7 October celebrations of the 40th anniversary of the founding of the

West Berliners partying on the Berlin Wall, New Year's Eve, 1989. One of the central figures brandishes a hammer he has been using to chisel away at the structure.

state. To the accompaniment of mass demonstrations, unseen in the country since the Berlin Rising of 1953, the heads of state went through the pantomime of 'celebration' while, behind the scenes, Gorbachev warned his host not to be too long about effecting the reforms. It was already too late.

Within days East Berlin and other cities witnessed thousands of demonstrators parading the streets, demanding reform and carrying banners with the slogan '*Wir Bleiben*' (We're Staying). If the authorities had hoped to rid themselves of a disaffected minority, expecting to be left with a docile majority, they had miscalculated. The police, supposing they were to follow standard procedures, reacted with violence. To the general astonishment of observers they were, instead, ordered to desist on instruction from Egon Krenz, the head of internal security. On 18 October President Honecker resigned and Krenz took his place.

If there was a conspiracy against the GDR by its own secret services, then so far so good. The populace, having cheered the fall of the hated Honecker, could now settle down peacefully to wait while the new dawn was ushered in by Herr Krenz. Unfortunately, the populace had not read its script. Demonstrations continued; emigration continued, if at a somewhat slower rate. Krenz offered dialogue; granted amnesties for any returning refugees; jailed demonstrators; and then made foreign travel easier. Presumably the deposed Honecker smiled sourly. On 7 November the government of three weeks resigned; on 8 November the entire Politburo resigned and was replaced; on 9 November the border with the West was thrown open and the partying began.

The next day President Krenz announced that he was working on plans for secret and free elections to be held in due course. On 13 November a new cabinet was sworn in under the premiership of Hans Modrow, Communist Party chief from Dresden. Seventeen of the 28-strong cabinet were Communists. The populace did not observe in this any significant change. In the first weekend after the opening of the Berlin Wall three million people crossed for a look at the other side. East Germans continued to stream west on a regular basis and it was estimated that up to 2000 people a day applied for permanent residence in the Federal Republic.

On 3 December the entire Politburo of 8 November resigned and Egon Krenz, until four weeks before head of the once dreaded internal security services, was replaced as head of state by a certain Manfred Gerlach, leader of the tiny Liberal Democratic Party. True, the Communist Prime Minister Hans Modrow remained in post but then, on 8 December, in a gesture which was astounding even in these eventful days, the East German Communist Party changed its name to the Party of Democratic Socialism. Exactly two months before, they had been nursing their hangovers from the celebration of 40 years of Communist rule of an independent East German state. But the real headaches had only just begun. Demonstrators were out again in force, and now it was a new slogan – 'Reunification with the West.'

Many incidents in the foregoing months had hinted at manipulation behind the scenes by elements in the regime itself. The theory of KGB collusion with its opposite numbers in other Communist Bloc countries has been convincingly advanced by respected commentators. On the other hand, the trail of blunders leads one to wonder whether professional services could really have been involved. Perhaps the first blunder was to ease the system in the slightest degree. Tyranny operates best when absolute.

...in Oneself – President Ershad of Bangladesh

In 1982 Hussain Muhammad Ershad won power in Bangladesh, following a bloodless coup. It was a popular victory and he at least seems to have remained convinced of his popularity with the voters. However, after nine years in power, he faced seemingly obvious discontent as thousands of people came out in street demonstrations, protesting against his regime as corrupt, dictatorial and authoritarian. On 6 December 1990 accordingly, President Ershad resigned, trusting his fate to elections scheduled to be held in February the following year, under the aegis of an interim president, who was charged with organizing the elections and instituting legal proceedings to investigate the charges of corruption.

Ershad seems to have believed that the unrest had been contrived and then orchestrated by his opponents in the Bangladeshi Nationalist Party and that the true sentiments of the people would be revealed in a massive vote in his favour. He had miscalculated. Not only did the elections return the BNP with a large majority, Ershad was sent for trial, the investigation claiming to have found him guilty not only of corruption but also of arms dealing. In

June 1990 he was sentenced to ten years in prison. Further accusations were to follow, so that in 1995 the ex-President appeared to be in jeopardy of his life on a murder charge.

...in Intrigue

Nicholas Fouquet, superintendent of finance for the 23-year-old King Louis XIV, was 46 when he fell from power; he spent the remaining 20 years of his life in prison. He is one of the candidates once identified by legend as the Man in the Iron Mask, but his real story was dramatic enough.

A younger son of the Vicomte de Vaux, Fouquet had held office for a decade when, in 1661, Cardinal Mazarin, the King's first minister, died. A brilliant conversationalist, a discerning patron of the arts and a man of versatile abilities both in law and diplomacy, he was, unfortunately, given the nature of his government responsibilities, less talented in money matters – except, whispered his enemies, when enhancing his own immense fortune. But now, Louis announced that he would take personal charge of the government of the country. Europe's most cynical court raised an eyebrow in polite disbelief as ministers adjusted themselves to the idea of making their reports directly to the youthful King.

In the first months of the new regime, Fouquet's arch-rival, Jean Baptiste Colbert, drew the King's attention to the parlous state of the national finances. By way of preparing his defences against accusations of defrauding the treasury, the finance minister used a courtier's manoeuvre and in so doing made a fatal mistake. He approached the King's mistress, Louise duchesse de la Vallire, and offered her money if she would speak on his behalf. The favourite of the King disdained the bribes and told him exactly what had been proposed. Louis, if he had had any doubt as to his course of action before, had none now. He determined to break the great minister.

Louis proceeded with care. As procurator-general of the parliament of Paris, Fouquet had the right to be tried only by his colleagues in the parliament and he had many friends in that assembly. Louis had good reason to fear the impact as well as the outcome of such a trial. With courtly deceit he persuaded Fouquet to sell the office, so that he might devote himself more completely to the interests of the Crown. How could the minister refuse? Next, Louis invited himself on a visit to Fouquet's great château of Vaux le Vicomte, not far from the royal palace of Fontainebleau.

The minister now made his second blunder. Seeing what he supposed was an opportunity to flatter and charm away any ill-will or displeasure the King might be feeling towards him, he laid on an entertainment that would become a legend in its own day. The immense palace, offset with acres of the most elaborate formal gardens, was in itself finer than anything the king then had. Six thousand guests were barely enough to fill the grounds, music performed by Fouquet's private orchestra was composed by his household musician. A play was commissioned from Molière and a thousand fountains cascaded in the grounds.

As he took his place at the dinner table laid with gold plate as far as the eye could reach, King Louis, far from being mollified, was confirmed in the suspicion that his minister of finance had indeed plundered the royal exchequer, and seemed intent on outshining his royal master. Two months later Fouquet was arrested on a charge of treason, his ministerial post of superintendent of finance abolished and a special 'chamber of justice' set up to try him and others accused with him of peculation.

There was never any doubt as to the verdict to be reached in the case of the fallen minister. Colbert took charge of his papers and suitably doctored them to build up the case. The commission was packed with Fouquet's rivals and enemies and when the president showed signs of impartiality and fairness, he was dismissed and replaced with one more aware of what his duty to the King required.

Even so, Fouquet defended his case with dignity and courage and in the end was acquitted of the charge of treason. Thus he evaded the death penalty and was sentenced to banishment for fraudulent maladministration. The King, who had been hoping for the death sentence, overruled the findings of the court and ordered the former minister be imprisoned for life. He was incarcerated in the fortress of Pignerol as far as possible from Paris, on France's border with Italy. The cynics at court took note that this King meant what he said.

But Louis went further. The extraordinary splendours of Vaux le Vicomte and the marvels of that last fabulous fête had fired him with the determination to put the royal magnificence beyond the reach of any possible rivalry. Over the coming years the modest little hunting lodge at Versailles, just outside Paris, would be transformed into the grandest royal palace in the Western world. The works were directed by the team which had created the glories of Vaux le Vicomte. The architect Louis Le Vaux, the landscape gardener André Le Nôtre, the painter Charles Le Brun, all had been 'discovered' by the fallen minister whose master of music, the gifted Jean-Baptiste Lully, became court director of music. Fouquet's blunders had cost him not only his job and his liberty but even his reputation as France's most discerning patron of the arts.

…in Your Allies

When the heirs of the Christian Visigothic King Witiza of Spain asked the Berbers of North Africa for help against the usurper Roderick in 711, the Berber chief Tariq led a Muslim force across the Straits of Gibraltar (i.e. *Jebel-al-Tariq*, Arabic for 'Tariq's mountain'). He defeated Roderick all right but did not restore Witiza's heirs. Instead, he sent for reinforcements and conquered most of the Iberian Peninsula. The results of this blunder, so far as Christian Spain was concerned, were not reversed until 1492, when the last Muslim forces were driven from Spanish soil.

In 1097 the Byzantine Emperor Alexius I Comnenus, in all the splendour of his office, received oaths of allegiance from Bohemond of Normandy and his crusaders, while their troops remained outside his great city of Constantinople. A successor of the first Christian emperor of Rome (Constantine the Great), Alexius saw himself as guardian of the Christian world against an encroaching tide of hostile tribes and infidels. Since taking power some 15 years earlier, he had been at war with Petchenecs, Cumans, Seljuk Turks and even this same Bohemond and his father Robert Guiscard. Nominally Catholics who had let their soldiers loose on a three-day sack of Rome, the Normans had had no compunction over making war on the booty-rich Orthodox empire of Constantinople. And now, though Bohemond was acting the part of ally and liegeman, Alexius was taking no chances. The western army was barred access to the great city and left to bivouac outside the massive ramparts, which for 700 years had been Christendom's eastern bastion.

Alexius had reason to be worried. The army was there largely because of a mistaken initiative he had taken. Over the centuries the empire's provinces in Palestine, Syria and Egypt had fallen to Islamic invaders. For example, Jerusalem had long been in Muslim hands, though pilgrims had been allowed access to the holy places. Recently, however, the situation had been destabilized by a turmoil of rivalries in the Islamic world and Alexius had looked for reinforcements and allies.

The Christians' pilgrim routes were in danger while, in 1085, treachery delivered the great imperial city of Antioch (Antakya, in modern Turkey) to a Muslim ruler. Alexius had sent messages to the west, offering good pay to knights and men-at-arms who would come to fight the infidel. The mail-clad heavy cavalry of feudal Europe were renowned as professional fighting men. But instead of disciplined, high-class mercenaries, Alexius got an army of fanatical pilgrims, camp followers and soldiers of fortune, officered by one or two devout warriors but also many adventurers ambitious to carve out principalities for themselves.

When he heard of the emperor's requests for military reinforcements, Pope Urban II had been inspired by quite a different idea. Let Christian soldiers unite to rid the Holy Land of the infidel hordes and reopen the pilgrim routes. Indulgence for their sins was offered to those who answered the call. The Pope's impassioned sermon delivered to the Council of Clermont in 1095 sparked the First Crusade. Men of every sort, from peasants to the landless younger sons of noblemen, joined the banner. When they reached Constantinople, Alexius was dismayed. It was his particular bad luck that his old enemy Bohemond should have decided to turn Crusader. The best the Emperor could do to retrieve his blunder in asking for assistance from the semi-barbarian west in the first place, was to hurry the army across the straits with money, supplies and transport, make the leaders promise to restore to the empire any lands they might conquer, and hope they would keep their oath.

The westerners had a triumphant campaign, recapturing Antioch, occupying much of Palestine and taking Jerusalem itself. To these conquests a flying column under command of Baldwin of Flanders added the important city of Edessa. Oath-breakers to a man, they held on to their conquests and for close on two centuries a cluster of Latin Catholic principalities (Crusader states) ruled what had been historic lands of the Greek Orthodox empire. But at least, Alexius could reflect, they had not sacked Constantinople, as the Guiscards had sacked Rome.

His descendants Alexius IV and V had even worse trouble with their Latin allies who, in 1204 diverted the Fourth Crusade to sack Constantinople, bundling Alexius IV off the imperial throne in rather less time than he took to blunder on to it.

The story begins in the year 1195, when the Emperor Isaac II was deposed by his brother, who became Alexius III. In time-honoured manner, to avoid the crime of regicide and in his case also fratricide, he had Isaac blinded and imprisoned. Isaac's son, another Alexius, who had been incarcerated with his father, escaped in 1201 and travelled to Germany where he joined his sister Irene and her husband Philip of Swabia. It so happened that, at the time, Pope Innocent III was sponsoring a Fourth Crusade to recapture Jerusalem. Chief among its military organizers was Alexius' brother-in-law, Philip of Swabia. Alexius persuaded Philip and other Crusade leaders to divert the Crusade to Constantinople to restore himself and his father. However, his approach to the Crusaders was to prove a fatal blunder.

The Crusaders were not independent agents, for they relied for their transport on the merchant city of Venice. She had no interest in land and little in money as such; what her merchant rulers wanted was market access – particularly in Constantinople, the richest city in the Western world and hub of traffic from the silk route. They saw their opportunity in the plight of the would-be emperors.

The deal was struck. Once the crusading army had restored Isaac and his son, the latter as Alexius IV, Venice would receive large trading privileges. The Crusaders' part in the bargain was to do their duty as soldiers – otherwise they would not get to be transported anywhere else.

The armies of Latin Europe might not be much of a match for Muslim Palestine – they never did reconquer Jerusalem – but they had no trouble at all with Christian Constantinople in 1203. The usurper Alexius III was easily turned off the throne, Isaac and his son restored, and the Venetians rewarded. But the Orthodox populace did not approve of the way the new court truckled to the Catholic westerners and Alexius IV had barely had time to regret his choice of sponsors before he, too, fell victim to yet another coup in January 1204.

Unfortunately, the players in these Byzantine games had forgotten that the great city was still ringed by a large army of loot-hungry Crusaders. With the pretext of the treasonable coup against their candidate, the leaders ordered the overthrow and death of the new usurper, Alexius V, and installed in his place a Catholic emperor of their own choosing, Baldwin of Flanders.

The Latin Empire of Constantinople, inaugurated with sack and pillage, survived some 60 years. It had been made possible by the blundering intrigues of the native rulers and carried through by a murderous army of Crusaders who did not once cross swords with enemies of the faith. Venetian trade moved up a gear, and the lions of St Mark, plundered from the great Christian metropolis, stand to this day in the Piazza, monuments to the cupidity of merchants and the stupidity of emperors.

...in Ideology

The new Latin states in Syria were not half a century old when the first of them fell to Muslim reconquest. In the autumn of 1144, after a four-week siege, Zengi Imad-ad-Din, Atabeg of Mosul and Lord of Aleppo, captured the city of Edessa, capital of Joscelin, Count of Edessa. The atrocities which followed almost matched the horrors of the Christian conquest of Jerusalem some 45 years before.

If the Franks of Syria were numbed with shock; the effect in Europe was little short of traumatic. The Count of Edessa was lord of some 10,000 square miles of territory straddling what is now the border between southern Turkey and northern Syria. The loss of his great city meant that the whole of this area of Christian hegemony was in danger if immediate military aid was not forthcoming. Zealots in Europe had long warned that without continuing assistance from the West, the Holy Land would be lost. Now the warnings struck home. Bernard of Clairvaux, mentor of popes and kings, preached the Second Crusade. In 1146 a great expedition, led by King Louis VII of France, set out.

Meantime the Muslim world was jubilant. Men said that Zengi would be pardoned all his sins for this one act and would be admitted at once to the joys of paradise. For years scholars and holy men had been preaching *jihad* (holy war) and now the army of the Faithful had knocked the coping stone from the Christian edifice in Palestine – it could only be a matter of time before the whole building crumbled. Two years later Zengi was dead, murdered by a servant he had insulted, and his lands divided between two sons. It was only a temporary setback for Islam. Nur-ad-Din, the son installed at Aleppo, soon proved a still more glorious champion of the Faith than his father – and a still more worrying menace to neighbouring Muslim rulers.

The Islamic Middle East was a patchwork of lordships centred on rich merchant cities, all admitting the supremacy of the Caliph in Baghdad, but each guarding jealously its independence of the others. The family of Zengi was as much feared for its expansionist ambitions by rival rulers, as it was admired for its warlike piety by their subjects. None had better cause to fear than the rulers of Damascus, Aleppo's rich and cultured neighbour to the south. Girdled by orchards and famed for its metal work and fine linen, this beautiful city, so close to Jerusalem, conducted an uneasy, and to good Muslims shocking, policy of tentative alliance with its Christian neighbours to counterbalance the threat from Aleppo.

For their part, the kings of Jerusalem and rulers of the other Christian states, responded to such approaches in a spirit of simple pragmatism. Fifty years overseas had taught them that survival depended on the mastery and manipulation of local politics. To newcomers from Europe, this cosy symbiosis with the infidel represented a betrayal of the faith. Thus when they finally reached the Holy Land, only to learn that the Christians they had come to save were wheeling and dealing with the very creatures of the Antichrist they had come to fight, King Louis and his captains were disgusted. The soldiery, as always on the look out for booty, wondered where it was to come from if they did not find some rich city to sack.

True, some of the lesser Christian lords of Palestine had themselves, more than once, looked with greedy eyes in the direction of Damascus. But the majority local view was to keep friendly with its ruler as a protection against the Aleppo of Nur-ad-Din. However, the King of France, at the head of a relieving army, could hardly be opposed by the 'Franks of Outremer'. And Louis had come to fight infidels. Accordingly, the crusading army marched against Damascus and in so doing forced its ruler to appeal for help to the man he feared most. Delighted, Nur-ad-Din prepared to come to the aid of his beleaguered neighbour.

Confident of relief, the Damascenes fought off attack after attack by the Christian besiegers. Whatever the policy of their ruler might be, the people of Damascus were proud to take their part in the holy war at last. Many deeds of heroism by civilians and fighters alike would be told in later years. An aged man of law seen marching towards the enemy lines was begged by a general to withdraw and leave the fighting to the soldiers. 'But,' he replied, 'I offered myself for sale and God bought me; I have not asked for the contract to be annulled.' With this he was alluding to the words [in the Koran]: 'God has bought the faithful ... and has given them paradise in exchange.' ... He was killed in battle not far from the city.

When news came that Nur-ad-Din was advancing in force to the relief of Damascus, the Crusading army retired. The siege, which had been undertaken for blinkered ideological reasons, had been a fiasco. A great Christian army had been forced into ignominious retreat. A city which, until now, had held aloof from the propaganda of the *jihad* had won its spurs, despite the wishes of its ruler; and its population now looked upon the most dangerous man in Muslim Syria as the champion of Islam. The fighting spirit of the Muslims, swelled by the triumph of Zengi, was fired still further by his son. Notable own goals for a campaign to restore the Christian cause in the Holy Land, and all traceable to the blunder of supposing that the only good Muslim was a dead Muslim, wherever he might be found.

...in Your Military

Muhummad Anwar Sadat, President of Egypt from 1970 to 1981, made the understandable but, as it turned out, fatal error of trusting the loyalty of his army élite corps, some members of which were religious fundamentalists dedicated to the overthrow of the head of state. For Anwar Sadat had committed what, in the political catechism of the Middle East, was a heinous crime – by making peace with the state of Israel.

His death, tragic for his family and mourned by the international community contained, it must be said, an element of black farce. Taking the salute as Commander-in-Chief at a military march past, he was assassinated by members of his élite corps while on parade.

The episode is reminiscent of the fate of the Dey of Algiers, as recorded in his journal by Captain Augustus Hervey for the year 1754. 'The Dey was sitting in a kind of alcove that was in a long gallery, and his kitchen at the far end of it. His head cook is the Prime Minister, which is by way of not being poisoned, and he was sitting a little way from the Dey ...' It would seem that the autocrat of Algiers had taken all reasonable precautions for his safety. But he, too, blundered, for Hervey tells as an aside: 'Poor man! he was murdered not many months after by his bodyguard as he was paying them, which he does himself every month.' When you cannot trust your own bodyguard, trust itself becomes a blunder.

...in Politicians

During the early 1990s it emerged that a British engineering firm, Matrix Churchill, had supplied quantities of arms-making equipment to Saddam Hussein's Iraqi government during the years before the Gulf War, in which British forces were to play a major role. In 1992 three directors of the company were charged with breaking government rules, said to ban such exports to Iraq. If convicted, they faced long prison sentences.

In fact, the rules had been reworded years before to allow just such trade to be conducted. The men's defence was denied access to this sensitive information by official orders known as Public Interest Immunity Certificates (PIICs), which five government ministers had signed under instruction from the Attorney-General. Unfortunately for the prosecution, the judge in the Matrix Churchill case refused to recognize these certificates. Various government ministers and also civil servants were obliged to give evidence and it became apparent that the directors had, in fact, been acting all along with government approval. The case collapsed in November 1992 when one of the witnesses, former Defence Procurement Minister Alan Clark, readily agreed under cross-examination that he had been aware of the matter all along. As other ministers struggled to distance themselves from a case which could easily have led to three men being unjustly sent to prison, interesting light was shed on the way the nation's business is conducted by the people supposed by the public to be in charge. Among those called to the stand was a man who had headed both the Foreign Office and the Treasury at the relevant time – the two departments which might have been supposed to have been closely involved in the trade – before going on to become head of government. On the 55th day of the trial, Prime Minister John Major, explaining that he had in fact had no idea about anything connected with the matter, had this to say: 'One of the charges at the time was that in some way, because I had been the Chancellor, because I had been Foreign Secretary and because I had been the Prime Minister, I must have known what was going on.'

Of course I was economical with the actualité.

ALAN CLARK
CONFESSES...
NOVEMBER 1992

At the end of 1992, a public inquiry into the matter was set up under Lord Justice Scott. Its findings – released on 15 February 1996 – did not do as much political damage to the Major government as the Conservatives had feared (and the Labour Party had hoped). But the episode had done little to persuade a sceptical British public of the trustworthiness of the party of government.

CHAPTER 12: BLUNDERING ROYALS

Until comparatively recent times most of the world's countries were governed by monarchs. Some were happy to leave the running of affairs to their ministers. Many were not. Queen Victoria, whose constitutional powers were supposedly very limited, in fact intervened time and again in the business of government to her ministers' despair. During the 1870s Edward Cardwell, Gladstone's minister for war, made major reforms in the structure and training methods, discipline and promotion pattern of the British Army. However, he was never able to modernize its command structure in line with the most advanced military practice by creating a general staff on the European model. The reason was quite simply the obstructionist George William Frederick Charles, second Duke of Cambridge, Commander-in-Chief. And nothing could be done about him as long as he wished to remain in post, as Queen Victoria insisted on a member of the royal family holding supreme command in her army. Her obstinacy amounted to a blunder of national policy. Cambridge finally resigned in 1895, and only then was it possible to initiate the necessary changes. Britain's humiliating record in the Second Boer War (1899–1902) owed much to the lack of a well-established general staff structure, and this in turn owed much to the refusal of the Queen to allow the appointment of a professional Commander-in-Chief.

The capacity of crowned heads for bungling incompetence has been the cause of more than one dynastic downfall as we shall see, but royal blunders were certainly not limited to high affairs of state. King Alfred the Great of Wessex and England famously blundered while he was on the run from England's Danish invaders disguised as a travelling minstrel, by allowing some griddle cakes to burn. Taking refuge in a peasant's cottage on the isle of Athelney, he was told to watch the bake by the busy housewife. Musing over the strategy for his counterattack, he forgot his kitchen duties and got a box round the ears for his incompetence. Alfred went on to defeat his Danish enemy, Guthrum. As a king, if not as a cook, he earned his title 'the Great'. He committed no blunders in government to match some of the more exotic errors of his successors.

Church and Marriage

There is a good case for arguing that England's break with Rome at the time of the Reformation, was the result of an arrogant blunder on the part of King Henry VIII. Wanting a divorce from his queen, Catherine of Aragon, he had petitioned the pope for an annulment. The situation was difficult

... the austere language of truth is rarely welcomed near the throne.

MADAME ROLAND, WIFE OF LOUIS XVI'S MINISTER OF THE INTERIOR, IN A LETTER TO THE ROYAL GOVERNMENT SHE DRAFTED OVER HER HUSBAND'S SIGNATURE IN JULY 1792 for the pope in so far as Rome was at the time dominated by Emperor Charles V, Catherine's nephew. Even so, the Church was accustomed to grant favours to kings and princes which it might withold from lesser mortals and Henry might have got his annulment, had he approached the matter in the right spirit.

However, Henry, whose main argument was that he should never have been permitted to marry Catherine in the first place, as she had previously been married to his brother Prince Arthur, prided himself on being a theologian. He based his case on his own interpretation of Church law and scripture, so challenging Pope Clement VII in his own specialism. No professional can concede a point to arguments advanced by an amateur, no matter how talented he might be. So Henry ensured his own defeat at the outset, whatever the rights or wrongs of the matter might have been.

More recently, it has been argued that Edward VIII made a strategic error in the matter of his marriage to Mrs Simpson. Edward's big idea was a morganatic marriage whereby Mrs Simpson could become his wife but remain commoner and thus never be queen as such. In fact, constitutional experts have argued that since, in English law, a wife takes her husband's title if he outranks her at marriage, such a solution was a legal impossibility. The wife of the king was ipso facto queen. In the fevered days of December 1936 such niceties of debate were steam-rollered when the King agreed to Prime Minister Baldwin's suggestion that before any decision was taken on the possibility of a morganatic marriage, the Commonwealth governments be consulted. Having agreed to seek his ministers' advice, the King was constitutionally bound to take it. He and Wallis had lost the debate before it began, his former charisma when Prince of Wales dimmed by controversy and constitutionalism.

Sixty years on and another Prince of Wales found himself entangled in the mesh of privacy and politics. In 1994, during a television interview with journalist Jonathan Dimbleby, Prince Charles startled British public opinion with an admission that he had been unfaithful to his wife Diana. Many traditionalists considered the very idea of a television interview containing personal revelations quite out of order in the heir to the throne. The public at large was, of course, fascinated at being party to such royal tittle-tattle. Nobody foresaw the depth-bomb consequences of the Prince's decision to grant the interview and bare his soul, for nobody foresaw that in November 1995 his wife, Diana, Princess of Wales, would in her turn grant a television interview.

In response to the measured questioning of journalist Martin Bashir she, too, confessed to having been unfaithful to her spouse. It can hardly be doubted that the line followed by the interview was the result of careful prior negotiation, for even without her official press adviser, the Princess proved a virtuoso manipulator of the small screen to match President Ronald Reagan. Assisted by master make-up artists who reduced her naturally radiant complexion to the rueful, almost haggard, mask of a woman older yet wiser, she presented well as a subject for public pity. Her mawkish plea to be 'queen of the people's hearts', produced instantaneous sighs of sympathy which drowned her steely assertion that she was determined to fight to maintain her royal role. From the psychology of 'cries for help', to voicing concern for the impact on her children in the most public forum that television had yet

I will govern according to the common weal, but not according to the common will.

JAMES I, KING OF ENGLAND, 1621

afforded to any public figure, she triggered every response button of a socially concerned age.

For Diana had developed from an engagingly honest naïve to be a natural media-performer. Almost without effort, it seemed, she had mastered the communication skill, which seasoned figures in the public eye give a lifetime to perfecting, of conveying the impression of sincerity and vulnerability, without for a moment losing sight of the priority interest of number one. In passing she managed, moreover, to appear to cast doubt on her husband's fitness and motivation for monarchy.

It was generally agreed that Diana had blasted her husband out of the water. Whether she had also blasted out of the water the British ship of state remained to be seen. One thing was sure. Few men have made a greater political blunder than Prince Charles when, in the era of TV monarchy, he opened the television channels to open royal hearts. His own patent dedication and sincerity was no match for the 'beautiful victim' image, so skilfully projected by his wife. Never underestimate the opposition, is a golden rule of all politics – and today, whether they wish to be or not, Britain's royals are very much involved in the business of politics.

Some people argued that the very future of the British monarchy was in jeopardy as a result of this public domestic slanging match. They could be right. The affair of the diamond necklace and the French Revolution (see pp. 5-6) suggest a dangerous precedent. But the House of Windsor seems to have the determination and dedication to survival and compared with the hazards faced by Europe's other royal Houses, this House has suffered comparatively little as yet.

Death at the Opera

On 1 March 1771, while attending a performance at the opera in Paris, Gustav, Crown Prince of Sweden, received a messenger with the news that his father, King Adolf Frederick, had died and that he, Gustav, had become king. An enlightened and talented man, Gustav was also a modernizer by temperament – it was he who founded the Swedish Academy for example, but, unfortunately, he could be headstrong and was liable to ignore warnings.

Like most reformers, Gustav III attracted enemies: among the nobility, when he arrested leading members of the House of the Nobility; and among a much larger constituency of his subjects when he banned home-distilling and made the production of aquavit a Crown monopoly. Although the latter was surely a serious blunder, he was able to ride the consequences of his autocratic policies until 1788, when he embarked on a war against Russia. Gustav thought he could win popularity and recover former Swedish territories on continental Europe by attacking Russia. A mutiny among aristocratic officers, who claimed the campaign was being mishandled, almost lost the war and gave birth to a committed opposition.

Victorious, Gustav contrived a second *coup d'état* in 1789 and the following year won another campaign against Russia. But his wars and his grandiose policies were now unpopular with the country while the opposition could

A crown is merely a hat that lets the rain in.

FREDERICK THE GREAT, KING OF PRUSSIA, 1740

see another royal coup on the cards, which would limit their privileges still further. A group of men formed a conspiracy with the aim of killing the King.

At the beginning of 1792, after 20 years in power, Gustav felt secure. Friends and advisers warned him there was danger afoot and specifically that trouble was brewing for the night of 3 March, when a splendid masked ball was to be held in the Stockholm Opera House. Ignoring all warnings, Gustav committed the cardinal political blunder of over-confidence.

That night, he entered the theatre with his entourage, wearing a tiny white mask and with a black venetian cloak thrown over his shoulder. The arrogant figure was of course unmistakable and when he strode unescorted on to the stage, he was quickly surrounded by a group of people in black masks. They were all members of the conspiracy. One tapped the King on the shoulder with the greeting: 'Bonjour, beau masque.' The playful formality was a signal to the chosen killer, Jacob Anckarström, who shot the King in the back. With a cry of '*Aie! Je suis blessé*' ('I am wounded') Gustav fell to the floor. He died in the royal palace 13 days later in extreme agony. It has been said of Gustav that he was a king 'made and unmade in an opera house'. His story provided Verdi with the plot of his opera *Un Ballo in Maschera*, his life and death a classic morality story of arrogance and over-confidence.

Untitled to Rule on Principle

The all-time champion for arrogance, a man who took the quality to almost mystical heights, was Henri comte de Chambord, the Bourbon pretender at the time of the fall of Napoleon III and the French Second Empire. On the face of it, the restoration of the French monarchy should have been a foregone conclusion following the elections of 8 February 1871. Out of some 630 *députés*, 400 were monarchists supporting one or other of the two lines descended from the pre-Revolutionary dynasty. But, although the Assembly retained its monarchist majority for two more years, a royal government was not restored. The stubbornness of the count was to ensure that all hopes of revival were still-born. In all conscience the situation was already difficult enough. Part of the explanation is to be found in a catalogue of political blunders; part in the historical circumstances, for this was an exceptional body, elected under exceptional conditions – Paris was surrounded by a German army and 40 French departments were occupied by German troops.

It was barely six months since France, under its Bonapartist emperor Napoleon III, had declared war on Prussia. Within weeks she faced humiliation. On 1 September 1870, Napoleon surrendered at the Battle of Sedan and went into exile in England (only four Corsican *députés* in the new assembly would confess to being Bonapartists). Three weeks later, the Prussian army began its siege of Paris. On 28 January 1871, terrorized by a German artillery bombardment that killed 400, the Government of National Defence agreed an Armistice: Paris would capitulate and a three-week suspension of hostilities would allow for the election of an assembly which could make peace. Many electors were prisoners or called up in newly formed armies. The bulk of the remainder followed the recommendation of local notables and clergy, hence in large part the preponderance of royalist deputies. Nevertheless, it was a massive majority and the new Assembly was established at Versailles, home of the Bourbons, and not at Paris, cradle of the French Revolution. A restoration of the old royal line seemed very possible.

The first negative indicators came with the election of veteran republicans, notably Adolphe Thiers, new head of the executive, to leading posts. True, they were experienced politicians, anti-Bonapartists and familiar figures in a time of crisis. Even so, it seemed to some an elementary blunder for a monarchist majority not to chose monarchist leaders. Then the Assembly passed two resolutions which demonstrated great common sense in the pursuance of class interests but made no political sense at all.

The first measure ended the moratorium on the promissory notes which had been the main Parisian currency during the later phase of the war and the subject of profitable speculation by financiers. The second measure was to make rents, which had remained unpaid during the war, immediately payable – which seemed only reasonable to the landlords and landed gentry. Together, the measures spelt ruin to the city's lower middle classes. When Thiers attempted to seize the 400 guns in the hands of the national guard of Paris, he faced riot and the refusal to capitulate as per terms of the Armistice.

Thiers now ordered the abandonment of the capital, not without too much regret perhaps since it was by now largely dominated by the left wing. The Paris Commune, formed in defiance, prepared for war to the death with the forces of the Assembly. The Second Siege of Paris, French against French while the German army surrounding the capital looked on, lasted from 2 April to 28 May and ended with the forces of the Assembly triumphant and some 20,000 Communards slaughtered – 50 times the number of Parisians killed by the German terror bombardment. This was clearly a triumph for the Assembly and Adolphe Thiers. It did not, however, mean the triumphant restoration of the monarchy. This was partly because Thiers was a Republican (cascades of French blood have, traditionally, been the lubricant of French republicanism); partly because the monarchist movement divided its loyalties between two branch-

He is a cretin whom we shall easily manage.

FRENCH STATESMAN ADOLPHE THIERS IN 1848, COMMENTING PRIVATELY ON LOUIS NAPOLEON BONAPARTE WHOM HE WAS PUBLICLY SUPPORTING FOR ELECTION AS PRESIDENT OF THE SECOND REPUBLIC. IN 1852 THE 'CRETIN' CARRIED THROUGH A COUP WHICH ESTABLISHED HIM DICTATOR AS EMPEROR NAPOLEON III

Far left: *Tsar Nicholas II of Russia (1868–1918).*

Left: *Napoleon III, Emperor of France (1808–73), the end of whose regime opened the possibility of a restoration of a branch of the old Bourbon royal family.*

es of the old royal house; but largely because of the political obtuseness of the senior 'Legitimist' candidate, who had the support of 182 *députés*.

The comte de Chambord had passed his life with a little court of exiles in a castle in Austria. He had learnt, in his own words, 'to expect everything from God and nothing from man'. Perhaps the noblest of his line and, being childless, certainly the last, he was also, unfortunately, the embodiment of the old gibe against the Bourbons that they forgot nothing and forgave nothing. Though he was willing to concede that the substance of power had fallen from the monarchy, there was never any prospect that he would accept the Revolutionary tricolour as the national flag, even though this was the obvious condition of government in modern France.

In the rival camp were the 214 *députés* who supported the claims of the House of Orléans represented by the worldly-wise comte de Paris. He had studied trade unionism in England and fought in the American Civil War and had some of the intuitions of a democratic politician. Moderate monarchists on both sides saw an obvious solution. Let the ageing Chambord ascend the throne as Henry V, to be succeeded at his death by the younger Orléanist line. But in July 1871 the legitimate heir to the Bourbon succession, never a man to do deals that impeached his dynastic past, declared that he would not let the white flag and the fleur-de-lys, 'the standard of Henry IV, of Francis I, of Jeanne d'Arc be torn from my hands'.

The presence of Joan of Arc in this list is interesting. In the aftermath of the national humiliation at the hands of the German empire and the loss of Lorraine, Joan, born in the lands of Bar and Lorraine, was rapidly advancing in cult status as the spiritual champion against the enemies of France. In the 15th century these had been the English, in the 1870s they were the Germans. Joan was not to be canonized as saint for another 50 years, but already the most Catholic of all the Bourbons cited her as a patron of the pure doctrine of royal legitimacy.

In May 1873, at last repudiated by a monarchist vote in the assembly, Thiers resigned and the Orléanist duc de Broglie replaced him as head of government under President MacMahon. Once again, prospects for a royalist restoration seemed promising. Unfortunately, the comte de Chambord seemed to believe the mere proclamation of his accession would rally national support. He visited France incognito in the autumn of 1874. But when he insisted that the country would have to surrender the tricolour to enjoy once again the blessings of Bourbon rule, the President persuaded him to return to his Austrian castle as secretly as he had come.

Without the support of the Legitimist deputies, there was no prospect of a restoration of the monarchy in France; without Chambord, that support would not be forthcoming; without the fleur-de-lys fluttering once more in the Place de la Concorde – formerly the Place Louis XV and site of the Revolutionary guillotine – Chambord would not return to Versailles. If the issue was monarchy versus republicanism, the comte and his supporters had made serious political blunders in their conditions and loyalties. But perhaps the issue had never been that simple, perhaps it had all along been about allegiances of a more impractical nature.

Strangely, King Henry IV who founded the Bourbon line in 1589, had proved much more of a politician than his otherworldly descendant. After all, to win the throne, Henry had surrendered not just a flag but his religion. A Protestant, he had turned Catholic with the cynical observation that Paris was worth a mass – for Chambord it was not worth even a tricolour.

An Honest Mistake

The master of the royal blunder in recent times was Tsar Nicholas II (see p. 167), an autocrat obsessed with his own authority to the exclusion of all else.

The case of Constantine II of Greece demonstrated that a throne can be lost even by the most constitutionally minded of monarchs and that to be unduly conscientious can lead one to fatal blunders. Constantine came to the throne at the age of 24, on the death of his father King Paul in March 1964. Handsome and personable he was, even so, held by many Greeks to be too attentive to the wishes of his mother, the German-born Queen Frederika, considered by some a near Nazi for her right-wing sympathies during the civil war against the Communists. When therefore, in July 1965, he dismissed the left-wing government of George Papandreou, the queen mother's influence was detected. Whether or not this was justified, the King was hardly himself of the extreme right. Some 18 months and a succession of ministries later, Constantine announced plans for full and fair elections to be held in May 1967. They were, ironically enough, forestalled by a coup from the right which, on 21 April, inaugurated the notorious regime of the Colonels. In December the King attempted a counter coup. It failed miserably. He settled down to exile in Rome, observing: 'I am sure I shall go back the way my ancestors did.'

The remark, hardly a clarion call of conviction politics, was characteristic of the man. And even had it been fulfilled, the omens would hardly have been auspicious. Ever since the founding of the Greek monarchy by the German prince Otto of Bavaria in 1832, Greek kings had blundered on and off the throne like solo performers in a cacophonous game of musical chairs.

Otto himself suffered two military coups. He was succeeded by a Danish prince who took the title George I – St George being a principal saint of the Greek Orthodox Church. He died to an assassin's bullet. His son, the German-friendly Constantine I was driven from his palace by bombardment from the Royal Navy during World War I. Constantine's son, Alexander I, died tragically of blood poisoning following a bite from his pet monkey. Recalled by a plebiscite, Constantine I was driven into final exile in 1922, following defeat in a war against the Turks. Another son, George II, reigned for barely two years before being in his turn forced into exile. Some ten years later he was restored and from 1935 to 1965, apart from the upheaval of World War II, the Greek royal house continued in power.

It was of course too good to last and as we have seen, Constantine II went the way of his ancestors. His failure to return like so many of them had done, was the result of a blunder of honour made by a constitutional monarch too conscientious for his own good.

In November 1973 the head of the Colonels' junta, Giorgios Papadopoulos, was ousted in a popular coup and in July 1974 the veteran republican politician Konstantinos Karamanlis became premier. By the terms of a gentleman's agreement it was understood that he was to prepare the way for a royal restoration and the King was to await his official invitation to return. The call never came. Instead Karamanlis, firmly in the saddle, called a referendum and in December 1974 the Greek electorate returned a majority of seven to three in favour of retaining the republican system.

Whether a determined move by Constantine in the first week after the ousting of the Colonels would have brought a surge in favour of the monarchy is not clear, but it is more than possible. There were royalists found to criticize what they saw as his indecision, some even a failure of courage to risk the venture. In the light of his family's history a certain hesitancy was to be expected, perhaps. Constantine, who surely felt betrayed by Karamanlis, insisted that even in exile he had to preserve his integrity as a constitutional monarch. He had, in other words, to await the advice of his prime minister. Yet in the context it was a blunder to adopt such text-book correctness.

To Ban or not to Ban a Royal Feminist

Constantine's moderation and determination to play by the rules may well have lost him his throne. A similar unkingly preference for reasonable behaviour by King Alfonso XIII of Spain had less dramatic, but nevertheless surpising results. In 1911 the court at Madrid was startled by rumours that Eulalia, Infanta of Spain and the young King's aunt, was just completing a book which it was said would prove politically controversial. Alfonso duly ordered the princess to halt publication or lose her royal privileges. But Eulalia, who lived in France, was a lady of independent mind and refused. Alfonso reconsidered and withdrew his threat.

But he could not withdraw the blunder. Whether or not his advisers had been right to fear damage to the monarchy from the contents of the book, controversy was now more or less guaranteed and on the international market. Nothing sells better than a banned book. Eulalia now had the court's grudging acceptance, it is true, but her English publishers knew better than to broadcast the fact. The book, its dust-jacket adorned with a sticker proclaiming 'The Book Forbidden by the King of Spain', enjoyed such roar-away sales that an American publisher later congratulated her on co-opting the King's help in a brilliant piece of marketing.

And what had been the cause of the trouble? The book's only political content in conventional terms was a few sentences mildly commending the humane ideals of socialism. Far more unacceptable to contemporary views were the comments the princess made on the status of women. 'For centuries,' she wrote, 'man has denied woman her finest qualities which are fearlessness and presence of mind, and the majority of women have come to be convinced that those qualities are unwomanly and to be reckoned faults.' A little further on in the text she deplored 'the lot of woman when, devoid of the means to free herself honestly from slavery, she was compelled to sell herself, by legal marriage or otherwise'. Bracketing, if only by implication, legal marriage with prostitution was well in tune with a militant tradition of feminism already flourishing in Britain and the USA, but according to the conventional wisdom of the day was subversive of society itself. The rumour of a royal ban was enough to ensure these feminist sentiments far wider currency than they could ever have expected.

He who would be king of the Hellenes had best keep his bags packed.

QUIPPED BY AN ANONYMOUS WAG ON THE BLUNDER-PRONE GREEK ROYAL DYNASTY

CHAPTER 13: BLUNDERS OF DESTINY

The history of the 20th century has been marked by so many and such bizarre terrors that from time to time supernatural causes are invoked. Both Adolf Hitler and later Ronald Reagan, it is said, consulted astrologers. In the 1960s both Washington and Moscow appealed to the same occult operators for advice in determining the most propitious dates for their space launches. In most of the non-Western world such lore is taken for granted Nick Leeson, the Singapore-based trader extraordinary whose blunders helped bust Barings, Britain's oldest merchant bank, in 1995, chose the Chinese lucky number 88888 for his secret account. His total failure, arrest and imprisonment might seem to be sufficient comment on the delusion of such ideas. But there are some startling coincidences in the concatenation of events to give us pause.

Two sensational assassinations are reasonably held to have had determining influence on the history of America; less well known are the eerie parallels

The assassination of President Lincoln in 1865, which found eerie parallels in the assassination of President Kennedy a century later.

BLUNDERS OF DESTINY

The blood-stained tunic of the Austrian Archduke Franz Ferdinand, whose assassination by a Bosnian Serb on 28 June 1914 triggered events which led to World War I.

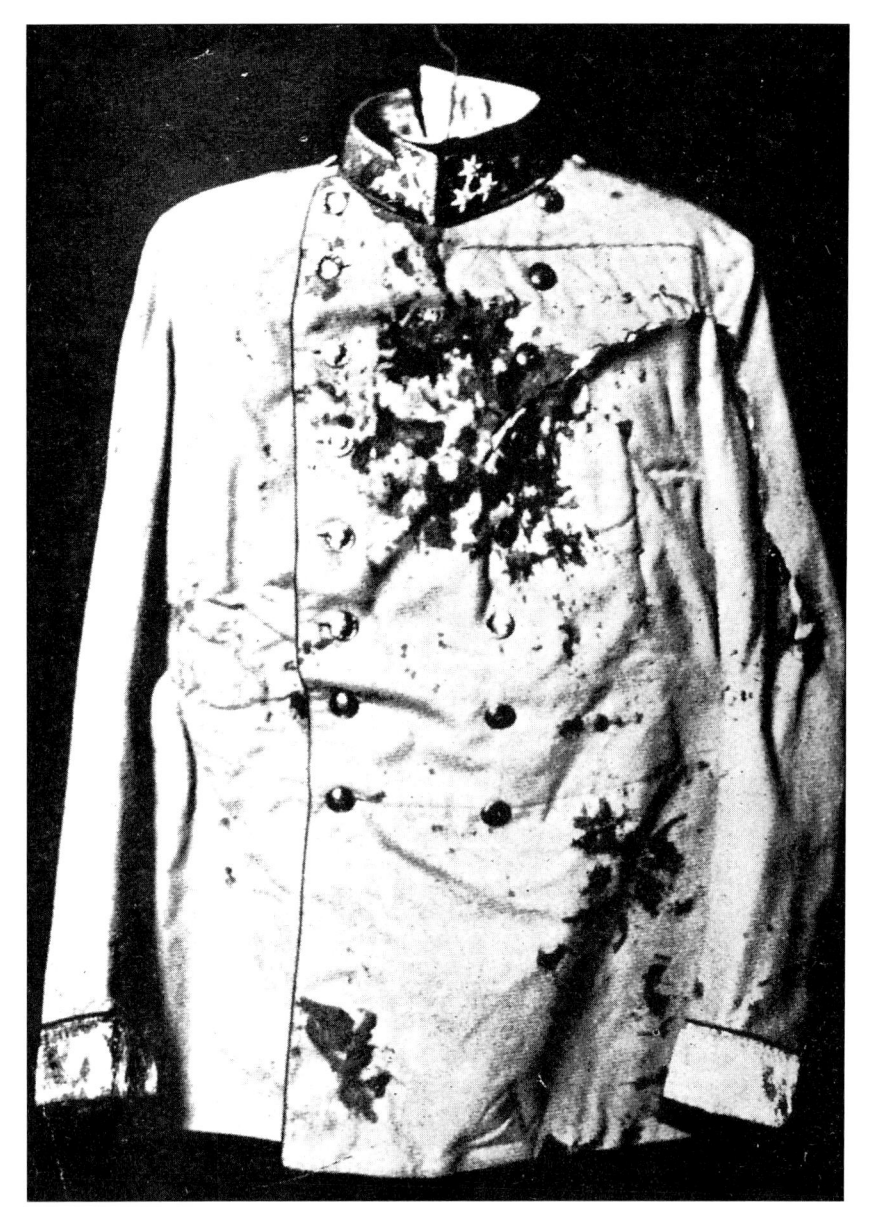

between the deaths of Presidents Lincoln and Kennedy. Both were killed by lone gunmen. Both were shot from behind. Both were shot in the presence of their wives. In both cases the victim was in a location against the wishes of advisers. President Lincoln's secretary was called Kennedy, President Kennedy's secretary was called Lincoln. The one urged Lincoln not to attend the theatre the night he was murdered; the other urged Kennedy not to visit Dallas. Both were killed in the seventh decade of the century. Both were succeeded by vice-presidents called Johnson, one born in 1808, the other born in 1908. Both Johnsons were Southerners. The assassin of Lincoln fled from the theatre where he had done the killing to a warehouse or barn where he was taken by the police, the assassin of Kennedy fled from a warehouse book depository to a theatre where he was seized.

In the 20th century events seemed to conspire to produce cataclysmic results on more than one occasion. The rise of Adolf Hitler (see pp. 176-180) is explicable in entirely rational terms, but his ultimate acquisition of power was made possible – at a time when his party's fortunes had already passed their peak – only by the sleepwalking stupidity of the leaders of Germany's political élite of the day.

As to the First World War, it seemed that Archduke Franz Ferdinand, whose death at Sarajevo precipitated the conflict, was in pursuit of his fate. His visit to the Bosnian capital on 28 June 1914 began ominously when a Serbian assassin made a failed attempt on his life with a bomb. The Archduke ignored warnings and advice to cancel his engagements. The route of his motorcade was diverted by chance into the street where a second assassin, armed with a pistol, was placed. The fall of the imperial house of Russia in 1917 was a more protracted affair but it, too, seemed to conspire in its own demise.

The Fate of the Romanovs

Nicholas II, Tsar of all the Russias from 1894 to 1917, has been traditionally regarded as a weak-willed incompetent; though recently historians have come to attribute his obsessive addiction to his own powers as autocrat to a reasoned assessment of the Russian character as incapable of government by any other system. Developments in the former USSR since the fall of the Communist dictatorship can certainly be seen as supporting such an analysis. However, the catalogue of blunders through which Nicholas logged his personal pilgrimage to destruction argues forcibly against the view that he was the man to save his people. Indeed, the events surrounding the fall of the House of Romanov can tempt even the most cynical to muse on the possibility of some extra-human intervention.

The charismatic charlatan Grigori Efimovich Rasputin, holy man and libertine who dominated the latter years of the reign, would certainly have agreed. His power derived from his apparent ability to staunch the haemophiliac flows of the tsar's son. Many saw this as a divine gift and his murder in 1916 by a group of nobles as the knell of doom for the dynasty.

Nicholas's catastrophic reign was inaugurated with a fatal error of judgement by his own father. Alexander III (1845–94), who viewed his weak-willed offspring with good-natured contempt, made the mistake of not once attempting to introduce him to the workings of government. Perhaps, though it is doubtful, he would have remedied the matter in due course. However, Alexander compounded this quite avoidable error with the possibly less culpable blunder of dying at the age of 49 when his intellectually challenged heir was just 26. Nicholas was frankly appalled. 'I have not been prepared to be tsar. I never wanted to be one. I know nothing of the business of ruling. What is going to happen to me and to all of Russia?'

The answer to the new tsar's question was simply that he was to be dominated by more powerful personalities, first his mother, then his wife. The tsarina's obsession with Rasputin, whom she regarded as the good angel of her son, was to cast a malign fog over the dealings between monarch and ministers. But long before the sex-charged mystic from Siberia arrived at court, the reign had opened with a thudding downbeat.

In January 1895, Nicholas met the representatives of Russia's provincial councils, bodies established some 30 years before to encourage the growth of local participation in the government of the country. In fact, they had been systematically obstructed by the ministry of the interior, determined to relinquish no jot or tittle of its authority. The accession of a young tsar seemed an omen of hope to the local worthies, ready to forget past humiliations and work with the new regime for a new Russia. In inimitable style, Nicholas off-handedly swatted their aspirations. 'It is known to me,' he announced to the assembly, 'that ... some persons ... have been carried away by senseless dreams of sharing in the affairs of government. Let all know that I shall preserve the principle of autocracy as firmly and as undeviatingly as my father.'

Little more than a year later another gesture signalled indifference to the mass of his ordinary subjects. In May 1896, four days after a coronation of fabulous splendour, some 500,000 people gathered to await the customary distribution of royal largesse on the Khodynka Field (now the site of Moscow's airport). Incompetent crowd-control ended with a stampede in which more than 120 people were killed. Following advice from a minister, Nicholas, though in his own words 'slightly unwilling', attended a ball at the French embassy. Public reaction was bitter.

It is hardly surprising that the turn of the century witnessed an epidemic of student strikes; these welded the rapidly growing Socialist Revolutionary Party into a real and dangerous force for change. In 1903, a quarter of a million industrial workers came out on strike, adding a call for a constituent assembly to their industrial demands. The royal family took time off for a wedding with their German relations in Darmstadt, only to find on their return that domestic politics were as troubled as ever. In January 1904, the tsar's chief minister observed to the minister of war: 'What we need to hold Russia back from revolution is a small, victorious war.' At the time the government was involved in protracted and hostile negotiations over disputed territories in Manchuria and Korea. Russia was inflexible and on 6 February, the Japanese delegation having withdrawn, their government broke off diplomatic relations, to the chief minister's delight. Two days later it seemed his prayer had been answered in full. Without any formal declaration of war, the Japanese attacked Port Arthur, Russia's naval base on the Liaotang Peninsula between Korea and China, aiming to bottle up the Russian fleet.

Rarely has a political prescription been so promptly filled nor, as it at first appeared, so precisely according to doctor's orders. Trouble had been brewing on Russia's eastern frontier for years and Nicholas had dreams of a grand imperial mission in Asia. How better to inaugurate it than with a short sharp war and a quick victory over the 'makaki' or 'little monkeys' as the tsar's courtiers dubbed the Japanese.

Certainly, Japan was a dwarf in world-power terms when compared with Russia. But she had the immense logistical and strategic advantage of being close to the theatre of war. Moscow and its troop concentrations were thousands of miles away, separated by the vast distances of Siberia from the scene of action. As at Pearl Harbor, 35 years later, Japan's chance lay in surprise attack. Hence the unannounced attack on Port Arthur. Where the Americans were outraged, the tsar and his court were delighted. Their inflexible diplomacy had contrived the outbreak of hostilities. All they needed now was the time to bring their immense forces to bear to finish the job.

Over the next few months, as the Russian war machine lumbered eastwards and the Baltic fleet steamed for Pacific waters, the Japanese won a quick series of victories which astounded the world community and it began to dawn on more thoughtful Russians that the policy initiative that sprang the monkey trap might have been something of a blunder. But nobody could imagine the extent of the disaster. In January 1905 Port Arthur fell to the Japanese. In March a vast Russian army was routed at the Battle of Mukden and in May the Baltic fleet, having at last arrived on station, was destroyed by Admiral Togo at the Battle of Tsushima.

The defeats were accompanied by the very scenario of near revolutionary unrest the war had been contrived to dispel. When Port Arthur fell that January, St Petersburg was wracked by industrial strife. On the first Sunday of the month, a demonstration thousands strong, carrying sacred icons and portraits of the tsar and singing the national anthem, had converged on the great square in front of the Winter Palace bearing a petition. The tsar and his family were not in residence but the marchers came cheerfully on through the snow. The minister of the interior had prepared a special welcome for them. By the end of 'Bloody Sunday' hundreds of men, women and children lay dead or wounded in the grey-red slush. Thenceforward, for many Russians, the 'little father' of all the Russias would be 'Nicholas the Bloody' and revolution was in the air in 1905. In June the crew of the battleship *Potemkin* raised the Red Flag in an eleven-day mutiny. Even the *corps de ballet* of the Maryinsky Theatre refused to take the stage. With the approach of winter came the October Manifesto which promised an elected,

A Japanese print depicting naval action against the Russian fleet in the Russo-Japanese war of 1904–05.

representative assembly to be called the 'Duma'. But it was packed with peasant deputies, traditionally pro-court. But in April 1906 the tsar promulgated new 'Fundamental Laws of the Empire' which reasserted the supreme autocratic power of the emperor and provided that only he could change them. By this simple and stupid act, Nicholas blocked off the constitutional road to change for his people. But then he would not allow the word 'constitution' to be as much as mentioned in his hearing.

That same month came the state opening of the Duma, calculated to intimidate its members. A tableau of ministers and courtiers, resplendent in uniforms and ceremonial dress, confronted the deputies dressed in a motley ranging from formal evening dress to peasant costumes or work clothes. Nobody was overawed. The Duma proved solid in its opposition to the tsar and his fundamental laws. In ten years of wooden and incompetent autocracy, Tsar Nicholas II had contrived the astonishing political feat of sapping the age-old loyalty of the peasants to the dynasty. The Duma was hastily dissolved and a second one convened. This was yet more hostile. Not until 1907 did government gerrymandering produce a sufficiently compliant, third Duma. Politically it was an irrelevance. It has been said that 'Nicholas was a negative character, commonplace in mind, ... saved from complete insignificance only by the macabre pathos of his end.' He and his family were to be murdered by the Bolsheviks at Ekaterinburg on the night of 15 July 1918. It is difficult to avoid the conclusion that the tragedy owed much to Nicholas's mismanagement of the government of his country.

The Case of the Austrian Corporal

On the morning of Monday 30 January 1933 Otto Meissner, state secretary to President Hindenburg, ushered the leaders of Germany's National Socialist and National parties into the President's office in the state chancellery in Berlin. Minutes later the two men emerged, Alfred Hugenberg, the industrialist founder of the National Party, as head of the Republic's key economic ministries and Adolf Hitler, the Austrian-born Nazi leader, as the newly appointed chancellor. It is usually thought that Hitler came to power on the back of a surge of national support for the Nazi Party which led to victory at the polls. In fact, his appointment was the consequence of a series of political miscalculations which added up to the most tragic blunder in 20th-century history.

The myth of the *Parteiführer* (leader) swept to power as *Reichskanzler* (chancellor) by mass popular support leading to electoral triumph, was itself a triumph of Nazi propaganda. In fact, the Nazi Party had not achieved a majority of the votes cast in any national election, and nowhere near a majority of the seats in the Reichstag. Moreover, the party leader had never stood as a candidate for the Reichstag. Until 1932, when he took out naturalization papers, he was not even eligible to stand, not being a German citizen.

In the elections that July, the Nazis' percentage of the vote was only 37.3. In the November elections the same year they lost 34 seats, while their chief rivals, the Communists, actually increased their representation. Shrewd

Adolf Hitler (1889–1945), newly installed as Chancellor of Germany and dressed for the part, with President von Hindenburg at a formal review in 1933.

observers reckoned their moment was past, as did many in the party. But Hitler, mindful of the humiliating failure of the attempted Munich Putsch of 1923, resisted all suggestions to seize power by force; even though in the Brown Shirt SA (*Sturmabteilung*) movement the Nazis commanded the largest and most brutal private army the world had yet seen and even though the party was the largest in the Reichstag, Hitler was determined that power should be won by constitutional means. Revolution would come after. Whoever blundered in the winter of 1932–3, it was not Adolf Hitler.

Altogether, 1932 saw four nationwide elections – two for the Reichstag and two for the presidency. At the age of 43, Hitler took German citizenship to enable him to stand for president against Hindenburg. He was defeated twice, just as his party failed twice to win an outright majority. Thus, four times in a single year the German electorate denied Hitler the mandate of majority power. He was eventually manoeuvred into office through back-stairs intrigues conducted by cynical professional politicians, mistakenly convinced they could control the 'Austrian Corporal'. Far from being inevitable, Hitler's success owed something to luck, but much more to the bad judgement of his political opponents.

Aged 85 and acting on the advice of the former Chancellor von Papen, President Hindenburg had discharged his constitutional duty with the utmost reluctance, for he disliked and distrusted Hitler. But the past three years had seen constitutional turmoil in which a succession of chancellors had all attempted to form minority governments, only to founder on the wrecking tactics of Communists, Nationalists or Nazis.

Apart from the Social Democrats, every major party in Germany was fervently anti-republican and anti-democratic. The right – aristocracy, industry and finance – was dedicated to the destruction of the republican 'traitors' it held to be responsible for the loss of the Great War, and to restoring their own power and privilege under the auspices of the monarchy. The Communists were dedicated to victory in the class war as directed by Moscow, the prerequisite for which was also the destruction of the 'bourgeois' republic which had been inaugurated at Weimar in 1919.

In the 1920s Germany was run by coalition governments often dependent for the implementation of policy on *ad hoc* majorities cobbled together by *Kuhhandel* (cattle trading) amongst the party leaders for specific pieces of legislation, or sometimes on the special emergency powers conferred on the President by Article 48 of the republic's constitution. From 1930 the aged Hindenburg was the constitutional focus of real power.

The power behind the scenes was Major General Kurt von Schleicher, the voice of the army without whose support no politician could hope to govern. On his advice, in March 1930, Hindenburg appointed Dr Heinrich Brüning chancellor. Unable to find a stable coalition, he went to the country in September but failed to win a majority, losing ground to the extremists. The Nazis became the second largest party in the Reichstag which, while it was welcomed by London's *Daily Mail* as a reinforcement of the defences against Bolshevism, was bad news for the republic.

More and more, Brüning fell back on presidential decree but von Schleicher began to toy with the idea of bringing the Nazis into government to establish a majority coalition. Though 'mere infants who must be led by the hand', they could be relied on to support government by their betters in the Reichstag while Corporal Hitler, flattered with some suitable government appointment, would drum up mass support as and when it was needed in the country.

The risible idea that Hitler would be content to serve as drummer boy for other parties was the first blunder of his 'betters'. Hitler's first objective was to persuade them to bring him in as chancellor, so that he could get access to presidential rule by decree. With that at his disposal, the overthrow of the republic could be achieved in short order by the use of its own constitutional procedures.

As has often been pointed out, Hitler had made his subversive intentions public knowledge as far back as 1925 in his book *Mein Kampf*, but few people of consequence read its turgid prose and no-one paid attention. In December 1931 he gave yet more explicit and public warning of what could be expected if the Nazis were allowed into a position of power; in an open letter addressed to Chancellor Brüning he wrote: 'If the German Nation once empowers the National Socialist Movement to introduce a constitution other than that which we have today, then you cannot stop it.'

Brüning, too, seemed to think he could manipulate the Nazis if only he could co-opt them into government on his terms. When invited to talks in January 1932, Hitler crowed: 'Now I have them in my pocket. They have recognized me as partner in their negotiations.' In fact, the talks failed and at the end of May, Hindenburg called von Papen to the chancellorship, persuaded by von Schleicher that this dapper cavalry officer and society gentleman would be able to deliver the Nazis in a majority coalition. In fact, since the Centre Party, furious at Brüning's dismissal, went into opposition, the Nationalists under Hugenberg felt themselves slighted and Hitler went back

> *Hitler is my prisoner, tied hand and foot by the conditions he has been obliged to accept.*
>
> Freiherr Franz von Papen, explaining to friends his decision to persuade President Hindenburg to appoint Adolf Hitler chancellor in January 1933, while himself accepting the technically subordinate but key posts of Minister-president of Prussia and Vice-Chancellor of the Reich. The plan was certainly subtle. He, aristocratic but at the same time sophisticated, would neutralize the Nazi threat while he flattered the Nazis with the illusion of high office.

Dapper Freiherr Franz von Papen (1879–1969) in full regimentals – the German Vice-Chancellor who reckoned he could manipulate Adolf Hitler.

on his vague promise of support, von Papen had to fall back on government by presidential decree backed by the army.

But Hindenburg did not lose faith in his ability to woo the Nazis. In June 1932 he called new elections for 31 July and lifted the ban on Hitler's SA Brown Shirts. Street murder and mayhem followed. Even so, the Nazis failed to win a majority at the polls. November saw von Papen renew his approaches to Hitler. Forced to resign in the face of a cabinet revolt organized by a jealous von Schleicher, he advised the President to invite Hitler to form a majority coalition, knowing very well that the idea was a non-starter because of the hostilities and rivalries in the Reichstag. Since Hitler was determined to rule by presidential decree, to appoint him in place of von Papen would mean that the constitutional position of the aged president would remain unchanged while his decrees would not even be implemented by a gentleman. If Hitler could not deliver the majority, then von Papen should stay. Such was the position when von Schleicher, angered that his agent von Papen appeared to have won the long drawn-out power-game, insisted that he himself be given the chance to form a majority government, believing that he could win Nazi support and knowing that he would have the support of the army. For Hindenburg this was the decisive argument and on 2 December he appointed von Schleicher chancellor.

The general, who for so long had operated behind the scenes, was no politician and made the fundamental mistake of assuming success before it had been won. Now it was true that in recent provincial

> *Herr Hitler is no longer a problem, his movement has ceased to be a political danger and the whole problem is solved. It is a thing of the past.*
>
> GENERAL KURT VON SCHLEICHER, EIGHT WEEKS GERMAN CHANCELLOR, TO AN AUSTRIAN VISITOR ON 15 JANUARY 1933
>
> **Thanks to Nazi non-cooperation, von Schleicher's government fell on 28 January and he was dismissed by President von Hindenburg. On 30 January Hitler was inaugurated chancellor.**

elections the Nazi vote had registered a drop of 40 per cent, that the party was in desperate financial straits and morale was at its lowest for years. But the Nazis still had their 230 seats in the Reichstag and when they refused to cooperate, von Schleicher's coalition plans collapsed. At noon on 28 January President Hindenburg entrusted von Papen with the negotiations which should bring Germany a new government. Now it was his turn to blunder.

Aware of the hostility of the Reichstag to himself as chancellor, and aware also that Hindenburg was still loath to appoint Corporal Hitler as a 'presidential' chancellor, von Papen proposed himself as vice-chancellor and Hitler as chancellor of a majority coalition. He assured the old man that the corporal was tied hand and foot by the conditions he had agreed to. As vice-chancellor he, von Papen, had the newly created right to be present on all occasions when the chancellor made his report to the president; he also held, *ex officio*, the key post of president of Prussia, the largest of the provincial governments. Apart from the chancellorship, the Nazis held only two minor portfolios in the eleven-man cabinet. The drummer boy had his glitzy title, the power lay elsewhere. This was *Realpolitik* in the classic mode.

It was also self-delusion on the grand scale. Over the next six months Hitler and his henchmen, chief among them Hermann Goering, Prussian minister of the interior, would demonstrate a cynicism and lack of scruple – qualities upon which von Papen and Hugenberg particularly prided themselves – which left these two politicians gasping. For Hitler had grasped the novel principle that revolution was best carried out with, not against, the power of the government. New elections were called for March 1933 and the Nazis harnessed the full machinery of the state, as well as the SA, to the business of terrorizing their opponents. Astonishingly, even so they won neither a majority of the votes cast (43 per cent) nor of the seats in the chamber, relying as before on the Nationalists under Hugenberg. However, this was enough. Before the month was up, by dint of proscribing their major rivals, the Communists, and by cheating, outmanoeuvring and/or simply brow-beating their coalition partners, Hitler and his lieutenants forced the 'Enabling Law' through the Reichstag. This authorized the government to legislate over the next four years without the cooperation of the Reichstag. It was, moreover, specifically authorized to deviate from the constitution as it saw fit. Government law was to be drafted by the chancellor and should come into effect the day after publication. Within a year, the democratic structures of the Weimar Republic had been dismembered.

Thus, when Hindenburg died on the morning of 2 August 1934, everything was in place for transition to a personal dictatorship by the despised corporal. News of the death was followed within the hour by an announcement that henceforth the office of president would be merged with that of chancellor. Adolf Hitler was proclaimed as well as head of state, the supreme commander-in-chief of the armed forces of the Reich. The dictatorship ended only with the death of the dictator himself in a Berlin bunker in 1945. Long before that it had become apparent that, when President Hindenburg made the fateful appointment of January 1933, someone had blundered.

Blundering towards Destiny

In France, the seizure of Louis XVI and his family at Varennes in June 1792, during their attempt to escape the country and the Revolutionary authorities who had taken charge of the government, was a tragedy that could have been avoided, had the King and Queen not committed a series of blunders. Unless, as some would say, it was written in the stars. The sequence of events is certainly remarkable.

The King's plan to escape from his hostile capital across the eastern frontier of France into the neighbouring German territories and thence to Vienna may, conceivably, have had a slim chance of success, but only on the condition that the planning was meticulous and security precautions complete. Anti-royal sentiment and particularly hatred of the Austrian-born queen, daughter of the Holy Roman Emperor, had been growing ever since the Revolutionary constitutional assembly had reduced Louis, God's elect, to the rank of a constitutional monarch.

Had the flight succeeded, he and his queen would surely have lived and the course of the Revolution would surely have been changed. It was also possible that, had it never been attempted, Louis might have retained the confidence of the people and so his head. As it was, the royals' bungled dash for freedom seemed to vindicate accusations that they were closet traitors to the new constitution, waiting only for the right moment to overthrow it in conjunction with support of other monarchs.

Whether the flight to Varennes need have failed is yet another question. The catalogue of blunders and delays in its planning and execution seem to go so far beyond the ordinary bounds of human stupidity and incompetence that even a sceptic might look for the hand of fate. To complete the aura of sleepwalking destiny which surrounds it, two eerie verse quatrains of the 16th-century prophet Nostradamus are claimed to foretell the event.

Preparations were discussed with the Marquis de Bouillé, army commander on the eastern frontier and coordinated by Count Axel Fessen, a Swedish officer in the French army and admirer of the queen. The obvious route, via Rheims, had regular relays of horses for through traffic. The King decided to go via Varennes, by less frequented roads and bypass Reims, despite objections that this would mean organizing a special relay team which would alert interest and possible suspicion. The advisers were next overruled on the choice of vehicle. They urged the use of two fast, standard long-distance passenger vehicles. The King ordered a special berline, a large luxurious, heavy and therefore slow private coach, bound to attract attention.

For things to run smoothly, an exact timetable was obviously essential. The planned departure date of 11 June was changed at the King's request to 19 June. Then, when everything was in place for the new schedule and the courtier in charge had lined up men and fresh horses to be ready on that day at Varennes, the King ordered a second delay. Although this time it was a mere 24 hours, it was quite enough for the orders and counter-orders of the rescheduling to alert those involved and any observant outsiders that important travellers were expected. But Louis had just remembered that he would draw his allowance on the new quarterly civil list on the morning of the 20th and thriftly decided not to go without it!

When the party finally got under way, it was a splendid and over-conspicuous affair. The coachman and flunkies, who should have been fitted out in nondescript uniforms, were instead garbed in splendid household livery. Thanks to the Queen's specially commissioned luxury travelling toiletry case, half the jewellers in Paris must have guessed she was planning a journey. M. de Choiseul, who was to leave twelve hours ahead of the main party to clear the route, was hampered by having to take the Queen's hairdresser whom she could not bear to leave behind.

In one respect the royal couple showed an element of good sense, agreeing to make their way separately and on foot, modestly dressed, to the coaches which were to await them at some distance from the palace. Their travel documents – absolutely in order since they were of course signed by the King himself – described the travellers as Madame la baronne de Korff (in fact the royal governess) and her children accompanied by their governess (in fact the Queen) and the baronne's *valet de chambre* (in fact the King).

They were to board the great berline on the northern outskirts of the capital. Thanks to the fact that her attendant did not know his way around Paris, the Queen very nearly missed the rendezvous. The King arrived without incident. He had shown surprising good sense in choice of clothes, being content with a grey coat and breeches, a satin waistcoat and grey stockings; unfortunately, he effectively abandoned the role of valet once the party was on the road. Instead of following in a second more modest coach, as would be expected by any normal lady of quality, this valet was placed with his supposed mistress, in the principal seat of her coach.

Still more calculated to draw attention to the travellers was the team of no fewer than six horses. Two horses might have had difficulty with the vast, well loaded equipage, but four would have done the job well enough; Madame de Korff and her party could not be content with less than six – the more usual privilege of royalty.

They had been recommended to take a M. d'Agout, loyal, determined and familiar with the route, they took the governess because her title outranked his. The coach was equipped with firearms, but these were stowed away in the luggage boot – the footmen being armed simply with hunting knives. Finally on the road, they were delayed for two hours by a broken axle. That perhaps could not be helped, but then the King delayed them another 30 minutes, so that he might contemplate a landscape vista which had taken his fancy.

At the next town they passed through, he showed himself at the window of the coach and was recognized. When they arrived at the first relay station, the troops detailed off to provide the escort were nowhere to be seen. They had waited two hours, attracting a growing crowd of suspicious and restive peasantry. Rather than risk involving the royal party in an ugly incident, the officer had ordered them back to barracks.

By this time the Queen was in despair, and with reason. At the little town of Sainte Menehould the King once more showed his face and this time was recognized by the alert postmaster Drouet in charge of the relay horses. He could not prevent the departure of the travellers, but he put his suspicions to the municipal authorities and they authorized him to go in pursuit.

At last, though long after nightfall, the royal party clattered into Varennes. It was the last stage before the frontier, but they were surely despondent. They had expected the fresh relay of horses to be at a farm on the near side of the town. In fact, by yet another blunder, the team had been placed on the far side. The road lay across a bridge and postmaster Drouet, galloping up ahead of his quarry who were still enquiring after their horses, blocked the route by overturning a cart of furniture which happened to be nearby. He next rode to the house of the *procureur*, or principal official of the commune, a grocer named Sauce.

Roused from his bed, the *procureur* at least knew his duty. Inspecting the travel documents, he found of course that they were in order as to the signature but, given Drouet's assertion that in fact the two travellers were the King and Queen, he instructed they spend the night in the town. Tragically, the captain of the troops posted with the relay horses on the other side of the bridge decided not to intervene. Bold action at this point might still have saved the situation but the captain appears to have thought he might risk the royal couple falling foul of mob action if he stirred up trouble.

The next day they were returned to Paris under armed escort. Both Louis XVI and Marie Antoinette were to meet their death beneath the slicing blade of the guillotine. Two hundred and fifty years earlier the Provençal

A dramatic reconstruction of the arrest of the family of Louis XVI in 1792 on the bridge at Varennes, the last stage of their flight from Paris to the German frontier. They were within reach of friendly troops who feared to intervene lest the royals be lynched by angry townspeople. It was the last in a fateful sequence of bungles and misjudgements.

doctor and seer Michel de Notredame had written, in the rigmarole of verses known as 'The Centuries', a quatrain which not only refers to Varennes, a town hundreds of miles to the north of his home in Montpellier and known for no other notable event in French history before or since, but also refers to a married couple coming into the town by night by a circuitous route; to blood and *tranche* (from *trancher*, to cut); to an 'elected Capet' (i.e. 'king of France'), and to 'a monk dressed in grey'.

Under the revolutionary regime, Louis XVI had remained king only by authority of the elected constituent assembly – and thus was the only member of the royal house of France who could in any way be referred to as 'elected'. He was commonly reputed to have the heterosexual urges of a monk and, as we have seen, he was dressed in grey. Fourteen quatrains further on we even find a still more startling group of references.

The four-line verse mentions 'a husband who alone will be mitred', a 'return', a 'conflict that will pass over the tiles by 500', a traitor who will be 'titled Narbon' and 'from Saulce we have oil', the old French spelling of 'Sauce', the name of the grocer who of course in his trade sold oil. The references to a 'mitred husband' and 'the 500 over the tiles' could mean a good deal to anyone who knew that, with Louis back in the palace of the Tuileries (built at the time of Nostradamus on the site of disused tile furnaces), the place was invaded by a mob who forced him to wear the red 'Phrygian cap of liberty' markedly similar to a bishop's mitre in appearance, and that two weeks later, the mob, now numbering 500, returned to the palace. No doubt the explanation is coincidence, but at the very least it proposes a remarkably high 'coincidence rate'. Louis' war minister, by the way, was the duc de Narbonne who was in secret contact with the revolutionary authorities.

A footnote on Nostradamus is perhaps in order. 'The Centuries' have been, subject of endless commentaries ever since their first edition publication in 1555. They are written in often turgid, always abstruse when not obtuse, verse. Anagrams, emblems, catch-phrases and mystic allusions are everywhere, none of the supposed subjects are specifically identified and no dates are given. The author himself claimed that he could have dated every prophesy had he had a mind to, and that he had deliberately garbled his message for fear of harassment by those in power in his own day for whom he foresaw bad fortune.

It could be said that he was wise to be cautious. The most famous astrologer of the previous generation, Luc Gauric, had been consulted by Giovanni Bentivoglio, the tyrant of the Italian city-state of Bologna; he foretold his exile and death. For this Gauric was sentenced to 'five turns of the strappado', a torture so terrible that it was years before he recovered. And yet, in 1506, Bentivoglio was indeed driven from Bologna, whose citizens turned the place over to Pope Julius II. The case was well known and Nostradamus evidently learnt the lesson of the strappado. But whether or not he foresaw the flight to Varennes, the astonishing sequence of blunders and accidents whether pre-destined or not that dogged the fugitives, remains one of the most bizarre episodes in history.

> *Here lies Joseph, who failed in everything he undertook.*
>
> JOSEPH II, HOLY ROMAN EMPEROR, SUGGESTING HIS EPITAPH, 1790

INDEX

Adolf Frederick, King of Sweden, 165
Agnew, Spiro T., 114-116
Aims of Industry, 90
Alcibiades, 99, 100
Aleppo, 160, 161
Alexander I, King of Greece, 169
Alexander III, Tsar of Russia 173
Alexius I, Byzantine Emperor 157,158
Alexius IV, Emperor, 158, 159
Alexius V, Emperor, 158
Alfonsin, President, 133, 146
Alfonso XIII, King of Spain, 170
Alfred the Great, 163
Algeria, 139
Algiers, Dey of, 161, 162
Anckarstrom, Jacob, 164
Antioch, 158
Arap Moi, President Daniel, 129, 130
Archer, Howard, 54
Argentina, 146
Arkansas, 35
Asquith, Herbert Henry, 65, 73-76, 129
Astor, Lady, 132
Aswan, 142, 143
Athens, 98-100
Attali, Jacques, 152
Attlee, Clement, 22, 23, 87-91
Australia, 146, 148, 149, 150, 151
Austria, 5, 149, 151

Babington, Anthony, 127-128
Badoglio, Marshall Pietro, 69
Baker, Kenneth, 48
Baldwin, Stanley, 42, 132, 140, 164
Baldwin of Flanders, 158, 159
Balfour, Arthur, 73, 74
Balladur, Edouard, 26, 27, 53, 54, 80-82
Ballot Act, 40, 41
Baltic Sea, 159
Bangladesh, 155
Bank of England, 45
Bashir, Martin, 164
Bastille, 7
Beaverbrook, Lord, 42, 88
Belgium, 131, 149
Belize, 145
Benes, Edward, 2
Benn, Tony, 118, 121
Bentivoglio, Giovanni, 184
Berchtesgaden, 3
Berlin Wall, 152, 154, 155
Bernard of Clairvaux, 160
Bernstein, Carl, 23
Bevin, Ernest, 23
Birkenhead, F.E. Smith, Lord, 76
Bishop, Sir Henry, 11
Bismarck, Otto von, 53

Blackpool, 116, 117
Blair, Tony, 31, 39, 112, 113, 121, 134
Boer War, 138, 163
Bohemond of Normandy, 157, 158
Boston, 62
Butt, Isaac, 40
Bouillé, Marquis de, 181
Boulay de la Meurthe, Antoine, 63
Bourbon family, 166-168
Boyne, Battle of the, 37
Bradlaugh, Charles, 9, 10
Brand, Speaker, 9
Brandenburg Gate, 152
Breteuil, Marquis de, 6, 7
Brittan, Sir Leon, 49
Broglie, Jacques Victor, duc de, 168
Brown, George, 129
Brownesville, 71-73
Bruce, Henry Austen, 39
Brüning, Heinrich, 178
Bruyère, Jean de la, 71
Buckingham Palace, 43
Budapest, 142
Buenos Aires, 146
Bulmer Thomas, Ivor, 43
Bundesrepublik, 147
Burke, Edmund, 62
Burleigh, Lord, 29
Bush, President George Herbert, 4, 134-5
Bute, Lord, 20, 22, 57
Butler, R.A., 117-118

Caillaux, Joseph, 14, 16-17
Caillaux, Berthe, 15-16
Caillaux, Henriette, (Riri), 15-16
Callaghan, James, 93, 119, 121, 134
Calmette, Gaston, 15-17
Cambridge, George William, 2nd Duke of, 163
Camisards, 36
Campbell-Bannerman, Sir Henry, 73
Canard Enchaîné, Le 18
Cannes, 32, 66
Cardwell, Edward, 163
Caroline Matilda, Queen of Denmark, 103-105
Carrington, Peter, Lord, 92
Carter, President James Earl, 133, 143-144
Casement, Sir Roger, 63, 65
Catherine of Aragon, Queen of England, 163-164
Chamberlain, Joseph, 138
Chamberlain, Neville, 2, 3, 34, 117, 141
Chambord, Henri, comte de, 166, 168-168

Charles I, King of England, 55-56
Charles V, Emperor, 164
Charles, Prince of Wales, 164-165
Charlotte, Queen of England, 19
Chatham, Earl of, 20, 22
Chatham, Lady, 22
Chile, 150
Chirac, President Jacques, 17, 18, 25-27, 53-54, 81-82, 147-15
Chirac, Bernadette, 26
Chirac, Claude, 26
Christian VII, King of Denmark, 102-103
Churchill, Lord Randolph, 9, 105-108
Churchill, Sir Winston, 2, 22-23, 42-43,69, 74, 86-91, 105, 107, 129, 132, 140-141
Churchill, Lady Clementine, 88
Civil War, English, 55-56
Civil War, US, 8
Clark, Alan, 19, 162
Clarke, Kenneth, 4, 31, 33, 86
Clement VII, Pope, 164
Clermont, Council of, 158
Clinton, President Bill, 35, 135
Clinton, Hillary, 35
Colbert, Jean-Baptiste, 156-157
Cold War, 143
Communist Party, 132
Community Charge, 46, 47 (see also Poll Tax)
Commune of Paris, 167
Condé, prince de, 182
Conservative Party, 1, 30, 32, 33, 40, 42, 47, 48, 79, 86, 91, 108, 116, 117, 122, 125, 131, 132, 162
Constantine I, King of Greece, 169
Constantine II, King of Greece, 169-170
Constantine the Great, Emperor, 157
Constantinople, 157-159
Coolidge, President Calvin, 126
Cooper, Alfred Duff, 34, 42
Copenhagen, 103
Count of Paris, see Paris, Henri d'Orléans, comte de
Cox, Archibald, 24
CREEP, 23-24
Croesus, King of Lydia, 152
Crossman, Richard, 97
Crusades, The, 158-160
Cuba, 136,
Curzon,, George Nathaniel, Lord, 106
Czechoslovakia, 2, 153

Dail, The, 28, 29, 30
Daily Express. 2, 125

185

INDEX

Daily Mail, 33, 178
Daladier, Edouard, 2
Dallas, 172
Damascus, 160, 161
Dashwood, Sir Francis, 22, 57
de Gaulle, President Charles, 26, 95, 148
Dean III, John, 24
Delos, Island of, 99
Delphi, 152
de Maistre, Joseph, 86
Denmark, 102, 103, 136, 137, 147, 149
de Valera, President Eamon, 3, 64, 65
Devaluation, 44, 45
Diamond Necklace, Affair of the, 5, 6
Diana, Princess of Wales, 164-165
Dilke, Sir Charles, 11
Dimbleby, Jonathan, 164
Disraeli, Benjamin, 1, 19, 28, 40, 105
Divorce, 10-11, 12-13, 15, 16
Douglas, Roger, 122
Douglas-Home, Alec, see Home, Lord
Drouet, Jean-Baptiste, 183
Dukakis, Michael, 134
Dulles, John Foster, 142
Duma, 176

Eagleton, Senator Thomas, 114
East India Company, 140
East Timor, 130
Easter Rising, 63-65
Economist, The, 49, 141
Eden, Sir Anthony, 90
Edessa, 158, 160
Edward VIII, King of Great Britain and Northern Ireland, 42-43, 164
Egypt, 142-143, 158, 161
Eisenhower, President Dwight D., 142
Ekaterinburg, 176
Eleanor of Aquitaine, 102
Elizabeth I, Queen of England, 29, 126-128
Elizabeth II, Queen of Great Britain and Northern Ireland, 43, 94, 118
Elizabeth, The Queen Mother, 93, 119
Eltham, 12, 13
ENA (Ecole Nationale d'Administration), 53, 54
Entebbe, 144
Erlichman, John, 24-25
Ershad, Hussain Muhammad, 155
Ervin, Senator Sam J., Jnr, 24
Eulalia, Princess, 170
European Parliament, 149
European Union, 146
Evening Standard, 134
Exchange Rate Mechanism (ERM), 78-80

Falkland Islands, 48, 119, 121, 145-146

FBI, The, 25
Fianna Fáil, 27, 29
Figaro, Le, 15, 16, 18
Financial Times, 49
Finland, 149
Fisk, James, 8
Focus, The, 42
Fontainebleau, Edict of, 36-37,
Foot, Michael, 92, 119-120
Foraker, Joseph B., 73
Ford, President Gerald, 25, 116, 132-133
Forsyth, Michael, 34
Fotheringhay Castle, 128
Fouquet, Nicholas, 156-157
France, 3, 5,25, 26, 54,69, 74, 81, 82, 92, 101, 126, 139, 141, 142, 148-151, 167
Franks Report, The, 145
Fraser, Hugh, 122
Franz Ferdinand, Archduke, 172-173
Frederick I Barbarossa, Emperor, 101
Frederick the Great, King of Prussia, 20, 165

Gaitskell, Hugh, 91
Galtieri, President, 146
Galway City, 13
Gandhi, Mahatma, 140
Gauric, Luc, 184
Gdansk, 97
Gérard, Dominic, 148
General Strike, 67, 132
George II, King of Greece, 169
George II, King of England, 19
George III, King of England, 19-20, 57, 59, 61, 63, 103
George V, King of Great Britain and Northern Ireland, 63
George VI, King of Great Britain and Northern Ireland, 23, 43, 88
Gerlach, Manfred, 155
Germany, 2, 3, 15, 83-86, 139-141, 147, 149, 152, 173, 178
Ghana, 130
Gibraltar, 146, 157
Giscard d'Estaing, President Valéry, 26, 82
Gladstone, William Ewart, 9, 11, 12, 13,14, 40, 41, 67, 105, 107, 163
Goebbels, Joseph, 135
Goering, Hermann, 180
Goldwater, Senator Barry, 94
Gorbachev, President Mikhail, 132, 153-154
Gordon, General Charles, 108
Gordon Riots, 62, 79
Gould, Brian, 134
Gould, Jay, 8
Grandi, Count Dino, 69
Grant, President Ulysses S., 8
Great Britain, 2, 3, 19, 140, 142, 145
Green, Sidney, 92
Greenland, 136, 137
Greenpeace, 148
Greens, 148, 151

Grenville, George, 57
Grey, Sir Edward, 73
Guatemala, 145
Guiscard, Robert, 158
Gummer, John, 52
Gustav III, King of Sweden, 165-166
Guthrum, 163

Hailsham, Lord, 118. 119
Haldeman, H. R., 24-25
Halifax, Lord, 58
Halys, River, 152
Hanley, Jeremy, 125
Harman, Harriet, 113
Havana, 136
Healey, Denis, 120, 124
Hearst, William, Randolph, 136-137
Heath, Sir Edward, 77, 90, 92, 94, 121-123
Hell Fire Club, 22, 57
Henry IV, Emperor, 102
Henry IV, King of England, 36
Henry IV, King of France, 168
Henry V, King of England, 102
Henry VIII, King of England, 163
Hermes, HMS, 145
Hervey, Augustus, 161. 162
Hertzog, President, 84
Heseltine, Michael, 31-3, 49, 52, 123
Hewson, John, 133
Hindenburg, President, Paul von, 176-180
Hiroshima, 149
Hitler, Adolf, 2, 69, 131, 135, 141, 161, 171, 173, 176-180
Home, Lord, 44, 95, 116-118
Hong Kong, 150
Honecker, Erich, 153-154
Houphouët-Boigny, President Félix, 130
House of Commons, 9, 10, 42, 43,51, 48, 61, 67, 74-76, 92, 106, 118, 129
Howard, Michael, 111-113, 134
Howe, Geoffrey, 78, 94, 122-124
Hogenburg, Alfred, 179-180
Huguenots, 36, 37
Hungary, 142-143, 153
Hurd, Douglas, 31, 79, 92
Hyde, Edward, Earl of Clarendon, 55

India, 140
Innocent III, Pope, 159
IRA, 28, 63
Iran 144
Iran-Contra Affair, 4, 156-157
Ireland, 28, 63, 65, 66, 149
Irish Home Rule 12, 40, 67, 73
Irish Volunteers, 63
Irwin, Lord, 140
Isaac II, Emperor, 159
Islam, 101
Italy, 149
Ivory Coast, 130

James I, King of England, 126, 128,

INDEX

James I, 164
James II, King of England, 37
Jameson, Sir Leander Starr, 138-139
Jameson Raid, 138-139
Japan, 174-175
Jaworski, Leon, 25
Jenkins, Roy, 65, 119-121, 134
Jerome, Jennie (Lady Randolph Churchill), 106
Jerusalem, 101, 159, 160
Joan of Arc, 168
Johannesburg, 137
John, King of England, 101-102
Johnson, President Lyndon Baines, 94, 114
Johnson, Samuel, 35
Jones, Sir William, 23
Joseph II, Holy Roman Emperor, 184
Jospin, Lionel, 18, 82
Joynson-Hicks, Sir William, 132
Julius II, Pope, 184
Juppé, Alain, 17, 18, 53, 54

Karamanlis, Constantine, 169-170
Kennedy, President John F., 25, 94, 171-172
Kenya, 129-130
KGB, 153, 155
Khodynka Field, 174
Khomeini, Ayatollah, 144
Kiel, Treaty of, 137
Kikuyu tribe, 129-130
Kilkenny, 14
Kinnock, Neil, 51, 76, 121
Kohl, Helmut, 83-85, 149
Korea, 174
Krenz, Egon, 154-155
Kruger, Paul, 138-139

Labour Party, 36, 39, 43-45, 51,74, 77, 80, 87-92, 94, 95, 119-121, 123, 131,134, 162
Lafontaine, Oskar, 85
Lalonde, Brice, 151
Lamont, Norman, 30-31, 80
Lange, David, 122
Lawson, Nigel, 1, 48, 78, 79
Le Blanc, Jacques, 148
Le Brun, Charles, 157
Le Notre, Andre, 157
Le Vaux, Louis,157
Leeson, Nick, 171
Leopold of Austria, 101-102
Lewis, Derek, 111-112
Liberal Party, 39, 40, 67, 73, 75-77, 105, 119, 131, 134
Liberal Democrats, 46, 123, 134
Licensing Laws, 39
Lilley, Peter, 34
Lincoln, President Abraham, 171-172
Lloyd George, David, 19, 65-67, 73-77, 88, 128
Local Government Finance Bill, 52
Lome, Enrique Dupuy de, 136
Louis XIV, King of France, 36-38, 156-157

Louis XVI, King of France, 1, 5, 6, 7, 181-184
Luttrell, Colonel, MP, 61-62
Luxembourg, 146, 147

Maastricht Treaty, 25
Macleod, Ian, 117
MacMahon, President of France, 168
Macmillan, Harold, 91, 116-118
MacNeill, Eoin, 63
Madelin, Alain, 53-54
Madrid, 78-79, 146
Mafia, 69
Major, John, 1,4, 30-34, 44, 46, 52, 69, 78-81, 83, 125, 133. 162
Mansfield, Lord, 60
Marshall, General George, 142
Marie Antoinette, 5, 6, 7, 181-184
Marshall Plan, 142
Mary I, Queen of England, 127
Mary II, Queen of England, 37
Mary, Queen of Scots, 126-128
Matrix Churchill, 162
Maurice, Sir Frederick, 74-76
Maxwell, General, 64
Mazarin, Cardinal, 156
McAlpine, Lord, 32
McCarthy, Senator Joe, 109-112
McCord, James, 23
McGovern, Senator George, 114
McKinley, President William, 71, 136
Mein Kampf, 178
Melbourne, Lord, 38
Melos, Island of, 99
Minneapolis Journal, 137
Mitchell, John N., 24
Mitterrand, President François, 26, 80,124, 152
Mobutu, President, 131
Modrow, Hans, 155
Monde, Le, 149
Morrison, Herbert, 22-23
Morrison, Peter, 125
Mukden, Battle of, 175
Mulley, Fred,145
Munich Agreement, 2-3
Mururoa, 148-150
Mussolini, Benito, 68, 69, 70

Nantes, Edict of, 36-38
Napoleon I, Emperor of France, 6, 7, 137, 149
Napoleon III, Emperor of France, 166-167
Nasser, President Gamal Abdel, 142
New York, 150
New Zealand, 91, 122, 134,148-150
Newcastle, Thomas, Duke of, 19-20, 22
Nicholas II, Tsar of Russia, 167, 169, 173-176
Nixon, President Richard Milhous, 1, 23-25, 94, 114-116
Norris, Steve, 69
Northampton, 9, 10

Norway, 136-137
Nostradamus, 181, 184
Nottingham Castle, 55, 56
Nur-ad-Din, 161

October Manifesto, 176
Open University, 43
Operation Desert Storm, 162
Ortiz, Frank, 133
Orleans, House of, 168
Otto of Bavaria, King of Greece, 169
O'Shea, Captain W. H., 12
O'Shea, Mrs 'Kitty', 12-14
Owen, David, 90, 119, 121, 124, 134
Owen, Robert, 38

Pahlavi, Shah Reza, 144
Palestine, 101, 158-161
Papadopoulos, Giorgios, 169
Papeete, 149
Papen, Franz von, 177-180
Paris, 14, 17, 18, 66, 124, 149, 150, 156, 157, 163-166, 182-183
Paris, Henri d'Orléans, comte de, 3
Paris, Peace of, 22
Paris, Siege of, 167
Parnell, Charles Stewart, 11-14, 40
Patten, John, 133
Pearl Harbor, 146,175
Pearse, Padraig, 64
Peasants' Revolt, 46, 50
Peel, Sir Robert, 10
Pericles, 99
Persia, 98, 100, 152
Philip II, King of France, 101-102
Philip II, King of Spain, 128-129
Phoenix Park, 12, 29
Pignerol, fortress of, 157
Pitt, William, the Elder, see Chatham
Pitt, William, the Younger, 129
Poland, 3, 141,
Politburo, 154
Poll Tax, 46-52
Polynesia, 148, 150
Pompidou, President Georges, 26
Pompadour, Mme de, 57
Port Arthur, 174-175
Portillo, Michael, 31, 33-34, 46, 47
Portugal, 130
Powell, Enoch, 100
Prussia, 20, 166, 180
Punch, 3

Rainbow Warrior I, 148
Rainbow Warrior II, 148
Ramsay Macdonald, James, 77, 140
Rasputin, 173
Reagan, President Ronald, 4, 116, 134-135, 153, 156, 157, 171
Redmond, John, 74
Redwood, John, 32-34
Reformation, 163
Reichstag, 176, 178-180
Revolution, 6, 149, 164, 181
Reynolds, Albert, 27-30
Rhineland, 2

187

INDEX

Rhodes, Cecil, 137-138
Richard I, King of England, 100-102
Richard II, King of England, 164
Ridley, Nicholas,145
Rifkind, Malcolm, 51, 52
Rights of Man, 149
Robespierre, Maximilien de, 7
Robinson, President Mary, 29
Rodgers, Bill, 119-121, 134
Rohan, Cardinal, 5, 6, 7
Roland, Madame, 163
Rome, 158, 169
Roosevelt, President Franklin Delano, 146
Roosevelt, President Theodore, 71-73
Rosebery, Lord, 73
Rothschild, 48
Rousseau, Jean-Jacques,5
Royalists, 55
Russia, 173-176
Russo-Japanese War, 175

Sadat, President Anwar, 161
Saladin, 101
Salisbury, Lord, 105-106, 108, 138
Sandwich, Lord, 57
Santer, Jacques,149
Santiago, 151
Saracens, 101
Sarajevo, 173
Sarkozy, Nicholas de Naga Bocca, 26, 27
Scharping, Rudolf, 83-85
Schengen Agreement, 146-147
Schleicher, Kurt von, 176, 178-180
Scotland, 126
Scott, Lord Justice, 162
Scottish Nationalists, 51
Schweicker, Senator Richard, 116
Second Empire, 166
Sedan, Battle of, 166
Séguin, Philippe, 148
Seven Years' War, 20
Shaw, George Bernard, 98
Short, Claire, 113
Shriver, R. Sargent, 114
Sicily, 99-100
Simpson, Mrs Wallis, 42-43, 164
Sinn Fein, 67
Sirica, Judge John J.,23, 25
Smith, Ian, 44
Smolko, Artur, 96
Smyth, Father Brendan, 28
Social Democrats, 119-120, 124, 134
Sons of Liberty, 62
South Africa, 98, 137-139
Souvigny, Charles Sorel Sieur de, 36

Soviet Union, 141-142, 144, 152-153 173
Spain, 20, 136, 146, 147, 157
Sparta, 99-100
Spiegel, Der, 149
Spring, Dick, 28-30
St George's Fields, 60, 62
St Petersburg, 175
Stalin, Joseph, 142
STASI, 153
Stevenson, Adlai, 126
Stockholm, 17, 150, 164
Straw, Jack, 112-113
Struensee, Count John Frederick, 102-105
Sunday Pictorial, 132
Suez, 142-143
Sweden, 136-137, 147, 149, 159, 163
Swift, Jonathan, 30
Syracuse, 100
Syria, 101, 143, 158, 160, 161

Taylor, A. J. P., 67, 132
Tebbit, Norman, 31, 125
Teheran, 144
Thatcher, Baroness Margaret, 1, 31-32, 46-52, 78-79, 92, 94, 110, 119, 121-124, 128, 145-146
Thiers, Adolphe, 167
Thomas, Ivor Bulmer, 43
Thorpe, Jeremy, 77, 94
Tiberi, Jean, 18
Tiger, HMS, 46
Times, The, 12, 49, 125
Tolpuddle Martyrs, 38-39
Tonkin Resolution, 94
Tory Party, see Conservative Party
Tumim, Judge Stephen, 112
Tower of London, 58
Transvaal, 137-139
Truman, President Harry S, 91, 109
Tsushima, Battle of
Uganda, 130, 144
Ulster Unionists, 65-67, 73
Un-American Activities Committee, 109, 112
United States, 1, 8,43, 47, 49, 64, 94, 115,126,136, 141-144, 151, 153, 161, 170
Urban II, Pope, 158

van Buren, Martin, 134
Vance, Cyrus R., 144
Varennes, 181, 183-184
Vaux, Nicholas, vicomte de, 156-157
Veil, Simone, 54

Venice, 159
Versailles, 2, 6, 163, 166-167
Victoria, Queen of Britain and Ireland, 10, 105, 108, 140, 165
Vienna, 5, 6
Vietnam, 43, 94, 115, 139
Vittorio Emmanuele III, King of Italy, 68-70
Volcker, Paul, 47

Wachowski, Mieczyslaw, 97
Waldegrave, Sir Richard, 48
Waldegrave, William, 48, 52
Walesa, Lech, 96-97
Walpole, Horace, 19, 20, 22
Walpole, Sir Robert,19, 22
Walsingham, Sir Francis, 127-128
Walters, Sir Alan, 1, 78
War of Independence, American, 145
Warsaw Pact, 152
Washington, 23, 24,149
Washington Post, 23
Watergate, 23, 24-25, 115
Watkins, Senator, 110
Weimar,178, 180
Weizsäcker, President, 84
Wellington, Duke of, 129
Wellington, New Zealand, 149-150
Welles, Orson, 136
Westland Affair, 49
Westminster Abbey, 19
Whelehan, Judge Henry, 28-29
White House, 71, 135
Whitelaw, William, 48, 122
Wilkes, John, 57-63
Wilhelm II, Emperor of Germany, 63-64
William III, King of England, 37
Williams, Shirley, 119-121, 134
Wilson, Harold, 36, 43-46, 65, 92, 94-96, 118, 119, 121
Winn, Godfrey, 2
Witiza, King, 157
Wood, Mrs. Benjamin,12-13
Woodward, Bob, 23
Wolf, Friedrich, 149
World War I, 2, 64, 87-89, 129, 172-173
World War II, 23, 69, 86-87, 129

Yeltsin, Boris,132
Yes, Minister, 143
Younger, George, 48, 124

Zengi, 160, 161
Zimbabwe (S. Rhodesia) 44, 46, 130